Peterman and Schmutzer have produced an insightful biblical theology of suffering that is impressive in its scope, depth, and fidelity to the biblical text. Every assertion is backed up with solid biblical evidence filtered through a well-designed hermeneutical-theological lens. Kudos to the authors for giving us such a relevant study.

ROBERT B. CHISHOLM JR., chair and senior professor of Old Testament Studies, Dallas Theological Seminary

Between Pain and Grace is a thorou~~gh~~ ~~dif~~ficult, but also very common, occurrenc~~e~~ a clear and nuanced presentation of ~~suffer~~ing. Extremely helpful are their discussi~~on~~ topics that are often avoided, rather than a~~ddressed~~

PAUL D. WEGNER, director and pro~~fessor~~ ~~Golden~~ Gate Baptist Theological Seminary

Between Pain and Grace is a remarkable book! The authors have laid a biblical foundation for a theology of suffering that is scholarly, yet engaging and easily understandable for a layperson. Particularly compelling is the distinction they make between pain and suffering, as well as godly and ungodly suffering. None of us are immune to pain, and all of us suffer to some extent, therefore the content is personally applicable to all readers.

HEATHER DAVEDIUK GINGRICH, professor of Counseling, Denver Seminary

The Bible teaches and experience confirms the reality that everyone suffers. Even so, when we suffer, it often surprises and staggers us. What does the Bible say about suffering? *Between Pain and Grace* is an incisive and profound exploration of the biblical theology of suffering. If you want fresh biblical insight on suffering, read this compelling and intelligent book.

TREMPER LONGMAN III, Robert H. Gundry Professor of Biblical Studies, Westmont College

Between Pain and Grace is certain to be of help to anyone who wants to understand more fully the impact of living in a fallen world that is filled with so much suffering. If you are walking through life with someone who is experiencing particularly difficult suffering, you will find the necessary guidance in the chapters of this book to become a more effective agent of the healing process in others . . . and maybe yourself.

DAVID TALLEY, professor/chairman of Old Testament, Biola University/Talbot School of Theology

For the church that is discovering anew the power and relevance of lament, this book offers a fresh study of the biblical dimensions of suffering that drive us to that expression of worship and the grace that draws us there. The reader will profit from a well-balanced presentation of theory and practice.

HASSELL BULLOCK, pastor of Warren Park Presbyterian Church, Cicero, IL

Our churches are full of Job's comforters, subtly telling us that we *must* deserve what we got. But our suffering, like the story of Job, is ultimately about the heavy, awesome reality of God, who does not often give us tidy answers or a bookend closure. Serious followers of Jesus need tools like this to bring holy perspective to the grief, pain, and tragedy we encounter and have experienced.

RAUL MOCK, editor at PneumaReview.com

Between Pain and Grace is a remarkable resource by an Old Testament scholar (Schmutzer) and a New Testament scholar (Peterman). It is Scripture-rich, thought provoking, and remarkably practical. Honestly, each chapter is worth the price of the book.

STEVEN D. MATHEWSON, senior pastor of CrossLife Evangelical Free Church in Libertyville, IL and author of *Risen: 50 Reasons Why the Resurrection Changed Everything*

Suffering pulls apart and tears the tapestry of human experience. *Between Pain and Grace* displays the colors of hope as Peterman and Schmutzer spread out the surprises of Scripture's message in the midst of our broken confusion. *Between Pain and Grace* is a book for the journey, not for the shelf.

GENE L. GREEN, professor of New Testament, Wheaton College and Graduate School

Between Pain and Grace is a wonderful integration of sweeping biblical analysis and emotional compassion, a theology of sin, suffering, and grace blended with knowledgeable understanding of how people really hurt. Schmutzer and Peterson show us a theology in which God's heart is very near to our suffering.

CLARK BARSHINGER, psychologist

Peterman and Schmutzer have given the Christian world a treasure in *Between Pain and Grace*. Examining suffering through a scriptural grid citing biblical narratives and references, they give hope to the hopeless and answers for those who are processing their own suffering. The book will be helpful for everyone from the professional addressing mental illness and family systems, the pastor ministering to a congregant, to the layperson looking for biblical answers.

MURRAY TILLES, founder and director, Light of Messiah Ministries

One of the few experiences shared by the entire human race is suffering. Hence, we need articulate guidance to help us understand and respond to the pain we have and will experience. This book is such a guide. It represents biblical theology at its finest—it is well researched, well applied, and bold. The chapter "Joseph's Tears: Suffering from Family Toxins" is worth the price of the book.

STEVEN R. TRACY, professor of Theology and Ethics, Phoenix Seminary, founder and president, Mending the Soul Ministries

What a powerful book! Peterman and Schmutzer have accomplished the rare feat of writing a book on suffering that is rich with biblical and experiential insight yet overflowing with pastoral sensitivity and relevance. The result is a potentially life-changing resource for pastors, students, and laypeople alike. If you live anywhere between pain and grace, you'll want to get your hands on this book! Better yet, you'll want to thoroughly digest its content and revel in its truth.

TODD WILSON, senior pastor, Calvary Memorial Church, Oak Park, IL

BETWEEN
PAIN &
GRACE

A Biblical Theology of Suffering

Gerald W. Peterman | Andrew J. Schmutzer

MOODY PUBLISHERS
CHICAGO

Edited by Jim Vincent
Interior design: Erik M. Peterson
Cover design: Design Corps
Cover image of clouds copyright © by Lilkar / Thinkstock (160058946). All rights reserved.
Cover image of texture copyright © by DavidMSchrader / Thinkstock (97493282). All rights reserved.
Cover image of crown of thorns © 2012 by Jill Battaglia / iStock (12236758). All rights reserved.

ISBN: 978-0-8024-0967-6

Library of Congress Cataloging–in–Publication Data

Names: Peterman, Gerald W., author.
Title: Between pain and grace : a biblical theology of suffering / Gerald W.
  Peterman and Andrew J. Schmutzer.
Description: Chicago : Moody Publishers, 2016. | Includes index.
Identifiers: LCCN 2016005772 | ISBN 9780802409676
Subjects: LCSH: Suffering--Religious aspects--Christianity.
Classification: LCC BT732.7 .P43 2016 | DDC 231/.8--dc23 LC record available at http://lccn.loc.
gov/2016005772

1 3 5 7 9 10 8 6 4 2

To
Bruce W. Winter
Scholar, Mentor, Friend.
With gratitude for our partnership

To
The believers of South Africa,
the land of my birth.
The beauty of your land is matched only
by the depth of suffering redeemed by
the people, pastors, and churches.
With gratitude for your early imprint

Contents

Introduction

A Different Approach

There are already many books on suffering, so why add another? Writing on suffering can seem rash or presuming, and we certainly do not claim to have the last word on this subject. Nor are we claiming that other books on suffering are flawed. We have learned valuable insights from many others who have written on pain and suffering.

Instead, we write to offer a different approach on this vital topic. In the next few pages we hope to introduce you to how this book is different, to what we will do—and to what we will not do.

This is not a book on philosophy. Philosophical discussions of suffering are important, but we will leave that discussion to those gifted in that area. Our discussion is biblical and textual; that is, we spend most of our time looking at particular passages of God's Word that help us understand suffering—his suffering and ours. Beyond understanding our suffering we are concerned with what Scripture says about suffering well and helping others in their suffering.

We have no illusions that the readers of this book will have all their suffering eliminated; nor do we intend to answer all questions. The end of suffering and the answer to every question is reserved for the new heaven and the new earth described in Isa. 65:17 and Rev. 21:1. But if the Lord is gracious, then some parts of the book will help you in living in and through your suffering with grace, maturity, patience, insight, and appropriate action (to hint that godly suffering is not to be thought of as passive). Likewise our discussion will help mold your thinking in order that you might be able to help others in the same process.

In this book we treat some aspects of suffering that are often left out of the discussion. For example:

1. We enter the debate over whether God suffers, answering that he indeed does (see chapter 3). This is also related to the ministry of Jesus himself (see chapter 4).

2. Although it may come as a surprise to many readers, we treat anger as a type of suffering (see chapter 6). Indeed the book as a whole emphasizes the emotional aspects of suffering.

3. We also treat sexual abuse and mental illness (chapters 10 and 11). We believe frank and biblical discussions of these subjects have come of age, and these discussions need to be set in the broader context of suffering throughout Scripture.

4. We also discuss how suffering is compounded by the damaged relational "bindings" of creation's relationships between God, humankind, and the earth (chapter 2).

Although we view these subjects as very important, we know we have not covered these topics completely; such subjects could have their own book–length treatment.

As with everyone else, we hold certain presuppositions. It may be helpful to mention a few in advance. On the one hand, we hold that God is omnibenevolent, omniscient, omnipresent, and omnipotent. Others have addressed the issue of suffering and concluded that although God is all–good, he is not all powerful and is therefore often not able to control or end suffering. That is the conclusion of Harold Kushner in his bestselling book *When Bad Things Happen to Good People*.[1] On the other hand, though God the Creator is sovereign, we do not appeal to God's sovereignty in a mechanistic or deterministic way. God's sovereignty does not eliminate free human action, does not remove secondary causality, and does not lessen human responsibility. We do not appeal to divine sovereignty in order to squelch the voice of human suffering.

As we mention the voice of suffering we should also mention that, unlike some books on suffering, we want to give sufferers a voice. Clearly Scripture does not silence the cry of the suffering. Instead it gives words to those who suffer, words they can repeat after God, after his Christ, or after God's holy people. We hope to show that "silencing or stifling the voice of suffering serves only to intensify it."[2] We are also aware of how the faith community often hears these discussions.

Our approach also speaks into the mindset of the unease our faith culture has toward pain and suffering. It is increasingly common to speak of constructing one's own truth. But we want to remind the reader that Christians have access to existing truths in Scripture that wait to be discovered.[3] As such, we are speaking into a postmodern mode of thinking that mistrusts the metanarrative of Scripture as well as its claim to a good God. So in these chapters, we want to identify some of these dislocated meanings and reconnect them to the grand sweep of Scripture's redemptive drama. God's Word has not left us without hope, illustration, or theological instruction.

We believe there is much to be explored in Scripture and affirmed for life, even as we suffer. Whether the reader is a layperson, leader, new believer, or pastor, we are aware that a cultural mindset surrounds all of us, and "claims of truth or value must be recognized by [the individual] if they are to lay any claim on [the person]. They cannot be leveraged on the basis of the authority of the meta-narrative."[4] We want to show that there is room for our personal "stories" of pain in God's grand drama. Whether it is the deep and painful struggles of leadership, the silence and stereotypes of mental illness, or the chaos that swirls around the fractured family, in this book the deeper truths of Scripture form the hub around which our discussions revolve. Frankly, this highlights the proclamation of the gospel, whenever one engages the dynamic metanarrative of its Redeemer.

We also realize that we have experienced certain kinds of suffering that qualify us to speak. We never forget that our suffering always has the community of Christ, his church, as the social context. We hope readers will lean more intentionally into their spiritual family, the body of Christ, the grieving community that is called to "rejoice with those who rejoice [and] weep with those who weep" (Rom. 12:15). We want others to talk about their pain and suffering, because we may have started a fresh conversation for them. Some problems we have named afresh, hoping to stimulate a fresh discussion and genuine healing.

Our hope is that those suffering will face their pain directly and find healing. As Henri J. M. Nouwen writes, "When Jesus says, 'It is not the healthy who need a doctor, but the sick' (Mark 2:17), he affirms that only those who face their wounded condition can be available for healing and so enter into a new way of living."[5]

GERALD W. PETERMAN
ANDREW J. SCHMUTZER
(Advent, 2015)

CHAPTER 1

The Grammar of Suffering

Basics of Affliction in Scripture

BY GERALD W. PETERMAN AND ANDREW J. SCHMUTZER

Hearing the terms *pain* and *suffering* makes many people uncomfortable, often evoking painful memories of experiences gone by or still being endured. Yet when we are talking about suffering, what really is the subject? This is an important question, and one we will return to below and several other times in the book. To begin, we assert that pain and suffering, although intricately related, are not identical.

There are several good books on the subject of pain and suffering, but with most the writers typically assume—in our view wrongly—that to talk about one is to talk about the other. For instance, in his excellent book on Pauline theology, Thomas R. Schreiner has a chapter entitled "Suffering and the Pauline Mission: the Means of Spreading the Gospel." He defines suffering as beatings, imprisonments, persecutions, and deprivations.[1] But by our definition, these things are pain, not suffering. What if Paul was deprived of food for two to three days but *gladly did this forced fast for the sake of the gospel*? Certainly he would experience the pain of hunger, but would he be suffering?

PAIN VERSUS SUFFERING

If the answer to this question is complicated, it just demonstrates that the relationship between pain and suffering is not straightforward but intricate and dynamic. It is important for us to ponder that dynamic relationship. So we will address pain and suffering from several perspectives.

Similar is Walter C. Kaiser Jr., who proposes "Eight Kinds of Suffering in the Old Testament."[2] But the kinds, as Kaiser describes them, would better be labeled "Eight Purposes for Pain in the Old Testament." The destruction of Sodom and Gomorrah is *retributive* suffering and the diseases of Job are *testimonial* suffering. In other words, Kaiser discusses the very important theological questions concerning what goals pain can have or what pain can accomplish. The chapter, however, has very little actual discussion of suffering.

What, then, are pain and suffering? The following two points will begin to answer this question and will continue to be important throughout the book.

Pain

We assert that pain is primarily *objective*, external, and typically social or physical as opposed to personal and mental.[3] That is, we will look at pain primarily as a thing or an event. A pain–event could be a betrayal, hunger, poverty, persecution, disease, a laceration, or a broken femur. These things can be viewed as events that are potentially damaging to the person, to the person's relationships, or to the person's cherished goals. The degree to which a person experiences suffering with these events is highly personal, and we will discuss this more below.

Suffering

We assert that suffering is primarily *subjective*, internal, and typically mental or emotional as opposed to physical or social. That is, we will look at suffering primarily as an experience. So, for example, one might have the same physical symptoms (objective) but vastly different subjective interpretation (that is, emotion). An example comes from Professor Patrick Wall, a medical doctor who specializes in the study and treatment of pain. He tells of interaction with a twenty–two–year–old female Israeli Army lieutenant with one leg blown off above the knee by a shell explosion. She "was in deep distress with tears flooding over her face. When asked about her pain, she replied, the 'pain is nothing, but who is going to marry me now!'"[4] Her suffering was related to her physical pain, but only indirectly. The suffering was primarily about the perceived loss of a cherished future goal (i.e., marriage), not about the pain in her leg. She suffered—and we suffer—when she interpreted her pain as destructive of her self or of the person she believed she should be. It is this interpretation that yielded acute emotional distress; that is, it yielded suffering. As Ferrell and Coyle assert, "Suffering results when the most important aspects of a person's identity are threatened or lost."[5]

THE RELATIONSHIP BETWEEN PAIN AND SUFFERING

From what has been said, we can see that the relationship between pain and suffering is highly complex. Hurding is correct when he explains that "not all pain, as a physical sensation, necessarily entails suffering."[6] Furthermore, just as we might have pain without suffering, so we might have suffering without pain.

Suffering without Pain

In their book *Pain: The Gift Nobody Wants*, Dr. Paul Brand and Philip Yancey tell of a rare disease called congenital analgesia, or congenital insensitivity to pain. One clinician had defined congenital insensitivity to pain (CIP) as "a rare inherited disorder of the hereditary sensory and autonomic neuropathy (HSAN) family. This disorder is characterized by a dramatically impaired perception to painful stimuli that leads to frequent trauma and self–mutilation."[7] In his medical practice Brand encountered a four–year–old girl named Tanya. Her insensitivity to pain meant regular repeated trauma to her body. It started in her crib when she bit off the tip of her finger and then "painted" with the blood. Her mother was horrified but, with her daughter's complete absence of pain, she had no way of convincing the infant Tanya that the behavior was destructive.

Seven years later Dr. Brand received a call from Tanya's mother. Brand reported:

> Tanya, now eleven, was living a pathetic existence in an institution. She lost both legs to amputation: she had refused to wear proper shoes and that, coupled with her failure to limp or to shift weight when standing (because she felt no discomfort), had eventually put intolerable pressure on her joints. Tanya had also lost most of her fingers. Her elbows were constantly dislocated. She suffered the effects of chronic sepsis from ulcers on her hands and amputation stumps. Her tongue was lacerated and badly scarred from her nervous habit of chewing it.[8]

Here we encounter a clear and tragic example of suffering without pain (that is, physical pain). Some forms of pain are a "gift." Tanya actually needed pain. But other examples could be included. Many of us have known people who, though generally wealthy, healthy, and loved, have suffered terrible mental trauma. Take Elliot Rodger. As reported in the online publication *Public Discourse,* Rodger had good looks, good health, above average intelligence, "a new BMW sports car, nice clothes, $300 Gucci sunglasses, college tuition fully paid for by his parents, and thousands of dollars in spending money."[9] Nevertheless he was tortured by his own jealousy and envy, resulting in a shooting rampage in which he killed seven and then took his own life.[10]

Pain without Suffering

But there is another angle to consider. Just as there can be suffering without pain, so there can be pain without suffering. Athletes know this. A gymnast preparing for the Olympics will invest long hours in her training, end all unnecessary relationships and social life, strictly schedule every hour of the day, and go through much pain in the form of sore muscles, short–term failures, and numerous minor injuries. But with most athletes in training, none of this pain is viewed as suffering. Of course, the pain–inducing workouts involve sacrifice and frequently lead to exhaustion. But it is not suffering. Similarly, a runner training for a marathon may log sixty miles in one week, tear a few toenails, and even fall hard, but claim not to be suffering.

When the goal is kept in mind and good progress follows, all the pain and exhaustion is a pleasure. It is the *meaning* that the athletes assign to their pain that allows them to consider it a stepping–stone to victory and achievement rather than a cause of torment and suffering.[11] In fact, some mothers make the same claim about the birthing process, because they are so focused on the goal of the precious child (cf. Isa. 66:7–10; John 16:21).

The Person's Perception of the Pain

What meaning do I assign to the pain I encounter? As we saw with the Israeli soldier earlier, the issue with her suffering was primarily a matter of interpretation or *assigning meaning* to her injury—her perspective on the pain evoked the suffering. The view we are describing here on the relationship between suffering and meaning is very similar to the view of Dr. Eric Cassell. In his excellent book *The Nature of Suffering and the Goals of Medicine*, he discussed this relationship extensively. He wrote, "Patients sometimes report suffering when one does not expect it or do not report suffering when it can be expected."[12] What makes the difference? It is the meaning assigned to that pain.[13] For the gymnast, a professional runner, or a woman in labor, the pain can be viewed as a means to a desired end rather than something that threatens them as persons. This is a significant issue of perspective.

The meaning assigned to pain is highly subjective. It will vary from person to person depending on a great variety of factors, including personality, individual history, theology, family background, community support, and personal desires and goals, to name but a few. In light of this, Cassell rightly comments, "The only way to learn whether suffering is present is to ask the sufferer."[14] The implications for empathy and response from others should not be missed.

When we say "assign meaning," it may sound clinical, calculated, or even detached. In truth, it might be anything but. For some of us, assigned meanings come quickly and subconsciously; for others deliberate, conscious thought may be required. And meaning is always very personal, context–specific, and rather dependent on a certain *relational ecosystem*. If a spouse betrays us, then certainly it pains us in ways that infidelity on the movie screen does not pain us. This infidelity of our own spouse takes on a certain meaning, such as:

"I can no longer trust anyone."
"I am damaged goods. I am second rate."
"My life can never be happy and fulfilled."
"My children will carry scars for the rest of their life."
"My reputation and community standing are permanently destroyed."

These statements are all emotionally painful and are the result of a highly personal *interpretation*. The interpretation—the assignment of meaning—depends on how personally one takes the pain. If the pain takes away a cherished expectation, if it ruins a career, if it threatens my sense of self, my physical, social, or emotional integrity, then surely it will result in suffering.

Our approach to pain, suffering, and emotions is based on what has come to be called a *cognitive theory of the emotions*. "Emotions are closely related to our thinking and especially to how we interpret events in our life, whether an event is good or bad, a blessing or a threat. But in order to interpret something, we need beliefs, convictions, or perspectives."[15]

Since beliefs and perspective vary from person to person and place to place, so will the assignment of meaning and thus, suffering.

A BIBLICAL EXAMPLE: PAUL AND JEREMIAH AS SERVANTS WHO SUFFER

Regarding the personal assignment of meaning, let us take an example from Scripture. We will compare the prophet Jeremiah (580 BC) with the apostle Paul (AD 50). We will look at the similar pains they encountered, yet the very different suffering they reported. Then we will attempt to explain the differences.

Similar Kinds of Persecution

First, Jeremiah and Paul were similar in their encounter with persecution. For example, on one occasion, after hearing Jeremiah's preaching, "Pashhur beat Jeremiah the prophet, and put him in the stocks that were in the upper Benjamin Gate of the house of the LORD" (Jer. 20:2). Paul experienced a similar persecution. As a result of freeing a demon–possessed girl, "the crowd joined in attacking [Paul and Silas], and the magistrates tore the garments off them and gave orders to beat them with rods. And when they had inflicted many blows upon them, they threw them into prison, ordering the jailer to keep them safely" (Acts 16:22–23).

The similarity between Jeremiah and Paul goes deeper than this one instance. Jeremiah is a prophet to the Gentile nations (Jer. 1:5) as Paul is the apostle to the nations (that is, Gentiles: Rom. 11:13). Both are set apart from the womb (Jer. 1:5; Gal. 1:15–16).[16] More importantly, Jeremiah is warned that his hearers will fight against him (Jer. 1:19). Paul likewise is one destined for suffering, as Jesus told Ananias, "I will show him how much he must suffer for the sake of my name" (Acts 9:16).

Different Responses to Persecution

Second, these men display vastly different responses to this persecution. Later in the same chapter we hear of Jeremiah's despair: "Cursed be the day on which I was born! The day when my mother bore me, let it not be blessed! Cursed be the man who brought the news to my father, 'A son is born to you,' making him very glad" (Jer. 20:14–15). In contrast, after their imprisonment, we find that about midnight "Paul and Silas were praying and singing hymns to God, and the prisoners were listening to them" (Acts 16:25).

Why the difference? We dare not oversimplify nor be reductionistic. There were times of trial and despair for Paul (Acts 20:17–35; 2 Cor. 1:8). Still, a reading of Jeremiah's book and Paul's letters verifies that their *responses* to pain, betrayal, and persecution were worlds apart. Certainly there is nothing like Lamentations for Paul; for him there was nothing like the self-reporting of a Jeremiah 20. If we look at the broad sweep of Paul's life, he appears much more positive. And just as certainly, if we consider the broad sweep of Jeremiah, he is a prophet immersed in tears. How do we explain this?

The Influence of Personality, Coworkers, Commission, and Understanding of the Messiah

Third, perhaps the following can set us in the right direction in explaining the differences between Jeremiah and Paul. Possible influences —that need not to be considered disjunctive—include the following:

Type of personality. For all we know, Jeremiah might have been a verbal processor and one given to melancholy. Paul might not have been. Some of us might have more of a tendency to retreat to our "cave" and think, while others are prone to vent their frustrations.

Coworkers. Friends help us deal with suffering. Who was there to support Jeremiah? It appears from his writings that there were few (e.g., Baruch). With Paul the reverse is the case. For the apostle the list includes at least Silas, Timothy, Luke, Prisca and Aquila, Apollos, Titus, Aristarchus, and Barnabas.

The nature of the commission. In Jeremiah's case, there is little hope for real change or repentance from Israel (see Jer. 1:17–19). He is told this up front and commanded to mourn (4:8; 6:26).[17] What about Paul? As an apostle to Gentiles he has a different commission (Acts 26:16–18), "to open their eyes, so that they may turn from darkness to light and from the power of Satan to God, that they may receive forgiveness of sins."

A Suffering Messiah. Even if Jeremiah understands the suffering Messiah as well as the prophet Isaiah (53:2–12), Paul is still at a great advantage. He can look back to the suffering of Jesus and interpret his suffering christologically. Jeremiah cannot do so. When it comes to pain and suffering, our life-setting matters.

The Holy Spirit. Paul had the new covenant experience of the Spirit. We must not fault Jeremiah for not having blessings and insight that can only come after Pentecost.

WAYS THE OLD TESTAMENT SPEAKS OF PAIN AND SUFFERING

Suffering within the Covenantal Relationship with God

Broadly speaking, the Old Testament offers no explanation for suffering. Instead, the Old Testament Scriptures *recontextualize* suffering by placing it inside a dynamic covenantal relationship with God. Entire communities could assign meaning to suffering (cf. Num. 11:3, 34; 1 Sam. 7:6). For relationship is, after all, the be-all and end-all of faith (Ps. 73:23–28). As such, it is relational trust and devotion that makes meaning of suffering.[18]

Beginning with Genesis 3, suffering is introduced by human rebellion—a profound breakdown of relational trust.[19] "Have you eaten of the tree of which I commanded you not to eat?" (3:11, 17). But the grand movement of the Old Testament focuses on the national sufferings of Israel, due to their disobedience. It is rare for the biblical text to ever explore the suffering of those "outside" Israel (e.g., Josh. 6; 1 Kings 17; 2 Kings 5; Matt. 15:21–28).[20]

Individual suffering is largely swept up in the larger social community that is never far away (Gen. 50:20). But it is in the Psalms where the most intense expressions of personal suffering are found (e.g., Psalms 39, 88). Whether caused by sin, enemies, or God himself, the prayers of lament "constitute Israel's primary faith strategy for drawing suffering into the orbit of YHWH's concern."[21] In the lament, Israel transposed suffering into a theological exchange to which God must respond.[22]

The Syntax of Loss

When someone suffers, they experience some kind of *loss* (cf. Job 1:13–2:7). This "tear" in the fabric of life can occur in a number of ways: a broken friendship, an abrupt transition, isolating circumstances, death of a close friend, a divorce, failed plans, or a life–altering diagnosis. In each, *something is pulled apart*, and the fullness of life is undermined. That is, some diminishment occurs—usually relationally—that formed the larger fabric of life: "You have caused my beloved and my friend to shun me; my companions have become darkness" (Ps. 88:18). Experiences of suffering are directly equated with the ruin of what is vital and dear to life.[23] That Job never cursed God (1:11, 22; 31:30) is not to say Job did not suffer greatly or even have anger toward God— "But it is God who has wronged me" (19:6a NLT; cf. v. 11). From the very beginning, however, Satan assumed Job would assign a negative–reactive meaning to his suffering (2:5). But the Accuser got this wrong.

Simple ideas need refinement, but healing is for broken lives. "And the LORD restored the fortunes of Job . . . the LORD blessed the latter days of Job" (42:10a, 12a). So declaring, "Well, that's life!" may describe the plight of humanity, but as an attitude *in* life, such comments repair nothing. Instead, they stifle empathy toward others, shun meaningful reflection, and promote cynicism within one's self. Growth comes from grieving our losses, not merely enduring them.

Sounds and Gestures of a Suffering Creation

Suffering itself has no "voice." No alarm is sounded for aid to come running. Instead, there are primal sounds and physical gestures that form the grammar of suffering. In fact, the initial stages of suffering often resist speech altogether.[24] Some forms of pain and trauma even switch speech off (e.g., torture, rape, shock).[25] We must learn to read and translate the grammar of suffering that we observe in the lives of people around us. Advocates, counselors, and healers understand the unique, "unlocking" gift of words and the power of speech (cf. Ezek. 24:25–27).[26] In Hosea, the prophet even commands the use of words: "Take with you words and return to the LORD" (14:2a). Until suffering is *translated* into a language form—even such things as art—neither processing (for the hurting) nor understanding (for the empathizing) can adequately occur. So candid prayer not only pleas for relief, it signals that a healing communication is alive!

From the very beginning, we should realize that the scale of suffering is more than global—it is *cosmic*. The Creator cares about his suffering world—not just suffering humans. The Old Testament is less interested in distinctions between the human and nonhuman. Because all creation is naturally dependent on the Creator (Job 12:10), biblical writers saw a plurality of relationships with greater association and intimacy (Jonah 4:11). For example, even the land responds as a sensate creature that "mourns" (Isa. 24:4; Jer. 4:28) and can be nauseated to the point of "vomiting" (Lev. 18:25, 28; 20:22) when it ingests violence.[27] Just as sin and contamination could defile the sanctuary, so wickedness could defile the land.[28] So Paul also declares that "the whole creation has been groaning *together*," waiting for God's future restoration (Rom. 8:22, emphasis added). In the Old Testament, the comprehensive connections of life go even further.

The Old Testament assumes we know that animals also cry out to their Creator: "How the beasts groan! . . . Even the beasts of the field pant for you because the water brooks are dried up" (Joel 1:18a, 20a). Job chastises his "counselors," challenging them to "ask the beasts, and they will teach you" (Job 12:7a). God also referred to a catalogue of animals who could instruct Job about suffering and dependence: "Who provides for the raven its prey, when its young ones cry to God for help?" (Job 38:41a; cf. Job 38:1–42:6). Jesus also mentions his care for simple birds: "Consider the ravens . . . and yet God feeds them" (Luke 12:24; cf. Ps. 147:9). Jesus tries to stimulate the faith of his disciples. If God cares for ceremonially "unclean" birds, surely he will care for ignorant people, who are worth more than animals (cf. Matt. 6:26).[29]

A person enters this world with a cry, lives amid wordless sighs, and then dies with a groan. Ecclesiastes and Lamentations do not hide these realities. But primal sounds also mix with gestures. In fact, physical gestures are an external expression of internal feelings.[30] Eyes can sparkle or shoot daggers; hands can go limp or fists can clinch; a face can beam or wince; a body can jump for joy or curl up in the fetal position.

Suffering ultimately finds its voice by drawing on the various "grammars" of a given culture: social, religious, and domestic.[31] Professional trades create with their own lexicons: writers tell stories, painters create portraits, and doctors read symptoms. These trades provide definition and context to understand suffering. Poets, sculptors, actors, and musicians offer aesthetic form, shape, and dignity to our losses, misery, and brokenness. They identify and interpret personal and collective suffering. But it is the community of faith that adds the authoritative Scripture, which invites the suffering to locate their distress within the context of shared faith.[32]

THE OT REGISTRY FOR EXPRESSING SUFFERING

Expressions of suffering in the Old Testament range from dire human experiences to a cacophony of sounds expressing the suffering of men and women. The OT registry is pervasive, indicating the ongoing dilemma of humankind.

Dire Human Experiences

People who suffer personal loss, economic poverty, physical distress, imprisonment, and various forms of oppression are numbered among the: poor (*dal*, Gen. 41:9; Amos 4:1) and needy (*'ni we'evyon*, Deut. 15:11; Ps. 35:10); the "faint and weary" (*'ayef, yagea'*, Deut. 25:18); the "crushed" and "broken" (*daka, shavar*, Job 20:19; Jer. 23:9); and the "shamed," "humiliated," and "disgraced" (*boshah, kherpah*, Lam. 2:1).[33] One reads: "She who bore seven has grown feeble; she has fainted away; her sun went down while it was yet day; she has been shamed and disgraced" (Jer. 15:9a).

Expressions of Human Sorrow

The verbal expressions of sorrow in the Old Testament are varied to reflect people's circumstances: "to grieve, suffer" (*yaghah*); "to be in pain, to grieve, hurt" (*kha'av*, Job 14:22); "to be bowed down, oppressed" (*qadhadh, khara'*); "to become dark, gloomy" (*qadhar*); and "to be devastated, frightened, troubled, in difficulty" (*pa'am, qashah*, Gen. 41:8; Josh. 10:2). One reads: "'Oh no, sir!' she replied. 'I haven't been drinking wine or anything stronger. But I am very discouraged, and I was pouring out my heart to the LORD'" (1 Sam. 1:15 NLT).

Intense Reaction to Pain

Some verbal expressions capture acute and instinctive human reactions to pain: "sigh, groan" (*'anaqah*, Ezek. 9:4); "weep" (*bakhah*); and "mourn" (*'aval*, Gen. 23:2; 1 Sam. 30:4; 2 Sam. 3:31). One reads: "As soon as Esau heard the words of his father, he cried out with an exceedingly great and bitter cry" (Gen. 27:34).

Sounds of Human Suffering

Some expressions of human suffering are taken from the world of animals: "howl" (Isa. 52:5), "roar" (Isa. 5:29), and "growl" (Isa. 59:11). In anguish, people "cry out" (Ex. 2:23; Job 35:12) and cry aloud (Ps. 3:4;

27:7). One reads: "Because of contention the oppressed cry out; They shout because of the power of the great" (Job 35:9, Tanak).

The "Twisted" Human Body

In various forms of suffering, the human body can "weaken" (Judg. 16:19), "fail" (Isa. 17:32), and "waste away" (Ps. 31:10). The effect of calamity and suffering means one's bones can "shake" (Job 4:14), "burn" (Job 30:30; Ps. 102:3), "scatter" (Ezek. 6:5), and be "out of joint" (Ps. 22:14). One's eyes can "grow dim" with grief (Job 17:7; Ps. 88:9). The heart can "melt" (Josh. 14:8; Isa. 13:7), break (Ps. 69:20), "throb" (Ps. 38:10), or become "hot" (Ps. 39:3). The heart also can become weighed down (Prov. 12:25), faint (Job 19:27), wither (Ps. 102:4), and be "stricken" (Ps. 109:22).

Like no other genre, the poetry of Scripture uses the vivid imagery of wounds. These are high–density expressions for pain and suffering that draw richly on the imagination and paint "loaded" pictures. While laments occur throughout the Old Testament (see Isaiah, Jeremiah, Habakkuk, Lamentations, Job), the laments of the Psalter are legendary for their candid use of somatic terms.[34] Whether protesting their innocence (Ps. 54:1, 3), confessing personal sin (Ps. 32:3–5), or calling God out for his inexcusable absence (Ps. 44:10–12), laments use imagistic representation for affliction, incapacitation, and diminishment.

While individuals may suffer, the family and community never sit passively by. The shame and social stigma of the suffering party forces friends to act in loyalty or betrayal. Whether in help or hindrance, suffering becomes a communal concern (Neh. 9:5–37). So in the Psalms, for example, the physical deterioration associated with pain and suffering always risks the social alienation of friends and family, who may "withdraw" (Ps. 38:11). At times, God himself seems to join those in flight from the hurting (Pss. 10:1; 22:11; 35:22; 38:21).

CONCLUDING OT OBSERVATIONS

Suffering etches deep marks in the people of the Old Testament. Old Testament accounts of suffering include: punishment, hardship, grief, disaster, loneliness, injury, shame, disgrace, disease, and death (Deut. 30:15–19). It has left an extensive lexicon that describes different "layers" of suffering. Suffering affects multiple realms in the *relational ecosystem*—sometimes several at once (e.g., physical + emotional + social).[35] Job's suffering illustrates this composite–dynamic (Job 1:6–2:10). From this discussion, we can make several concluding observations.

First, the issue of *innocent suffering*, and its accompanying protest to God, is far more prominent in the Old Testament than the New (see earlier comments on Jeremiah and Paul). While the Old Testament writers struggle with *theodicy*[36] (e.g., Habakkuk) and the prosperity of the wicked (cf. Ps. 73:3–13), the New Testament emphasizes the transformative power of Christ's innocent suffering for the redemption of others.[37] Even substitutionary suffering (e.g., Isa. 52:13–53:12; Zech. 11:4–17) is not understood in Old Testament theology as a challenge to the justice or goodness of God. Every expression of evil and suffering is matched by a corresponding certainty that God will vindicate (Ps. 94:1–3; Isa. 57:17–21; Hab. 3:12–15).[38] The contemporary reflex of "daring" God or holding him hostage to reason devoid of mystery is a foreign and foolhardy response by biblical standards.

Second, the Old Testament portrays suffering as a *depth of loss* that resists any moralizing explanations.[39] Instead, story after story in the Old Testament faces the bald reality of someone's *guilt* that shows up in social *grief* and typically climaxes in community *fragmentation* (Gen. 44:16; Lam. 3:49, 51; 2 Sam. 13:37–39). That other people can act cruelly is a loss of nurture and shalom (Pss. 55:2–5; 59:3–4); but the abusive silence of God is utterly destabilizing (Pss. 44:10–12, 18, 24; 88:6–9a). Life cannot sustain both vertical and horizontal separations. Such loss is a rupture in the relational ecosystem of the most devastating kind

(Ezra 9:6–15; Neh. 9:5–37). Nonetheless, suffering people cry out *because* God is mighty, not in challenge of it.

Third, grief and mourning were not stoic, brief, individualistic, or of one gender. As we have seen, pain was expressed vocally and communally, and often ranged from inarticulate groaning to artistically written compositions, even intended for the teaching of the community (2 Sam. 1:17–27; Ps. 73:26a, 28b; Lamentations). Voicing one's pain was not viewed as *un*masculine.

> That the expression of grief should be brief, relatively dispassionate, and primarily characteristic of women was a Greek development that entered the church through people such as Augustine, who, for example, felt grieved that he had very briefly grieved the loss of his mother.[40]

Communities of faith that are committed to addressing a fuller spectrum of suffering must intentionally name the real ills of real people living among them, then listen to the pained testimonies of these people's suffering. Real words matter when facing real pain. Too often, the contemporary church has struck not only "sin" and "brokenness" from its working vocabulary, but also grief from its corporate expression that is needed to face suffering on personal and global levels. The Old Testament displays far greater candor and complexity when facing corporate sin and pain (Isa. 15:3; 2 Chron. 34:19; Joel 1:13). But the contemporary church, often more concerned with marketing an image, refuses to guide people into genuine lament over the effects of sin or a collective embrace of sorrow, outside twelve–step programs and "underground" accountability groups.

Fourth, within a distinctly theological worldview, the Old Testament affirms that any description of suffering and evil must factor God into the equation. Without a *theo*centric worldview, neither suffering nor evil necessarily calls the *meaning* of suffering into question.[41] Rather, they become experiences to be endured; somewhere between "That's life!" and "YOLO" (You Only Live Once). But because God defines the beginning ("In the beginning, God," Gen. 1:1) and the end of all Scripture ("the beginning *and* the end," Rev. 22:13, emphasis added), the simple conjunction "and" calls all who suffer to locate the vocabulary of life within the grammar of faith.[42]

HOW THE NEW TESTAMENT SPEAKS OF PAIN AND SUFFERING

Here we will not engage in detailed exegesis of any particular New Testament passage. Instead, we will be looking at the types and distribution of words the New Testament uses, taking a broad look at how it discusses threats to us and the suffering that can result.

Our discussion is representative, not exhaustive. Here we merely intend to illustrate the breadth of suffering in the New Testament and begin classifying pain and suffering into types for the sake of our discussion.

We will talk of external or objective threats (sources of pain) and personal or subjective suffering. As we said earlier in the chapter, these two are not equivalent, although they are related. We do not assume that the external is always disjunctive from the personal and the like.

Physical Sources (Nature and People)

The world we live in sometimes threatens us, doing so in a great variety of ways, some personal and some impersonal. New Testament writers know this quite well. Five examples follow.

Storms

A windstorm came down on the lake while Jesus and the disciples were in the boat. They were in danger of drowning (Luke 8:23). Likewise Paul had already been shipwrecked three times (2 Cor. 11:25) before he and Luke were violently storm tossed for two weeks on the Mediterranean Sea (Acts 27:18–27).

Famine

"And one of them named Agabus stood up and foretold by the Spirit that there would be a great famine over all the world (this took place in the days of Claudius)" (Acts 11:28).

Disease/Illness

Near the pool of Bethesda Jesus saw "a multitude of invalids—blind, lame, and paralyzed" (John 5:3). Matthew summarized Jesus' ministry, writing, "His fame spread throughout all Syria, and they brought him all the sick, those afflicted with various diseases and pains, those oppressed by demons, epileptics, and paralytics, and he healed them" (Matt. 4:24; see also Matt. 9:35; Mark 1:34; 3:10; Luke 4:40; 6:18). Christians also suffer illness, since Paul reports that Epaphroditus "was ill, near to death" (Phil. 2:27; cf. Gal. 4:13).

Accidents

On the one hand, there is no word in the New Testament that exactly corresponds to our use of the term "accident."[43] On the other hand, Jesus spoke against the view that there is a one–to–one correspondence between disaster and sin, saying, "Or those eighteen on whom the tower in Siloam fell and killed them: do you think that they were worse offenders than all the others who lived in Jerusalem?" (Luke 13:4). The point is that "natural calamities afford no proof that those who suffer in them are any worse sinners that anybody else."[44] Rather, they suffered an accident.

Abuse, Violence, or Oppression

This category is large, probably owing to a variety of factors such as the writers' sensitivity to evil and the church's encounter with persecution. Here we find the rich dragging the poor into court (James 2:6), Christians being slandered (1 Peter 3:16) and deprived of property (Heb. 10:34), Herod slaughtering innocent children (Matt. 2:16), Stephen being executed unjustly (Acts 7:57–58), Paul beaten by Romans and from Jews receiving "the forty lashes less one" (2 Cor. 11:24–25; cf. Acts 21:30–32), and preeminently the brutality that Jesus faced (Luke 18:32–33; Matt. 27:28–31).

Spiritual Sources

The external threats we considered above do not require that we have a Christian worldview. The following, however, differ in that they presuppose a spiritual world. From a New Testament perspective, threats from the spiritual world are just as real as those from the physical world.

Demons, Demonization

This threat is commonly found in Matthew, Mark, and Luke. Thus Jesus' "fame spread throughout all Syria, and they brought him all the sick, those afflicted with various diseases and pains, those oppressed by demons" (Matt. 4:24; cf. Matt. 8:16; 10:8; Mark 1:34; 7:29–30; Luke 4:33–35; 8:2; 13:32).

The Enemy

The enemy is Satan himself—the devil who first appears in Scriptures as a serpent (Gen. 3:1–5; cf. Rev. 12:9). Because of his threat Paul urges the Ephesians to put on "the whole armor of God, that you may be able to stand against the schemes of the devil" (6:11; cf. 2 Cor. 2:10–11), and Peter warns, "Be sober–minded; be watchful. Your adversary the devil prowls around like a roaring lion, seeking someone to devour" (1 Peter 5:8). Acts tells us that Jesus "went about doing good and healing all who were oppressed by the devil, for God was with him" (10:38).

False Teachers

Even when a threat is "spiritual" we should not think that natural means are never used. So we are told that, for his pride, Herod was struck by the angel of the Lord. That is a spiritual cause. Nevertheless, the same verse says "he was eaten by worms and breathed his last"

(Acts 12:23). That is a natural means. So also those who teach a false gospel are willing human agents of the enemy. Thus Paul says that false apostles working at Corinth are "deceitful workmen, disguising themselves as apostles of Christ. And no wonder, for even Satan disguises himself as an angel of light. So it is no surprise if his servants, also, disguise themselves as servants of righteousness" (2 Cor. 11:13–15).

Subjective/Personal Sources

Here we talk of suffering as we have defined it earlier. That is, the inner, subjective experience of a person in pain. Primarily we can see that suffering occurs by the emotional words that are used.

Anger

One may wonder why anger is included with suffering. We will explore this further in chapter 6. In short, anger is included since it is always a *secondary* emotion following from some other pain. Thus when Herod was tricked by the wise men, he was furious (Matt. 2:16). Jesus displayed anger toward the Pharisees because he was grieved by their hard–heartedness (Mark 3:5). Because of his pastoral love, Paul burned with indignation when Christians were abused by false teachers (2 Cor. 11:29).

Anxiety/Distress

During Zechariah's time of temple service, the angel Gabriel appeared to him, and the temple servant became "troubled when he saw him, and fear fell upon him" (Luke 1:12). After listing his many trials such as shipwreck, persecution, and deprivation, Paul crowns the list with the daily pressure on him of his anxiety for all the churches (2 Cor. 11:28). Epaphroditus has similar distress on behalf of others. Concerning the believers in Philippi, "he has been longing for you all and has been distressed because you heard that he was ill" (Phil. 2:26), Paul wrote. In chapter 4 we will speak more of the distress of Jesus in the garden of Gethsemane (e.g., Mark 14:33).

Agony/Anguish

When the church in Caesarea urged Paul not to depart, he answered, "What are you doing, weeping and breaking my heart?" (Acts 21:13). Concerning unsaved Jews, Paul reports having great sorrow and unceasing anguish in his heart (Rom. 9:2; cf. Gal. 4:19). Although it does not use a specifically emotional word, a heart agony is probably reflected in Jesus' cry of dereliction: "And about the ninth hour Jesus cried out with a loud voice, saying, 'Eli, Eli, lema sabachthani?' that is, 'My God, my God, why have you forsaken me?'" (Matt. 27:46).[45]

Grief/Sorrow/Tears

We have already mentioned the grief and sorrow of Jesus, one caused by the hard-heartedness of the Pharisees, the other occurring in the garden as he anticipates arrest (Mark 3:5; 14:34; cf. John 13:21). In addition, Paul was grieved by a visit to the Corinthians (2 Cor. 2:1), by a subsequent painful letter to them written "out of much affliction and anguish of heart and with many tears" (2 Cor. 2:4), and by his situation at the time of writing to the Philippians (2:27). Peter speaks of being grieved by trials (1 Peter 1:6). Tears also appear in the life of Peter (Mark 14:72), of Mary (John 20:11), and of Jesus (Heb. 5:7–8).

CONCLUDING NT OBSERVATIONS

Our summary above has been cursory. Much more could be found to study. This selection is meant to show the broad representation we find in the New Testament. Much could be said in summary of the evidence but we restrict ourselves to the following five points:

First, the pain and suffering are both physical and emotional, including but not limited to: disease, grief, storms, exploitation, accidents, shame, slander, torment, brutality, terror, frustration, despair, murder, abuse, and betrayal. By definition, life in this age—although it has many joys—is in constant threat of pain and suffering.

Second, consider who suffers. In the New Testament we find preeminently the suffering of Jesus. His is innocent suffering, and suffering that redeems. In Luke 9:22 Jesus says, "The Son of Man must suffer many things and be rejected by the elders and chief priests and scribes, and be killed, and on the third day be raised." The phrase "suffer many things" has to do with "the entire process of rejection and persecution," since we see that there is a specific reference to crucifixion later.[46]

But in addition to the suffering of the Messiah, we find secondarily the suffering of the people of God—first predicted by Jesus (e.g., Matt. 10:16–22; 24:9–13), and then experienced by the early church (e.g., Acts 8:1–3; 1 Peter 4:12–13). And, as with the Old Testament (e.g., Jeremiah 20), the suffering affects the individual, as we see especially with Paul in the latter half of Acts and in some of the letters (e.g., Acts 14:19; 2 Cor. 11:23b–27).

Third, a key feature of suffering is hinted at: desire. It is not a feature that encompasses all suffering; nevertheless it is repeatedly seen. Because we have desires and goals, we suffer. Jesus desires the repentance of Jerusalem and it will not receive him. So he laments its rebellion (Luke 13:34) and weeps over it (Luke 19:41). Herod wants the sole enjoyment of kingship's power. Consequently, he kills all the male babies of Bethlehem so that no newborn king might be a threat to him (Matt. 2:16). If we had no desire, no longings, and no goals, we would have a significantly reduced liability to suffering. This has long been recognized by Buddhism. Its "Four Noble Truths" say: (1) suffering exists, (2) suffering arises from attachment to desires, (3) suffering ceases when attachment to desire ceases, and (4) freedom from suffering is possible by practicing the Eightfold Path.[47]

But a life without desire is not a godly life as described and prescribed by both Testaments. Indeed a life without desires, goals, and relationships is not even a human life.

Fourth, if we take all the evidence into account, we see that *the New Testament gives us not a two-dimensional presentation, but rather an emotionally rich picture filled with intricacies and tensions.* Jesus rejoiced in the Spirit (Luke 10:21) and had compassion (Matt. 9:36), but also grieved (Mark 3:5) and wept (Luke 19:41).[48] Similarly, on the one hand, Paul calls the Philippians to rejoice always (4:6); yet in this same letter he reports his own sorrow (2:27) and tears over enemies of the gospel (3:18). Paul also has unceasing anguish over unsaved Jews (Rom. 9:2), even though he describes himself in 2 Cor. 6:10 as "always rejoicing."[49] This tension has much in common with the experience of Old Testament saints.

Fifth, and following from the above, we find a certain perspective on emotion. *It is common to hear it said that emotions are neither right nor wrong, "they just are."*[50] *The New Testament—indeed all Scripture— takes a different view.* It does not deny emotion. It does not, for instance, tell someone who is angry that he is not angry. It does, however, praise certain emotions and not others depending on their basis (e.g., Ps. 97:10; Amos 5:15; Rom. 12:9). It does make clear that some emotional reactions are "wrong" in the sense that the emotion is based on a culpable misunderstanding, sin, rebellion, selfishness, or the like.

Thus in certain contexts certain emotions may be appropriate or inappropriate. For example, Jesus rebuked those in the synagogue at Capernaum (Luke 4:24–27). But when they heard his words "all in the synagogue were filled with wrath" and tried to kill him (vv. 28–29). We can rightly say this anger was sinful—that is, wrong. Similarly, the Corinthians were proud of a man in the congregation who had an incestuous relationship with his stepmother (1 Cor. 5:12). Paul says that instead of pride (a wrong emotional response) they should have mourned (a correct emotional response).[51] We note here that the correct emotional response was to suffer.

AMID PAIN AND SUFFERING

1. Reflect on the distinction drawn between pain and suffering. Have you seen the distinction borne out in your life? In the lives of others? Discuss particular examples where you have had pain without suffering and suffering without pain.

2. Ponder the following statement: "Suffering is primarily emotional and the emotion needs to be given a voice." Do you think the statement is helpful or harmful? Explain your answer.

3. The "grammar of suffering" in the Old Testament includes cries, groans, and pained prayers written to God. Because pain and suffering still exist, what do you think are some stereotypes or myths that contemporary believers live with that are hindering their ability to face their suffering?

4. Suffering can be described as *deep loss*, resulting in serious diminishment to one's life. What kinds of loss have resulted in diminishment and suffering in your life?

5. If a good friend *assigns a meaning* to their suffering that you are not familiar with (or even uncomfortable with), what do you think would be the wisest response to your friend?

CHAPTER 2

Groaning Together

The Relational Ecosystem
of Sin and Suffering

By Andrew J. Schmutzer

L ooking across the landscape of God's creation, one has to agree
with the poet William Blake:

> *Everything that lives*
> *Lives not alone, nor for itself.*[1]

All created life is interconnected. It is a grand web of relationships
that reflect God's design for our world. It is richly ironic that not only is
the function of creation cohesive, but so is its brokenness.

In this chapter we will consider several aspects of God's symphony–
like created order. Then we will consider the terrible effects of sin that
now reverberate throughout this created order. We will investigate what
we call the *relational ecosystem* of God's creation. Like the roots of a massive tree, we are forced to recognize sin's amazing ability to penetrate deep
into the crevices of human life, especially the relational tissues of our
lives. Suffering is intricately woven into the fabric of our relationships.

CREATION AS A RELATIONAL ECOSYSTEM

Based on creation theology, the relational ecosystem refers to the interrelationship of all created life. We can identify four key areas in this relational ecosystem:

1. God with humankind;
2. man with woman;
3. humankind with animals; and
4. humankind with the ground.

Some core texts here are Genesis 1–3; Psalms 8, 104, and 148. Creation texts reveal the "core bindings" that define personhood, the function of relationships, ethics, and our human stewardship that is grounded in the creation mandate (Gen. 1:28). With so many stories illustrating the horrors of sin in Scripture, it is refreshing to know other texts celebrate what God *intended*. So the salvation that God provides in Christ has more to do with healing and restoration than mere rescue and deliverance. As we will see, sin's consequences tear apart the relational ecosystem (cf. Rom. 8:19–22). Our suffering is the relational *alienation* that sin causes.[2]

The Divine–Human Encounter

A personal God necessarily works relationally. From the character of his inner–trinitarian fellowship to the *functional* outworking of relationships in human culture, relationships are primary to the divine–human encounter. This relational substructure is evident in Israel's *Shema* about loving God and serving neighbor. What emerges is an inseparable pairing of divine and human interaction. Worship and ethics are indivisible (Deut. 6:5; Lev. 19:18; Mark 12:30). Our relating is very Godlike. It was always meant to work that way. I agree with the claim of Thiselton, "God created humankind because God loves us and chose to reach forth, as it were, out of himself, to create beings 'other' than himself, *to commune with them and enjoy fellowship with them.*"[3]

This relational God constructed creation to function relationally. When we view creation through this relational lens, God's words, actions, pain, and promises take on a new significance. In creation, *what* God does is a reflection of *who* God is. Now we can appreciate, in a fresh way, the unique relationship God has with his image bearers and "the implications this divine–human encounter has for relationships between human beings" (Gen. 9:5–6).[4]

To contemplate suffering is to reflect on personhood as God intended, and so life as God intended it to be. MacMurry rightly observes that "personal existence is *constituted* by the relation of persons"—the personal self has "its being in relationships."[5] These implications run deep, both for suffering and healing. *Being–in–relation* is how life is wired. Even in our pain and suffering, "individuals do not remember alone but as members of a group."[6] To find healing and closure is to find community. What God orchestrated to work together, sin has shred apart. Can a good God really let this happen? Acknowledging these realities, we turn to some specific observations in Genesis 1–3.

The Doxology of Creation (Gen. 1:1–2:3)

Genesis 1:1–2:3 depicts God's creative acts through majestic separations (vv. 3–31), with humankind as the eighth and climactic creative work of God (1:26–31). Repeated refrains include: *announcement* ("and God said"), *divine decree* ("let there be"), *report* ("and God made"), *evaluation* ("and it was good"), and *temporal frame* ("there was evening and there was morning").

The cumulative effect of these refrains reveals: (1) only through the agency of God's "word" does anything take form (cf. John 1:1–18); (2) the world is created according to divine will or "moral imagination" of the Creator[7]; (3) *Elohim* is transcendent over his creation, not co-extensive with what he makes—he is the universal ruler (cf. Ps. 95:3–7); (4) God's creation was "good," fulfilling God's divine intention (cf. Ps. 104); (5) God created the world in a logical and orderly manner, from distant (Gen. 1:2) to the dearest (1:26), inanimate to the animate, chaos to rest, silence to blessing; and (6) God's realm and the realm of humans are not radically distinct. This means that "divine sovereignty in creation is understood, not in terms of absolute divine control, but as sovereignty that gives power over to the created *for the sake of a relationship of integrity*.[8]

So the first exposition is potent *theocentric* doxology. A testimony of world–making overtures clearly lies at the foundation of this portrait, one capable of spawning numerous creation psalms (see Psalms 8, 19, 65, 104, 148). The first exposition highlights several significant themes.

God's Act of Speech

In the first exposition, the speech of God (Gen. 1:3, 6, 9, 11, etc.) is the work of God.[9] Whatever *Elohim* commands is enacted; to speak is to manifest. The Creator's mighty acts are recounted as God's declaration of "good" (vv. 10, 12, 18, 25, 31). This is life–nourishing functionality, not mere aesthetic quality. "Good" and the culminating "very good" (v. 31), after human creation, is the divine *evaluation* that the divine intention has been achieved. A few canonical steps away, the great doxology calls: "Praise him in his mighty heavens. Praise him *for his acts of power*" (Ps. 150:1b–2a NIV).

In the first triad of days, God's speech–work separates formless chaos into *static spheres* as "space is arranged into vertical layers."[10] The second triad populates the first, the entire week of which establishes the theological and cosmological basis for Israel's religious calendar: "lights in the vault of the sky" to "serve as signs to mark sacred times, and days and years" (1:14 NIV; cf. Ex. 16:22–30; 20:8–11). The seven days of God's creative work represent the liturgical week of Israel, the day beginning in the evening and the week crowned by the Sabbath. The seven–day format models the core sacral structures of both time and space, reflecting that of the temple, with the final day representing a temporal "holy of holies."[11] John Goldingay helpfully observes:

> The importance of time is not its speed in reaching a goal, *but its rhythm in relationship* with objects in creation. Thus time highlights

interrelationships in creation. . . . The ideal rhythm of time is woven into the pattern of creation, including day and night (Gen 1:3–5), Sabbath (Gen 2:1–3), and months and years (Gen 1:14–19). These rhythms are not obstacles to be overcome by humans. On the contrary, human life is enriched when it corresponds to the temporal patterns of creation.[12]

God Sustains What He Makes

Though *creatio ex nihilo* is important to Christian doctrine, Genesis itself does not contain this fully developed doctrine. We must realize that "darkness" and "the deep" are present when the first exposition comes "on line" (1:2). We have seen that God's creation was a series of separations—*only performed through divine speech.* God's work is always toward that which fosters life. For this reason, neither "darkness" nor "water" is called "good" until those respective domains are ready to nurture life (vv. 4, 10). Now we can appreciate the various elements of the relational ecosystem as they interconnect: God with humankind, man with woman, humankind with ground, and humankind with animals.

Humankind Is "Bound" to the Earth in Service

Alongside the significance of the creation mandate for humankind to be fruitful and multiply, subdue and rule (1:28), we must observe the parallel theology of *creatio continua*. This is the ongoing creative governance that is also a core theological reality. The report of God's performative speech includes: "separated" (1:6, 7, 14, 18), "made" (1:7, 16, 25), "set" (1:17), "created" (1:21, 27), and also his attentive seeing (1:4, 10, 18, 31),[13] "form[ing]" (2:7), "plant[ing]" (2:8), and "install[ing]" (2:15). However, neither creation nor its development flows in one direction. Necessary for ongoing creative governance is *a mutuality of vocation*; human vocation also includes the nonhuman.[14] Days Three and Six, for example, are unique: the *land*, a secondary agent, actually produces vegetation (Day Three, 1:11) and then produces living creatures (Day Six, 1:24).[15] Calling this *an interdependent mutuality of vocation*, Terence E. Fretheim explains:

> In these cases, God speaks *with* that which has *already* been created
> and involves them in further creative activity. This is mediate rather
> than immediate creation; it is creation from within rather than cre-
> ation from without; God's creating is not unilateral, it is multilateral.
> *The nonhuman creatures have a genuine vocational role...*the waters
> and earth do actually participate with God in acts of creation.[16]

In the creation mandate, the power of blessing is heard in the direct
discourse of God's first words to humankind. Here is felt the obligation
of task, the privilege of royal assignment in the sanctity of a creative
work with a partnering–God. Ironically, the verbs "to serve" and "to
keep/guard" require that humankind (the subjects) expend their efforts for the well–being of the object (the ground). Humankind was
not installed in the garden to indulge himself, but, as Block puts it, "the
purpose clause of Genesis 2:15 reverses the roles; he was put into the
garden to serve it and to guard it, presumably to protect it from inside
and outside threats."[17] Goldingay summarizes these important points:

> God's making the world was like a king's planting a farm or park or
> orchard, into which God put humanity to 'serve' the ground and to
> 'serve' and 'look after' the estate. . . . Serve, service/servitude, servant
> are thus relational or social terms, pointing to the worker's relation-
> ship to the boss rather than to the activity of the work or the end
> result. . . . By implication all human beings are servants of God, and
> there is no suggestion that they are designed to be under each other's
> mastery. Explicit 'service' starts in the second story, where humanity
> is created to 'serve' the ground (2:5, 15).[18]

God included humankind in service that he could have done himself, but chose instead to incorporate other agents for creation's development. Clearly, Gen. 2:5, 15, and 3:23 "assume that the earth *needs
work*; the earth was never designed to be on 'auto–pilot.'"[19] In fact, Gen.
1:28 is framed by reference to the "earth/ground." For humankind, the
realm of their stewardship remains distinctly earthbound. Genesis 1
represents a *tripartite* cosmology (cf. Pss. 8:7–8; 148):

Domain #3:	*Sky*	(Day 1 [vv. 1–5], Day 4 [vv. 14–19])
Domain #2:	*Water*	(Day 2 [vv. 6–8], Day 5 [vv. 20–23])
Domain #1:	*Earth*	(Day 3 [vv. 9–13], Day 6 [vv. 24–31])

Significantly, we find all three domains in Gen. 1:28. ("sea, sky, earth"), but their very order is rearranged relative to the creative process in Genesis 1 (i.e., "sky, sea, earth"). This emphasizes the solidarity of humankind with the *earthly* domain and its creatures of Day Six.[20]

This raises several implications for a theology of suffering, agency, and restoration. The Creator's presence is not coextensive *with* nature (i.e., pantheism), nor is his transcendence detached *from* his creation (i.e., deism). In both extremes, suffering remains unaddressed! Because of various pagan notions, Christian tradition has, unfortunately, emphasized an unaffected and impassible deity. In turn, this has separated nature from humankind, work from worship, temporal from eternal, and so creation from restoration.[21] For so many faith traditions, this has resulted in a dualism of spirit versus body. The effect is one that minimizes the reality of pain and suffering, resulting in a *fragmented universe* and a muted doxology (cf. Psalms 145–150; Phil. 2:10–11). But the very laws of nature are a sign of God's faithfulness in upholding his creation.[22] God did not prevent Adam from making certain choices, nor does God suspend moral or natural laws today. God continues to work within the relational ecosystem he initiated in creation.

Humankind is "Bound" to God in Stewardship

Human agency is clearly seen in the creation mandate (1:28; cf. 1:26–28).[23] God is the cosmic King (Deut. 4:32; Rev. 4:11) and his speech to his heavenly court (Gen. 1:26) reveals his creative intention (1 Kings 22:19–22; Isa. 6:8).[24] Only with humankind does God talk this way as "Let us" replaces the impersonal "Let there be." Humankind is the terrestrial counterpart to God's heavenly gathering (cf. Pss. 29, 148).[25] Patterned after God, humans serve their King by modeling the divine to the world (Ps. 115:16). In the biblical theology of Genesis, being an image bearer is primarily *functional*—there is a royal task entrusted to people (Ps. 8:5). But being an image bearer is also *relational*.[26]

Notice how humankind serves in the middle of this dynamic relational ecosystem that is bound to God (the commissioner), marriage (the partner), the earth (the cultivated), and the animals (the ruled). From Genesis to Revelation, these are intended to operate together. Image is tied to "ruling" (Gen. 1:26b NIV, *radah*), but never as a commission to rule other people. This is the purpose expressed in the phrase: "so that they may rule" (v. 26a, cf. NIV).[27] Humankind serves as God's *under-king*, charged with the care of creation, care of neighbor, and worship of God. Humankind's mission is a merging of two primary elements: *endowment* (for reproduction) and *commission* (for governance). Notice, however, that "ruling" envelope this entire passage as the divine discussion about rule (v. 26b) then echoes in God's audible blessing to rule (v. 28b). Here, "subduing" (*kavash*, v. 28a) is the task of earthly *development*, through domestication and cultivation.[28] Humankind is called to a royal imitation of their Creator through production and care—"When Adam had lived 130 years, he had a son in his own likeness, in his own image" (5:3 NIV). In the context of the creation mandate, "subdue" is not oppressive, but indicates the use of all the economic and cultural potential associated with land.[29]

The divine image founds a unique relationship between the Creator and his agents. It is their image as under-kings that gives humankind both moral vision and functional capacity to achieve an order worthy of their Creator. They *cocreate* with God (4:1; 5:3). Theirs is not a dominion of power, but power for dominion. So the psalmist knows well: "You have given him dominion over the works of your hands; you have put all things under his feet" (Ps. 8:6).

Three Key Observations

Again, we can make some significant observations at the intersection of suffering and image bearing. First, notice that the pronoun "our" (v. 26a) underscores *a theomorphic perspective* (i.e., humans in the form of God), as "our image" and "our likeness" fix their point of reference in God, not in "him" or "herself."[30] As a result, how humans treat each other really matters—we are emblems of God! Suffering and criminal treatment matter to God. He knows when humans oppress each other (Gen. 4:10–11). Not surprisingly, human pain and suffering deeply affect the life of God, throughout all of Scripture (Gen. 6:5; Acts 9:4). Furthermore, immoral actions can "pollute" the ground in the relational ecosystem (Num. 35:33–34).

This passage also portrays *a holistic personhood.* We do not *have* God's image, we *are* God's image. But gender is not image, nor does God have gender. *Rather, we are image bearers who have gender, not genders who have image.* In fact, the narrator's report culminates with the genders in unity ("them," Gen. 1:27c). Notice that *God addresses them as persons, not genders.*[31] This holism has been lost in contemporary thought. In society today, gender and sexuality are horribly skewed, because gender has been isolated from accountability to all parties in the relational ecosystem: isolated from a Creator's design, from community, cordoned off from personhood, and even separated from self! But creation theology never sanctions mere human love toward anything, be it a rock, a computer, or one's same gender. God's boundaries are good and intended to foster life on the Creator's terms, not human notions of "designer-sexuality" or *omni-affection* (Gen. 1:26; 2:23–24). Jesus makes this clear in the way he quotes Gen. 1:27 and 2:24 (Matt. 19:4–5). The role of marriage in the relational ecosystem remains.

A further observation is about *the danger of immaterial personhood.* We lose all bases for addressing the *physical* aspect of suffering if we define image without any embodiment. A theology of suffering must work with the entire embodied experience of personhood. After all, it is the body, not the soul, that is the temple of the Holy Spirit (1 Cor. 6:19–20). Suffering marks our bodies, so healing must also work with the physical realities of our bodies, with the dignity and design that creation gives it.

CELEBRATION, DISRUPTION, RESTORATION

The second exposition (Gen. 2:4–4:26) is a "close–up" of the relational, covenant making "Lord God," who "forms" the man from the dust (2:7). God did not rest from creating by withdrawing from creation or dominating it. Rather he genuinely feels a need in the man's life (2:18). God "allows himself to be affected, to be touched by each of his creatures. He adopts the community of creation as his own milieu."[32] Given the image of God that defines the royal status of humankind, the relational ecosystem is a binding force, intended for the betterment of all life.

The relational ecosystem of creation "assumes from the start that it is together and only together that human responsibilities . . . can be carried out."[33] It is together that man and woman find identity, and it is together that their identity is fractured. In the second exposition, moral cohesion is brought through divine law (instruction, 2:16–17). These are God's boundaries for a community under obligation (Gen. 2:15). Within the relational ecosystem, law actually fosters relationship.

Sadly, human rebellion will permanently change relationships within the ecosystem, but not terminate relationships. As Kessler insightfully explains, even at a national level, "Israel's inability to keep the law flawlessly does not take Yahweh by surprise. . . . *Torah* was given as a means of *maintaining* rather than *establishing* a relationship."[34] So Genesis can be viewed as a "prequel" to Israel's Sinai instruction with God. At Sinai, national values extend the cosmic principles God already started in creation. Not surprisingly, then, there is provision for *relational repair* with individuals or groups who fail to abide by God's standards (Gen. 9:5–6).[35] For God's creation, the law renewed to Noah (vv. 1–2) assures that moral order reflects the created order, thereby sustaining and extending God's creative work.

Using Wisdom, Knowledge, and Understanding

God was the Master–Workman from the beginning (Job 38:4). So we read in Proverbs: "Then I was constantly at his side. I was filled with delight day after day, rejoicing always in his presence, rejoicing in his whole world and delighting in mankind" (8:30–31 NIV).

Humans truly partner with God in his rule over creation. Personified wisdom "rejoices" in his entire world and "delights" in the contribution of humankind, who mimics God's creative–workmanship (Ps. 8:46). In fact, the core ingredients of *wisdom, understanding,* and *knowledge* that God used in the creation of the cosmos (Prov. 3:19–20) are precisely the same three "tools" that people use when they build (Prov. 24:3–4; cf. Ex. 31:1–11).[36] With obedience, human work matches God's designs, achieving dynamic quality through God's Spirit (Gen. 1:2; Ex. 35:30–35). Small wonder that man celebrated in God's design of woman!

Man Is "Bound" to the Woman in Celebration

Upon God's creation of woman, the man uses the instrument of speech to display, to some degree, the image of God in poetic celebration (Gen. 2:23):

> This one is finally bone of my bone . . . this one shall be called "woman," for from man was taken this one. (author's translation)

On the one hand, the man's words are a testimony, an exuberant announcement in the very presence of his attending Creator. With the woman now in the relational ecosystem, she is a source of utter delight. But notice, this is also the man's *evaluation*—this time God gives the assessment of divine creation over to the man! The serpent got it wrong, God does not hoard his power (3:5); instead, he shares necessary power for interdependent relationship.

Only with someone like him is the man heard speaking, for the first time! This reveals the richness of the relational ecosystem. Sharing and receiving someone's voice forms a special connection (Song 2:14; John 10:27). What the reader hears is the *sacrament of surprise*, necessary for healthy sexuality in marriage. In sexual deviance, it is precisely the lack of created boundaries that no longer brings the delight of "this one"—Adam's sacrament of surprise. In the Old Testament, the face (*panim*) could be the most important part of a person's body. The "face" was a relational concept referring to the entire person.[37] In the Song of Songs, one hears the "lover" declare, "Let me see your face, let me hear your voice" (2:14). By design, intimacy was stirred in these gardens (Song 4:16; 6:2).

The Seventh Day, God's Rest, and Humankind's Example

On the seventh day (2:1–3), "the heavens and the earth were completed" (2:1 NASB; cf. 1:1). While the creation of humankind is the climactic work of God (1:26–31), the Sabbath rest is the climax of God's creative week (note "seventh," 3x). For several reasons, this day is special. First because it is called "holy" (2:3), a sacred time, not the standard "good." This day is unique also because the usual *temporal frame* is absent—there is no "evening and morning." This sets up some crucial implications for relationship amid struggle. As Dumbrell explains:

> The rest on the seventh day into which God enters is given implicitly to humankind (since the end of the day is not noted). Such rest cannot be achieved by toil or by trial; indeed, humankind's rest in Genesis 2 simply cannot be rest from work already done. . . . The Sabbath day provides the *ongoing context* in which the ideal life of the garden takes place *and is to be perpetuated*. God's own rest is the divine endorsement of creation, and *God's willingness to enter into fellowship with humanity*.[38]

God's rest establishes ordering and worship as a cosmic ethic, a partnership with humankind that leans into the eschatological future. As Fretheim notes, "Creation may be 'finished' (2:1), but that does not mean that God's work has come to an end."[39] Israel's national Sabbath of cessation from work (Ex. 20:8–11) "is grounded in the very structure of creation as ordered and blessed by YHWH" (cf. Ex. 16:27–30; 31:12–17).[40] Inclusive of all life, Sabbath rest also extends to the animals from the very outset (Ex. 20:8–11). Created on the sixth day with the animals, humankind is bound to the care of the animals. One even reads in Proverbs, "A righteous man has regard for the life of his animal, but even the compassion of the wicked is cruel" (12:10 NASB). In fact, so dynamic is this Sabbath movement, it culminates in the tabernacle construction (Ex. 31:3–17), connecting "world–building" and "sanctuary–building." The tabernacle is even announced on the Sabbath by Moses and "filled" in six days, all under the active agency of the Spirit of God.[41] Israel's Sabbath functioned as a temporal shrine, a weekly place of intimate communion with God.[42] But the Sabbath also fueled an ethic of intervention for the suffering of others as Israel's spiritual *celebration* became Jesus' opportunity for physical *restoration* (Luke 6:6).

The Relational Ecosystem Breaks Apart

In the garden–sanctuary, foundational "bindings" are broken by human rebellion (Gen. 3:1–19). Relational fracture is evident in every part of created life: spiritually, socially, environmentally, and even with the personal self. Profound shame now stifles life. We must see these fractures more closely.

In the theology of creation, one's place of origin determines character and purpose.[43] With "no man to work the ground" (2:5b), cultivation awaited the cultivator. So the "human" (Heb. *'adam*) is extracted from the "humus" (Heb. *'adamah*, 2:7). With the earth as his point of reference, the earthling is installed in a particular place "to work it and take care of it" (2:15 all NIV). Adam cultivates the fertility of the soil. Similarly, the woman is "taken out of the man" (2:22); hers will be a fertility of the body—"for she was taken out of man" (2:23). The animals are also "formed out of the ground" (2:19), and they are "creatures that move along the ground" (1:25, 30). Humankind and animals are created on the same day, from the same source, and share the same sweeping blessing tied to the earthly domain of Day Six, the realm of human stewardship.

In truth, "sin" is not even mentioned until Cain's exile (4:7, 13–14). Instead, it is rebellion that shatters the relational ecosystem; it is a loss of relational trust that shatters the harmony in the web of relationships and brings God's judgment on all relationships. Both functional and relational, the *compensatory judgments* of 3:14–19 follow the order of transgression (serpent → woman → man; 3:1–7). Over twenty plural verbs and pronouns fall silent in 3:8–19—community among God, man, and woman clearly has been shattered! Sarna helpfully observes that the judgment for each party not only (1) affects what is of central concern in the life of that entity, but also (2) regulates an external relationship.[44] So there is some measure of correspondence between the offense and the judgment; between the point of origin and the future orientation. Further, relational hostility will now exist between humans and the serpent (3:15). For her part, the woman will pursue fertility amid relational antagonism with the man (3:16b). Similarly, the man now pursues the soil's fertility amid its antagonism (3:17–19). Their points of origin no longer offer security or fulfillment. Though Adam and Eve are exiled from the garden–sanctuary, Kaiser rightly claims that the mandate to work the ground is "intact."[45] That said, caring–work (2:15) has degenerated to "painful toil" (3:17; 5:29 NIV); horticulture has diminished to exhaustion, regardless of one's profession.

While the creation mandate remains in effect, pain and alienation now bind the relationships (Gen. 5:29; Eccl. 2:23). Their collective pain and suffering is staggering. The man's "painful toil" (*'tsabon*, 3:17) working the ground repeats her "pains" (*etseb*) enduring childbirth (3:16a). A final bond is ruptured when the couple is "banished" from the presence of the Lord (3:23). Once Abel's blood soaks into "the ground" (4:10), it "will no longer yield its crops" for Cain (4:12 NIV), and ultimately a pervasive "wickedness" reigns in "the human heart" (6:6), stunningly matched by the "pain" (*atsab*) of the Lord's grieving "heart" (6:6). There is no domain of life that is not marred by the effect of human sin and rebellion. Sin has ecological and cosmic effects—from Creator to creature, the entire relational ecosystem now suffers (6:7; Rom. 8:22).

Evil and Suffering in the Sin–Portfolio

In order to address the extent of brokenness in the relational eco-system, we must move beyond notions of sin as some isolated "event." This means we must also rethink the autonomous self and the legal equation of "sin–as–crime." Sin is *anti–creation*. As Plantinga states it, "Sin is disruption of created harmony and then resistance to divine restoration of that harmony."[46] There is a complex "sin–portfolio" that must be faced. Significantly, sin and suffering have a life cycle, an environmental logic that moves from:

1. the *act,*
2. through the resulting *guilt,*
3. to the perversion that is brought to others as a *consequence.*[47]

While sin operates in its own portfolio, it is important to realize that not all sin is equally devastating. The effects can be construed as: *sin (act) → corruption (evil) → pollution (spoiling).* The devastation factor depends on the nature of the sin and the life cycle it unleashes in the social environment. *Evil is the resulting corruption of that environment,* the exploding and imploding of the ecosystem that follows a despoiling act.[48] "Moral evil is social and structural as well as personal: it comprises a vast historical and cultural matrix" of derived effects—"*we both discover evil and invent it; we both ratify and extend it.*"[49]

Pollution follows on corruption. So for example, a father's incest of his daughter not only damages his child, it also pollutes his own marriage bed. Sex has been perverted at numerous levels, now. There is no private sin. The effects of sin can ripple out like shock waves. When one considers the larger relational ecosystem, there is no "contained sin."

Facing Sin's Organic Continuum

The practical implications of sin living on in the relational ecosystem must be understood and not avoided. Long after sin may have been forgiven, the consequences can live on as part of the *organic continuum* of sin. This points to the shortsightedness of the "blame–justification" model to address the multilayered nature of evil. As Mark E. Biddle explains:

> The biblical notion of sin as a mishandling of the uniquely human calling to bear the image of God in creation implies responsibility not only to God—first and foremost, of course—but also, in fulfillment of the call, to other people and to the created order. *Forgiveness must, therefore, include remedy and healing . . . [for] the real injury that outlives the act of wrongdoing.*[50]

When it comes to suffering there are usually ambiguities related to sin that simply do not fit with a juridical model of "sin–as–crime." The more pervasive danger of postmodernism's "turn to the subject"—the preoccupation with "I"—runs aground here: when the autonomous self remains unaccountable or some consequences of evil are minimized because the harm was "unintentional," then that act is placed beyond the realm of redemption.[51] The "I" acknowledges no "we." The reality of suffering consequences, even after forgiveness, is a tough biblical truth that contemporary faith struggles to accept.[52]

Sin "Matures"

Sin must be checked or it will "mature." From Cain's "banishment" beyond even his father's exile (3:23; 4:14, 16) to stories like the rape of Tamar (2 Samuel 13), the continuum of sin naturally matures into further results—like the "sin of the Amorites" that had not yet *matured* (Gen. 15:16; cf. Rom. 1:18–32). Evil's corrupting effects twist and pervert reality. So the escalation of sin and suffering in Genesis 1–11 illustrates:

(1) children impacted by a parent's sin,
(2) creating conditions that negatively affect the children's options, and thus
(3) predispose the children toward certain choices,
(4) which contribute destructively to their personal lives.[53]

In summary, God is eager to forgive, but he does not suspend the moral and physical principles that are built into the fabric of the relational ecosystem. Sin twists reality and passes on a contorted environment to those who come after. This, in turn, limits their freedom to choose rightly.[54] Is anybody prepared to say that Lot's daughters and their incestuous relationship with their father was *not* related to their exposure to horrific sin in Sodom? As Biddle notes, environment is not destiny, but it is predisposing.[55] What we see today is sin lingering in the world, distorting perceptions, clouding perceptions, posing inauthentic possibilities, skewing systems, and perpetuating itself. God's grace and forgiveness given to one generation does not simply halt the sequence of effects brought into the next generation.[56] Think of how racism, alcoholism, or cultic perversions leave their mark on people in the ensuing generations.

The Distortion of Worship

When creation reverberates with doxology throughout Scripture (e.g., Ps. 95:3–7; Rev. 4:11), it is important to pause and consider how sin distorts our worship. When it comes to sin and suffering, pollution corrupts by *addition*, actually combining what should be kept apart.[57] This polluting effect inhibits worship through idolatry. "In idolatry a third party gets in between God and the human persons, adulterating an exclusive loyalty."[58] Like image bearers calling animals their god or the Israelites worshiping a golden calf, the intruding dynamic compromises the intended relationships with God by contaminating individuals, severing communities, and so *distorting the proper orientation to the Caring King*.[59] Whenever personhood is misplaced, the symphony of doxology is muted. This is described well by Alistair McFadyen:

> Sin is hence, not so much free choice, as spiritual disorientation of the whole person at the most fundamental level of life–intentionality and desire. . . . In all our relations, we live out an active relation or misrelation to God, we enter the dynamic of worshipping God or

other forces and realities. Sin is therefore living out an active misrelation to God. . . . Genuine transcendence, and so the grounds for genuine joy, are blocked.[60]

GOD'S GRACIOUS INVOLVEMENT, SIN'S TERRIBLE TOLL

Looking at creation reveals the identity of God, his mission for humankind, and the depth of human community that comprises the relational ecosystem. Our analysis of this relational ecosystem has helped us, in turn, face the sobering aftereffects of sin—what has dismantled these relationships. We must learn to speak of *actual sin*—pain and suffering in our lived experience—not just original sin. In conclusion, we should note several key points.

First, far from being aloof, *God is caught up with all of his creatures in the relational ecosystem*, constantly moving toward his purposes of renewal.[61] Observe the following events from Genesis:

- God involves humankind in caring responsibilities for creation (1:28; 2:15).
- God dialogues with humankind (3:8–13).
- God gives counsel to help humans avoid their own destructive behavior (4:6–7).
- God regularly ameliorates judgment (3:21; 4:15, etc.).
- God suffers a broken heart (6:6).
- God chooses Noah, guides the building process, brings the animals, and even closes the ark's door (6:8, 13, 14–16; 7:9, 16).
- God hangs his war bow in the sky (same Hebrew word) upside down, away from people—that he "will see" (8:16)—in covenant disarmament for "all living creatures of every kind" (8:15).
- God promises not to add to human suffering and limits his divine options for addressing sin and violence (8:21–22).

Second, *wisdom is part of the very character of God*, who works with skill and beauty. God remains relationally active in world-renewal, but God does not do what his image bearers can accomplish in his power (Ex. 31:2; 35:30; 36:1–2). So one can look to this wise Creator for needed wisdom and skill in living (Prov. 8:1–21) and to creation itself for lessons in wisdom (Prov. 6:6).[62] Even when people cannot understand God's activity, God's wisdom invites a response of confident trust despite the sin and suffering in life (Job 38–41).

Third, *human beings are God's unique representatives within God's creation.* Only with them does the Creator interact in speech (Gen. 1; 3). Sin twists the most majestic aspect of being image bearers: the capacity to form relationships. "There is no true being without communion."[63] Humans rule for God and are to extend his created order, pushing back the effects of suffering. Humankind is to respond to its Creator with celebration and worship. As Gen. 1:14–15 anticipates festivals in the Israelite calendar, so Gen. 2:1–3 anticipates Sabbath relationship. In short, God's representatives are to express rich relationship to God through work, rest, and worship.[64]

Fourth, *believers in the community of faith are called to not only live in* eager anticipation, *but also adopt a stance of resistance to oppression, evil, and injustice.* God's creation is still afflicted with profound suffering. One day this suffering will be removed and creation will be characterized by peace, harmony, and the knowledge of God (Isa. 11:6–9). Then, alienated nations will rejoice in God's goodness and justice (Isa. 42:4; 52:10).[65]

Fifth, *sin is like blindness: it brings additional constraints to the liveliness of living that should be normal.* Sin is *not* "doing no harm to anyone," as the popular idea states. Sin is better seen in its destructive effects. Ultimately, sin is a self–destructive breach of fellowship with God and consequent alienation from God and other people.[66] The implications are significant: beyond a mere act, *sin is an attitude toward God that paralyzes obedience, fellowship, and worship.* This also means that *sin is corporate alienation and destruction of the relational ecosystem, and not an individual act,* in the popular moralistic notions of sin.[67] God watches his children like a concerned (and angered!) parent, watching their child in the process of destroying him or herself.[68]

Sixth, *the effects of sin also manifest themselves* in our bodies, *not just as a legal form to be "deleted" in forgiveness.* Even personal and social distresses are written in bodies. The ability to discern others and oneself in relation to others is deeply connected with embodiment—"Persons are bodies with a first-person perspective."[69] In the words of Elizabeth Boase, "Somatic expressions have communicative power. The Body acts as a 'mediating symbolic device. ' . . . [E]mbodied language forms a bridge between the personal and the transpersonal, the bodily and the cultural."[70] We must learn the body's language of suffering and employ this suffering in spoken and written metaphors—just as the book of Lamentations does. *We must listen to various forms of physical suffering and learn the language of the diminished and overwhelmed body.*

AMID PAIN AND SUFFERING

1. Why is the reality of the *relational ecosystem* so important for understanding God's creation (positively) and the character of sin (negatively)? How does viewing God as *relationally engaged* affect the way you can relate to God?

2. Terence E. Fretheim referred to the way creation is connected to man and woman and responds to God as *an interdependent mutuality of vocation.* What do you think are the strengths and weaknesses of this?

3. If humankind had "served" and "guarded" the garden as God intended, how might relationships look different than they do now? Why do you think God gave humankind opportunity to rule and develop his creation, when God could have done it all himself?

4. When we explored the nature of the image of God, it was stated: "We are image bearers who have gender, not genders who have image." What are some concrete examples of how society has switched these two?

5. We observed that popular faith has abandoned a relational view of sin, and only sees individual acts. Why is this such a dangerous misunderstanding of sin? What personal example can you give?

CHAPTER 3

The Suffering of God

Compassion in Vulnerability

By Andrew J. Schmutzer

Nothing illustrates or honors suffering like a story. And, when we are trying to understand our pain and our trials, we look for a story that will be revealing.[1] Some define life, God, and suffering through empirical information or an "act of God." Others use cultural stories and myths. Most importantly, we need to understand how Scripture presents its redemptive drama.

If, instead, we allow the Scripture to become fragmented, it is in danger of being diluted and absorbed into our individual narratives.[2] To be sure, suffering always "writes" a powerful personal story—which Christians need to hear in far more testimonies!—yet stories are not what redeem people's lives. Stories show how lives are redeemed. Understanding the Bible's story of the suffering of God is all about how God presents himself in Scripture, and this is a *theo*–drama far more riveting than most know! To get here, though, we need to do some digging.

EXPLORING STORY

In the Greek play *The Frogs*, Aristophanes writes about the god Dionysus and his slave Xanthias. They embark on a trip into the underworld to resurrect a skilled poet. As they are passing through Hades, they both claim to be gods. So they construct a decisive test: both of them will be flogged, and they conclude, "Whichever of us squeals first or even bats an eyelid isn't a god at all."[3] In other words, true deity is defined by freedom from pain and suffering.[4] But is God really this unresponsive and sealed off from pain? Is the life of God really detached from the pain of his own creation? Is this really the God of the Christian Scriptures? Assuredly not!

As one of the leaders in the anti-apartheid struggle in South Africa, Allan Aubrey Boesak discusses another kind of illustrative story. In his book *Dare We Speak of Hope?* he describes the Khoi people of the Eastern Cape. He notes three distinctives of their faith: (1) a supreme being, named Tusi-Goab, is the Giver, Protector, and Sustainer of all creation; (2) the people depend on and resonate with nature; and (3) they are aware that their "human-being-ness depend[s] on the life-giving interrelationships with other human beings."[5] Tusi-Goab fights on behalf of his creation and helpless people, not just for himself. In Tusi-Goab's fight against evil, Boesak explains:

> Though God was victorious, they say in that ancient and ongoing battle God was wounded in the knee. That is why the supreme being is called Tusi-Goab, which literally means 'wounded knee.' . . . Tusi-Goab was in the first place not a God of power and might, but of woundedness and empathetic solidarity, a God who fought on behalf of God's creation and children, and who was willing to be wounded for their sake. . . . Because Tusi-Goab is wounded, the ancients go on to say, God understands the woundedness and woundability of God's creation, of God's children. . . . It may well be that this is the answer to the oft-debated question why the Khoi in South Africa so

easily opened their hearts to the Christian gospel. . . . The lure of the Christian faith could only have been in the fact that they discovered in the crucified Jesus, with the wounds in his hands, feet, and side, so much of the image of Tusi–Goab, the God whose name is 'Wounded Knee.'[6]

Boesak poignantly argues that we can speak of hope "only if we speak of woundedness."[7] Because of the profound evil, systemic suffering, and social injustice that Boesak lived through under apartheid, he concludes, "Hope is fragile, for it is the hope of the vulnerable, of those at the bottom of the well."[8]

SERIOUSLY . . . A SUFFERING GOD?

Though hardly the theological scandal it was once, the idea of a suffering God still runs up against several roadblocks. On the one hand, these two illustrative accounts need not be multiplied in order to show how intellectually postmodern and un–omnipotent a suffering God can seem to some. On the other hand, it is stunning that some ancient non–Western religious traditions can be so richly oriented around a "wounded deity."[9] Simon Chan noted how European reflection moved sharply toward a theology of a suffering God after World War II, as a countermeasure to the unprecedented mechanized evil of the twentieth century. By contrast, Asian theology moved decidedly in the opposite direction, cordoning God off from human pain and brutal regimes, in order to oppose the fear of ancestral spirits and demonic oppression more common in Asian cultures. The transcendence and immanence of God find different emphases, depending on the *cultural codes* of a group and the meaning they attach to their suffering. Western theology has prioritized objective certainty, and this has led to a dogmatism ill equipped for the dialogic categories of a *relational* theology.

Much of the problem has been the tendency of Western Christian theology to view God in categories of *rational abstraction and political triumphalism*—categories that cannot accept the affectability of God or the Khoi people and their God with a "wounded knee."[10] Regarding this, Markos makes a keen observation:

> We post–Reformation, post–Enlightenment Christians are too often uncomfortable with such nature talk. On the one hand, we fear that our doctrines will become so diluted with pagan elements that Christianity will fade into the realm of myth. On the other hand, we are suspicious of any language that resembles pantheism—*not so much because we are Christians as because we are children of a modernist world that has defined nature as a thing to be studied rather than loved, and the unseen world as a non-thing to be explained away or, better, ignored.* Our fears are not totally baseless, but fears they are, and they often prevent us from understanding the deep hunger that draws so many into the precincts of the New Age.[11]

But the God of biblical orthodoxy functions at neither end of this spectrum: New Age vagueness or classic austereness.[12] The way men and women within the laity long to relate to their approachable God seems ultimately dashed to the ground beneath a menacing "bar–of–justice" theology. Where is the tender "Shepherd of the sheep" (Heb. 13:20 NIV) who "gathers the lambs . . . and carries them close to his heart" (Isa. 40:11 NIV)? This same paradigm is charged to church leaders, "being examples to the flock" (1 Peter 5:3). This is the same God of *both* Testaments, and he still comes to the aid of frail sheep.

THE VULNERABLE GOD

It is our contention that God relates to his creation in willing vulnerability. From his committed relationship with his rebellious creatures God experiences an inevitable emotional pain. Further, we claim that a *theology of the suffering of God* is evident throughout the testimony of Scripture, not just in the passion of the crucified Lord Jesus, God's Son.[13] This chapter will explore numerous biblical passages, rather than pursue abstract philosophical or metaphysical arguments for divine perfection, simplicity, ultimate power, or perfect freedom—arguments that take on a logic of their own, usually detached from the real drama of biblical texts.[14]

Observing the suffering of God in Scripture is not a simple enterprise. Considering the relational life of God—within the inner–Trinitarian relationship and among God's standard human agents—requires a hermeneutic of *discernment*, not *deduction*; a relational theology, not objectivist epistemology.[15]

Metaphors have raised another problem. The claim that metaphors are simply accommodative language to speak of God is linguistically and hermeneutically naïve. As Caird points out, "We have no other language besides metaphor with which to speak about God."[16] Fretheim helpfully explains, "Metaphors do reveal an essential continuity with the reality which is God." The real danger, however, "is either interpreting metaphors literally in every respect or (more commonly today) *denying any essential relationship between the metaphor and God.*"[17] The interpreter must determine where the point of comparison lies. "But to conclude that such language reveals nothing of God's essential personhood makes all such language pointless."[18] When God is given human characteristics, it reveals a God who is living and personal— One who is committed to interaction with people. As Fretheim states:

> Christians should have no difficulty using such language for God, *for in Jesus Christ God has acted in a remarkably anthropomorphic way.* A direct line connects this kind of language for God and God's becoming flesh in Jesus Christ, "the image of the invisible God" (Colossians 1:15). In this human being God reveals to us most supremely who God is, how God relates to us and the world, and the depths to which God will go for our salvation.[19]

Unfortunately, classic epistemology is embarrassed by the anthropomorphic aspects of God—in both Testaments. In fact, such language has been transposed or explained away in generic notions of God.[20] But this dismissal of emotional aspects in the language for God runs into the *fallacy of circular logic*, as Kevin J. Vanhoozer explains. This hermeneutic assumes that the interpreter already knows either what God is like, or what the author of the biblical text knew God to be like, and can thus differentiate between the language that is intended to correspond to God's true nature and actions, and that which is not.[21] So any biblical text that speaks of divine possibility is simply dismissed. *But no biblical text or passage argues divine impassibility*, that is, God cannot experience emotion or suffering.[22] Broadly speaking, classical theism is itself a hermeneutic "on guard." Again, Vanhoozer explains:

> In the classic theological paradigm, the Bible and classical philosophy are seen to agree: a perfect being who has life in himself cannot suffer. Where the Bible appears to ascribe emotion or suffering to God, the tradition quickly concluded that such language must be figurative. *Classical theism thus functions as a theological hermeneutic for construing what Scripture says about the love of God.*[23]

A TRANSCENDENT YET IMMANENT AND RELATIONAL GOD

"God is love, and whoever abides in love abides in God" (1 John 4:16b). What this love requires of God toward his wayward creatures we shall have to explore.

Sadly, some "frozen categories" of biblical orthodoxy have stressed the *legal* work and *transcendent* life of God to the exclusion of his immanent presence and *relational* pain over the rebellious humankind that he came to save, through Jesus Christ. But the profile of God, popularized within every generation of theologians and pastors, is often a God who is stubbornly "other," above the fray of human ills, ablaze in glory and power—completely apart and unaffected.[24] In effect, God has been marooned on an island of unapproachable sovereignty by his own image bearers, stripped of his emotions, addressed by abstract titles, hailed in monikers of "victory," and defined by terms that are offensively negative to seeker and saint alike: *im*mutable, *im*passible, *im*peccable, *in*effable, and so on. So much definition—*via negativa*—shuns the vulnerable love and emotional spectrum of God's own person. This is not the portrait of God in Scripture.

KEY QUESTIONS

We must pause and ask some vital questions:

- *Question 1:* How does God relate to human pain, injury, violence, and involuntary suffering?
- *Question 2:* Can a God who does not or cannot experience suffering in some sense really be said to "know" the tides of pain that sweep through his own world?
- *Question 3:* How are humans to enter a genuinely personal relationship with a secluded God?
- *Question 4:* Can a God who is unable to sympathize—at cost to himself—really be said to love?
- *Question 5:* Because humans are made in the image of God, can our unique connection with God be limited to emotion or reason, or does God relate more holistically with us?

Our response to these questions: Scripture reveals great breadth and depth in the life of God. From Creator to Savior, God has always chosen to be vulnerable. In the freedom of his love toward all creation, especially humankind, this results in a spectrum of his own suffering.

These questions capture the weight of what is at stake with a God who is relationally intimate with his creation.

SOME TERMS AND TENETS

While most of these topics of our study could be expanded further, our purposes require us to at least consider some of the primary terms and tenets in this relational theology of God. First, several important terms must be defined.

- *Impassible:* used in classical theology to claim that God cannot suffer, since he cannot be affected by anything external to himself.

- *Passibility:* refers to God being affected by and responsive to the external world.
- *Pathos:* both suffering (= pain) and passion (= emotion), capable of "disturbing" pure reason.
- *Apatheia:* divine impassibility; divine constancy, expressed as immutability (= static).
- *Patripassianism:* the idea that the Father suffered with Christ.[25]
- *Panentheism:* God eternally exists in a mutually interdependent relationship with creation.[26]

Most significant is the term *impassibility*, meaning God does not experience emotion or suffering. As Placher explains it:

> Divine impassibility served two functions. It ruled out vulgar passions: no more rapes, no more private vengeance. At the same time, it preserved divine power. Part of what power seemed to mean, after all, is that one can affect others for good or ill but yet remain unthreatened by them, invulnerable. It is the most powerful ruler who is safe and secure from external threat.... For God, then, impassibility guarantees omnipotence.[27]

In other words, God feels neither pain nor pleasure from the actions of another being. But Scripture, as we shall see, actually shows otherwise. In the end, terms such as *impassible* are not helpful, as the profile of God is far more complex and interactive than such negative terms even allow. *God's love makes him willingly involved in the lives of people*—God is not stoic and unaffected. Again, however, there was a rich cultural backdrop that fueled this stoic worldview. Richard Bauckham explains the Greek philosophical thought that shaped classic theology's aversion to a suffering God:

> For the Greeks, God cannot be passive, he cannot be affected by something else, he cannot (in the broad sense) 'suffer' (*paschein*), because he is absolutely self–sufficient, self–determining and independent. . . . The connecting thought is passivity. Suffering is what comes upon one, against one's will. It is something of which one is

a passive victim. Thus suffering is a mark of weakness and God is necessarily above suffering. . . . To be moved by desire or fear or anger is to be affected by something outside the self, instead of being self-determining. . . . God cannot be subject to anything.[28]

More accurate to the biblical testimony is the claim of Thomas J. Oord, when he writes, "God acts intentionally and sympathetically" toward his creation.[29] Yet the Council of Chalcedon dismissed a God who is passible as "vain babblings," condemning those who held it.[30] But even some of the greatest creeds of contemporary faith obscure this biblical truth.

The Westminster Confession of Faith states that God is "infinite in being and perfection, a most pure spirit, invisible, without body, parts, or passions; immutable, immense."[31] This is a proud statement of *apatheia*. The intent of such platonic declarations is to "preserve" God, keep him entirely "other," and in no way subject him to suffering. But how does a "pure spirit," devoid of "passions," actually rescue his impure and frightened image bearers? What does this mean about God's relationship to the brokenness of his world and the suffering of his creatures? Even Erickson shows an unfortunate retreat into more stoic conceptions of divine personality when he speaks of God engaging in "reciprocal relationship," only to conclude: "It seems best to think of God having empathy, rather than sympathy, for humans and their feelings. In other words, he knows what we are feeling, *but does not necessarily experience that same emotion himself personally.*"[32]

Is that it? Are we left with divine cognition? Hardly. Christians of all theological stripes are rethinking the impassibility of God, for several reasons, and now argue that God is the "deeply moved 'First Mover.'"[33] Roger Olson states:

> Some evangelical theologians believe that the God of classical theism is not much better than the God of panentheism; if the latter is too dependent and weak, the former is too impersonal and despotic. How can the God of classical theism be the compassionate God of the biblical narrative, they ask?[34]

John Feinberg expresses similar dissatisfaction. For him, the claims of both classic theism and process theism are inadequate. On the one hand, the self–sufficient, immutable sovereign God of classical theism, he claims, is "too domineering, too austere, and too remote to be at all religiously adequate."[35] On the other hand, the adapting, power–sharing God of process theology, Feinberg claims, is not strong enough to sustain and revitalize hope that all things will be well. He proposes a third model: the *King who cares*. D. A. Carson also registers his methodological disagreement with impassibility:

> The methodological problem with the argument for divine impassibility is that it selects certain texts of Scripture, namely those that insist on God's sovereignty and changelessness, constructs a theological grid on the basis of those selected texts, and then uses this grid to filter out all other texts, in particular those that speak of God's emotions . . . *impassibility is seeping over into impassiveness.*[36]

The roots of contemporary impassiveness reach back into philosophical commitments of impassibility in an earlier era. Nicholas Wolterstorff describes the stance of the early Christian church: "God dwells eternally in blissful non–suffering *apatheia*," which in the end, makes Augustine's God "remarkably like the Stoic sage: devoid of passions, unfamiliar with longings, foreign to suffering."[37] So actually, *passibility*—i.e., "passionate love"—straddles the two doctrinal extremes of *apatheia* and *pathos*. This discussion illustrates how these terms have been used, most often, to isolate God from any "outside" suffering.

FIVE CORE TENETS OF A SUFFERING GOD

While we have briefly touched on some "strands" comprising a theology of the suffering of God, we can also list some core tenets of a suffering God, of a God who is actively engaged in vulnerable relationship with people.

A theology of the suffering of God draws on some core realities of

God's emotional life and activity, as portrayed in Scripture.

1. God maintains his *compassionate-love* toward people (Ex. 34:6b–7; James 5:11).
2. God is in constant *relatedness* with his creation. God's life with his creation is always incarnational. From the highly relational metaphors (Isa. 42:14; 66:13) to his theophany in human form (Gen. 18–19), God is constantly interacting, drawing himself into potential pain (Hos. 11:8).
3. God is *willingly vulnerable* toward people (Gen. 6:5–6). Jesus Christ is the fullest expression of God, and he suffered greatly (John 14:9; Phil. 2:7–8). Far from divine child abuse, Jesus Christ gave up his own life (1 John 3:16).
4. God is *affectable*, evident in his emotional life. God freely loves, and in that love is willing to risk great anguish and suffering (Ps. 78:40–41; Jer. 18:7–10).
5. God is personally *consistent*, amid great pain (Pss. 90:2; 95:9–10; Heb. 13:8).

God's availability to his creation results in a rich vulnerability matched by new initiatives of discipline and restoration. God's dialogic commitment causes him to be impinged upon—brought to areas of agony, grief, and joy.[38] However, the emotional life of God does not diminish the unchanging character of his promissory purposes.[39]

KEY BIBLICAL PASSAGES INVOLVING GOD'S SUFFERING

Here are six key passages from the Scriptures that help us to explore God's suffering.

1. Genesis 6:5–6

The LORD saw that the wickedness of man was great on the earth, and that every intent of the thoughts of his heart was only evil continually. The LORD was sorry that he had made man on the earth, and He was grieved in His heart. (NASB)

From creation onward, God is affected by the events in his world. What the Lord saw (v. 5) counters the "sons of God" who "saw" (v. 2). God is no robot or some static principle. Rather, God engages intimately with his creation, to further his transcendent purposes.[40] "Sorry" describes the emotional anguish of God (cf. Ex. 13:17; Jer. 31:19), which is further explained by the final clause: "and He was grieved in His heart" (v. 6b). God's "pained–heart" ('*atsab libbo*, v. 6) responds to humankind's "wicked–heart" (*libbo ra'*, v. 5), and recalls the first judgment involving the woman's "pain" ('*atsab*, 3:16) next to the man's "pain" ('*itsebon*, 3:17).

The *relational ecosystem* described in chapter 2 includes the pain of the brokenhearted Creator toward humans who were intended to act differently. As Fretheim writes, "God's judgment is not a detached decision . . . the judgment is a very personal decision, with all the mixed sorrow and anger that go into the making of decisions that affect the people whom one loves. Grief is always what the Godward side of judgment looks like."[41] While pre–flood humanity has a scheming heart, God responds with a wounded heart, filled with pain.[42] As Walter Brueggemann observed, God's commitment is costly:

> It has effected an irreversible change in God. . . . It is now clear that such a commitment on God's part is costly. The God–world relation is not simply that of strong God and needy world. Now it is a tortured relation between a grieved God and a resistant world. And of the two, the real changes are in God.[43]

2. Exodus 3:7–10

I have surely seen the affliction of my people . . . and have heard their cry. . . . I know their sufferings, and I have come down to deliver them. . . . The cry of the people of Israel has come to me. . . . Come, I will send you to Pharaoh that you may bring my people, the children of Israel out of Egypt.

God addresses Moses as his chosen agent, the means of Israel's deliverance. But Moses will force God into a compromise in his divine plan

(4:14). Alongside this portrait of resistance from Moses, there emerges a profound revelation of God's intimate attention.[44] In 3:7, three key verbs highlight God's full engagement on their behalf: "*seen . . . heard . . . know.*" What the narrator notes about God in 2:24–25 is *now stated from God's own mouth.* This is God's first speech since he gave Jacob permission to descend to Egypt (Gen. 46:1–4). They are not merely "sons of Israel"; instead, their "affliction . . . cry . . . and sufferings" have arisen to God as "my people"—noted twice (3:7, 10; cf. Gen. 18:21)!

There is a new level of *knowing* for God (3:7; cf. 33:12–17) that changes his relationship with his people and incites a dynamic act of redemption: "Come, I will send you" (v. 10).[45] With this spectrum of God's senses activated (v. 7) he is now physically mobilized into the very midst of their trouble.[46] The severity of Israel's oppression provokes a radical intervention from God.[47] This is a God who "come[s] down to deliver" (v. 8), incarnated in the mouth of Moses (4:11) who even has "the staff of God in his hand" (4:20)!

3. Numbers 14:2–5, 9–13, 19–20

All the Israelites grumbled against Moses and Aaron, and the whole assembly said to them, "If only we had died in Egypt! . . . We should choose a leader and go back to Egypt". . . . Then Moses and Aaron fell facedown. . . . "Only do not rebel against the LORD." . . . But the whole assembly talked about stoning them. . . . The LORD said to Moses, "How long will these people treat me with contempt? How long will they refuse to believe in me? . . . I will strike them down with a plague and destroy them. . . ." Moses said to the LORD, "In accordance with your great love, forgive the sin of these people, just as you have pardoned them from the time they left Egypt until now." The LORD replied, "I have forgiven them, as you asked." (NIV)

The grief and fear that Moses and Aaron show by falling facedown (v. 5) sets the stage for the sudden manifestation of God's glory in his wrath (v. 10; cf. Ex. 16:7). God's glory is his royal grandeur, and in the context of his anger it can appear in a storm–like theophany (1 Sam.

7:10; Ps. 29:3, 7). While God desires fellowship from his people, he does not force their obedience. So, for good reason, Joshua and Caleb passionately try to avert God's anger (v. 6). God's anger appears over five hundred times in Scripture, precisely because people use their freedom to act in rebellion and defiance against God's tender love and instruction (cf. Ex. 34:6–7; Ps. 95:8–11).

What God does next is stunning—he laments! "How long . . . contempt"; "How long . . . refuse" (v. 11); "How long will [they] grumble against me?" (v. 27). "Lament is always an integral part of the wrath of God."[48] God uses the very language of his servants who cry out to him (Pss. 6:3; 13:1–2). This is not a quest for information, but combines divine (1) *complaint* with (2) *anguish* (cf. Ex. 16:3, 7–9).[49] In fact, God's memory of past actions only intensifies the painfulness of the present. God is not a dispassionate accountant. On several occasions he genuinely struggles over what shape the people's future will take: "Why should I forgive you? Your children have forsaken me. . . . Should I not punish them for this?" (Jer. 5:7–9 NIV; cf. 2 Sam. 24:11–13; Joel 2:12–13).

Of course, it is entirely God's prerogative to activate their punishment through the standard *cause–consequence* sequence; that is, moving from announcement of judgment to *execution* of judgment. But Moses intervenes at this key juncture with a three–part plea:

1. God's reputation as a powerful deliverer is at stake (vv. 13–14).
2. Mass destruction lets the wicked determine the fate of the righteous (vv. 15–16).
3. God's revealed nature requires that God be motivated by grace as much as the need for justice (vv. 17–19).[50]

This three–part argument forms the foundation for Moses' dire request that God "forgive the sin of these people" (v. 19).[51] Observe that *Moses's request is not based on any repentance from the people*, just the magnanimous character of their covenant–keeping God (cf. Ex. 34:6–9; Neh. 9:17–19).[52] God's response to Moses is immediate and positive:

"I have forgiven them, as you asked" (v. 20). Unlike humans, God's pain and emotion do not incapacitate him. Nevertheless, forgiveness does not preclude punishment.[53] But death will come only to those who maintained disbelief in the face of God's mighty acts of deliverance (cf. Ps. 95:9). God will not "put all these people to death" (v. 15). Moses succeeded in changing God's course of action, and no priest was involved. Though still angered by their collective rebellion, this text illustrates how God "invites participation in the accomplishing of divine will."[54]

God's judgment is viewed in terms of a breakdown in personal relationship, and all the accompanying effects of anger and pain. At stake is a relationship, not a contract. "To bear the suffering, while making continuing efforts to heal the relationship, means at least that God chooses to suffer for the sake of the future of that relationship."[55]

4. Hosea 11:8–9

How can I give you up, O Ephraim? How can I hand you over, O Israel? How can I make you like Admah? How can I treat you like Zeboiim? My heart recoils within me; my compassion grows warm and tender. I will not execute my burning anger; I will not again destroy Ephraim; for I am God and not a man, the Holy One in your midst, and I will not come in wrath.

There is no greater display of God's pathos in a parent's love than Hosea 11. Not surprisingly, this is a suffering love. God's love has been obstinately shunned—past and present (vv. 1–2a). So Israel's judgment is now inevitable. Of all ironies, Israel will "return" (*shub*) to Egypt, because they refuse to "return" (*shub*) to God (v. 5; cf. 2:6–7)! Their rebellion has forced God to activate their means of destruction through Assyria (vv. 5–6). God's pain is acute: "My people are determined to turn from me. Even though they call me God Most High, I will by no means exalt them" (v. 7 NIV).

In verse 8, God begins intense self-questioning. His words are soaked with wrenching emotion. Four rhetorical questions occur in one verse, highlighting a rich paradox—he is the sovereign–broken,

God! This is turmoil, not timidity. God reconsiders the *extent* of destruction. Whereas Admah and Zeboiim were destroyed with the cities of Sodom and Gomorrah (Gen. 19:21, 25; Deut. 29:23), God's parenting–love will curb the degree of Israel's judgment. The reference to these ancient cities highlights both precedence and manner. While the wickedness of these cities caused them to be "overthrown" (*hapak*, Gen. 19:21, 25), now it is God's caring heart that is "overthrown" (*hapak*, Hosea 11:8b)! The daring use of this verb (*hapak*) describes the sudden agitation and "shake–up" of God's heart.[56]

While God begins by "pouring out his heartfelt agony" (v. 8a), he concludes by describing the sharp emotional effect Israel's pending judgment has on him—the heart of God "recoils" or "is torn" (NLT).[57] The sharp justice of the Judge is overwhelmed by the tender compassion of the Parent (cf. 1 Kings 3:26). God maintains his mysterious freedom that willingly stoops to the messiness of his wayward child. The rebellious son will not be stoned (cf. Deut. 21:18–21). The declaration that "I loved him" (Hos. 11:1a) is also mingled with persistent sorrow and, together, will prevent the final ruin of his loved ones.[58] God does not suffer as mortals do. He does not lash out to destroy the deserter, venting frustration. God's anger is restorative, not revengeful. So the boundaries represented in his "I will not" statements (three times) distinguish the balanced emotional life of the "Holy One" from humankind.[59]

Again God's pained memory shows through (Hos. 11:1–8), and causes profound suffering for God (v. 8–9).[60] In God's love, the destruction is drawn down, though they have not even repented!

5. Jeremiah 5:9:1, 10; 13:7; 14:17–18

O that my head were waters, and my eyes a fountain of tears, that I might weep day and night for the slain of the daughter of my people! (9:1)

Weeping is a social behavior, utilizing tears that are meant to be *seen*.[61] Tears are standard fare in laments (cf. Pss. 6:8; 39:12; 102:9), and this pain is evident in the book's beginning (Jer. 3:21; 4:19; 6:26; 7:29). In the "weeping poems" of Jeremiah, the parent–child relationship illuminates God's behavior and deep emotion.[62] In his ministry, Jeremiah finds God to be patient, compassionate, merciful, and long–suffering (3:12; 13:14; 15:15). Yet because God is the agent of destruction as well as lover of the nation, love and anger mingle in God's tears (cf. Jer. 31:20; Isa. 63:15).

While it can be difficult to determine *who* the speaker is in these biblical texts, if God speaks in *any* of them, then God weeps.[63] Roberts argues persuasively that God's weeping is couched in the form of "city laments" common to Mesopotamia. These laments depict deities weeping over their precious cities.[64] (The parallel to Jesus weeping outside Jerusalem should not be missed [Matt. 23:37–38; Luke 19:41–44].) In the case of Jeremiah, I believe the prophet is expressing *God's suffering*. Terence E. Fretheim's comment is a helpful guide:

> The suffering prophet and God are so interconnected that it is difficult to sort out who is speaking in many texts. Nor should one try to make too sharp a distinction. As if with one voice, prophet and God express their anguish over the suffering of the people.... These texts should be interpreted in terms of the prophet's embodiment of God's mourning.... At least, Jeremiah's mourning is an embodiment of the anguish of God, showing the people the genuine pain God feels over the hurt that his people are experiencing.[65]

The movement of Jer. 8:18–9:1 has one speaker, arguably YHWH. There are not multiple voices here (*contra* 12:1–6; 15:10–21), though the *persona* of both prophet and God may be present. Emotive phrases like "O that" (*mi–natan*) connect the close of chapter 8 with the opening of chapter 9. "Day and night" underscores the depth and duration of grief. The speaker wishes to continue weeping, uninterrupted (cf. Ps. 42:4; Lam. 2:18).[66]

The God who "exult[s]" and sings over restored Israel (Zeph. 3:17) also weeps over Israel's pending destruction. The tears are a plea for the people to turn around: "I will take up weeping and wailing for the mountains, and a lamentation for the pastures of the wilderness" (Jer. 9:10).

Again, there is no change of speaker surrounding verse 10. The people's fear of abandonment (8:19) is actually what God is about to do (12:7–8)! But rather than their leaving Jerusalem and fleeing to the wilderness (9:2), God makes a wilderness out of Jerusalem (cf. Luke 19:41–44).[67] The people "are so deeply enmeshed in evil that they lack the will to repent."[68] God is weeping and lamenting over the loss of a treasured relationship.

"But if you [pl.] will not listen, my soul will weep in secret for your pride; my eyes will weep bitterly and run down with tears, because the LORD's flock has been taken captive" (Jer. 13:17). Here the weeping, though "in secret," is noted for the entire community. Reference to "life/soul" (*nephesh*) adds to the sincerity of "secret" tears that affect the innermost parts. "They arise from an interior emotion rather than an insincere display."[69] Again, the goal is to prompt the people toward restoration of the relationship—even as Jeremiah's tears embody God's: "You shall say to them this word: 'Let my eyes run down with tears night and day, and let them not cease.... If I go out into the field ... and if I enter the city ...'" (14:17–18).

In verses 17–18 God commands Jeremiah to quote a message to his people: "Say to them this word" (17a). This means that the following first-person pronouns ("my, I," vv. 17–18) refer to God and his lament. God's tour of his royal city and its adjacent territories prompts God's weeping, as he mourns in a communal lament. Like Jer. 9:10, the text of 14:17–18 singles out the weeping of God. But as Roberts observes, "The anthropomorphisms involved in such a portrait of God are simply too striking for most commentators to entertain seriously."[70] God's sorrow is intensified because of the false optimism of the wayward prophets. The response of the people is too little, too late.[71] This is the portrait of a God in deep sorrow for the "blows" of punishment that he must bring, and the devastation that follows. As David A. Bosworth notes:

Tears signify deep distress, especially when an important relationship is threatened or terminated. . . . Weeping is a powerful non-verbal expression of distress and need, and the weeping of YHWH is revealed to the people. . . . They should respond with empathy for a suffering God and seek to soothe YHWH's pain by their own repentance. . . . The revelation that YHWH's experience of the punishment is sorrow rather than satisfaction serves an important function.[72]

6. Revelation 5:6

And between the throne and the four living creatures and among the elders I saw a Lamb standing, as though it had been slain.

While it is common for Christians to comfort each other with the words "He's still on the throne," that is only where John begins (4:2). A passive appeal to God's sovereignty may sound good (e.g., "Turn it over to God"), but these words offer no care to the rape victim, no reprieve for the depressed, no intervention for the starving, and bring no solace to those betrayed by their spouse.[73] A "bigger" picture is needed for our profound stories of suffering.

Seeing a heavenly throne room (cf. Isa. 6:18) and a sealed scroll in his vision, John fears no one can break its seven seals—until he is informed that the "Lion of the tribe of Judah" and the "Root of David" is qualified to open the scroll (Rev. 5:1–5; cf. Gen. 49:9; Isa. 11:1–5). Both titles identified the Messiah as the conqueror of the nations, one ready to destroy the enemies of God's people. These were standard texts and titles for Jewish messianic hope in the first century (cf. 1QSb 5:24, 29).[74] At one level, this is imagery of a new David who secures a military victory over Israel's enemies. But this scene is actually not about the slaying of the wicked (cf. Isa. 11:4).

John *hears* about the conquering Lion, but when he turns to look, he *sees* a slaughtered "Lamb" (v. 6; cf. Isa. 53:7)![75] For John, the auditory is often redefined by the visual (cf. 1:10–12; 7:1–2, 9; 9:16–17).[76] John makes this identification by the ritual marks of slaughter. Neither the Lion nor the title will appear again in the book. The Lamb, however, will appear over twenty-eight times to designate the exalted Christ.

Resurrected, the Lamb now stands. This highlights his sacrificial role. The scene climaxes with the Passover Lamb (1 Cor. 5:7) ready to lead a new Exodus (Rev. 5:9–10; cf. 17:14). Taken together, the mix of titles for the Lion and Lamb forms a new symbol—conquest by sacrificial death![77] This composite now explains *how* the ancient Scriptures are fulfilled.[78] Jewish expectations have been changed. Evil has been defeated by a sacrificial death, not military conflict.[79] And those delivered are from all nations (5:9–10).

This is a stunning picture of power redefined in weakness![80] "The Lamb is the *embodiment* of the Lion, not its replacement."[81] This is Revelation's most lingering image. On the historical horizon, this is a scene of impressive might, especially for those who have "little power" (3:8)—like the Philadelphian believers (3:7–13). To the eyes of faith, the cross is not victimization or "divine child abuse," but the willing choice of the "Lamb of God" (John 1:29), who reigned from the cross (John 19:19). Christ joined humanity, in his suffering. Suffering, not force, was key to his victory.

The death of the Passover Lamb was so significant that this sacrificial image was permanently taken up into heaven. This is what Peter Hicks calls "the eternal scarring of God."[82] I agree with Hicks when he states: "Somehow, evil in all its forms—sin and suffering and death—has been taken eternally into the Godhead; the marks of slaughter on the Lamb are eternal; there is blood on the throne of heaven."[83] John's vision of the wounded Lamb goes well beyond the notion of Christ's death as an event in history; he transforms the crucifixion into a principle of cosmic proportion, which, in turn, serves as a starting point for understanding what it means to live faithfully in a world characterized by profound suffering (cf. 6:9–11).[84]

SIX GUIDELINES AS WE STUDY
THE SUFFERING OF GOD

At present, I believe biblical studies are making the freshest contributions in the study of the suffering of God.[85] That said, several points, theological and practical, should be made.

1. Avoid Philosophical Theism

First, so much interpretation has been afraid of the emotional and verbal particularity of God in Scripture, and so interpreters resorted to a philosophical theism. I agree with Timothy Wiarda, who observes, "Apologetic and theoretically oriented interests drive much of the modern discussion of divine passibility."[86] Such interpreters are conditioned by the social concerns that drive their contemporary thinking, although they tacitly deny their approach is hermeneutically socialized at all. Yet there are clearly certain rationalistic and triumphalist categories that prioritize power and autonomous sovereignty, particularly in the Western tradition. Jürgen Moltmann observes that the church fathers mistakenly saw only two alternatives: (1) essential incapacity for suffering, and (2) fateful subjection to suffering. However, *willing vulnerability*—expressed in passionate love—is the excluded third alternative.[87] The net effect is the loss of biblical metanarrative to rationalism. In this case the *story* of suffering in the life of God is actually the meaning of doctrine, and following his suffering will press us closer to God's *theo*-drama.[88]

2. Recognize the Paradox

Second, the suffering of God also dips deeply into paradox: "The weakness of God is stronger than men ... though he was rich, yet for your sake he became poor" (1 Cor. 1:25b; 2 Cor. 8:9). Elevating power as perfection, we have missed the majesty of a God who "stoops" to humankind in frail flesh (cf. Ps. 113:6), living in scandalous weakness. Or, as Michael S. Horton puts it, "Christ's will to weakness is stronger than modern humanity's will to power, and that which the supermen of our age regard as opium for the masses."[89]

God's love precedes power, rightly argues William C. Placher. "A God defined in terms of power is precisely not a reliable rescuer, because power provides no guarantee of concern. . . . It is his silent suffering that paradoxically confirms his identity as the true Messiah."[90]

3. Accept Our Own Weaknesses

Third, we noted at the outset that we would have to dig, and that includes staring into the darkness of our own hearts. We are petrified of weakness! Manipulation and violence are the false alternatives to real power, where we turn when we are too weak to risk vulnerability.[91]

> Human beings seek power because they are afraid of weakness, afraid of what might happen should they be vulnerable, and so the drive for power that looks like the purest expression of freedom proves in significant degree inspired by an enslaving fear that dares not risk vulnerability. . . . Probe violence and the quest for domination far enough, and one always finds the fear of weakness.[92]

We have projected an "isolating" power onto God that he never claims for himself. He prefers the company of orphans, widows, and the poor (Ps. 113:5–9)—the weaklings of the world. Only a God who stoops in His power is really strong enough to take on the pain of the world.[93]

4. Understand That His Suffering Helps Mend Our Lives

Fourth, understanding the suffering of God helps mend the shattered lives of believers who have known painful and alienating suffering. For broken, betrayed, and persecuted lives, a suffering Savior makes following our Lord credible, not just possible (cf. Heb. 2:17–18; 4:15–16). Being a disciple of the "First Wounded" creates a new reality through a fresh view that many Job-like believers need. The wounded redeemed can follow this kind of Shepherd.

Personally, I'm drawn to pain in ways I'm simply not drawn to praise. Being a disciple of one who does not hide his sorrow or wounds is beyond comforting; it calms the deep–down places that have no words, only groans (cf. Rom. 8:26–27; Heb. 7:25). This relationship of the scarred Lamb to his suffering sheep helps us say "No" to surrogate attachments that promise relief, but only enslave.

This "man of sorrows" (Isa. 53:3) does not ask us to go where he has never been—this is a precious discipleship, indeed. He not only died *for* us, he is willing to suffer *with* us.

5. Let the Suffering God Draw Us into Profound Relationship

Fifth, embracing a suffering and scarred God draws human affliction into the context of a profound *relationship*, not membership. This provides a nurturing point of departure for the hurting—beyond "divine knowledge." This relationship draws from a shared place of suffering that is capable of calling believers out of their *commodified* lifestyle and their addiction to technology.[94]

Mechanical solutions to suffering have seduced the contemporary church to shun the rawness of pain, to shun the gift of communal grief–sharing and our basic need for human community. The suffering of God can stimulate a practice of bearing others' pain that we might rather deny as unspiritual or unproductive. But this is no pill or program. It is all about following the wounds of our risen Lord in a time when affliction is increasingly something of an embarrassment to "refined faith."

6. Embrace Music That Recognizes the Suffering of God

Sixth, we need to reacquaint ourselves with the tradition of hymns that tapped beautifully into the suffering of God. Hymns like "O Sacred Head, Now Wounded," or "Arise, My Soul, Arise" that contains the lines:

> Five bleeding wounds He bears,
> Received on Calvary;
> They pour effectual prayers,
> They strongly plead for me.[95]

This connects divine and human suffering. "It is said of God that no one can behold his face and live," Wolterstorff writes. "I always thought this meant that no one could see his splendor and live. A friend said perhaps it means that no one could see his sorrow and live. Or perhaps his sorrow is his splendor."[96]

AMID PAIN AND SUFFERING

1. From authors like Joni Eareckson Tada, Nicholas Wolterstorff, Timothy Keller, Alister McGrath, John R. Stott, Warren McWilliams, D. A. Carson, and Kevin J. Vanhoozer—to say nothing of Christian songwriters—many write about aspects of God's suffering. Why do you think this topic is increasingly being addressed today?

2. Do you feel that emotion is still viewed as second-rate to reason, in the Christian faith? What are the implications of a God who can or cannot experience emotional pain?

3. This chapter argued that God has always related to people in willing vulnerability. What are the implications of this for the coming to earth of Christ, who died for rebellious sinners?

4. In what ways have people projected their fear of weakness on an all-powerful God?

5. In what ways does a suffering God offer meaningful "connections" to various ways you are suffering?

CHAPTER 4

A Man of Sorrows

Emotions and the Suffering of Jesus

By Gerald W. Peterman

O ne of the most brutally honest depictions of the suffering of Jesus came in the movie *The Passion of the Christ*. This highly popular movie earned $370 million when released in 2004, but its R rating (for "sequences of graphic violence") made many viewers uncomfortable.[1]

Typically when we speak about the passion of Jesus, we mean the violent events depicted in the film: his arrest, interrogation, beating, and brutal crucifixion (Mark 15:15–25). These things were passion in the sense that they were both physically and emotionally painful and evoked passionate responses both by Jesus and all who watched his suffering.

As we mentioned in chapter 1, we should not simply equate physical pain with suffering; the two are closely related but not identical. In this chapter we will consider the emotional suffering of Christ, or what we might call his negative emotions. Of course, these emotions were not isolated to Passion Week. On the contrary, there is evidence that our Lord, as is the case with us, also experienced painful emotions on a regular basis. According to Isaiah, "He was . . . a man of sorrows, and acquainted with grief" (53:3). If Paul had "great sorrow and unceasing anguish" in his heart concerning unsaved Israel (Rom. 9:1–2), then surely our Lord carried with him this pain also, for "he came to his own, and his own people did not receive him" (John 1:11).

As we explore Jesus' emotions, we should be clear about three things. First, *Jesus is fully human*. John asserts that "the Word became flesh and dwelt among us" (1:14). Likewise Paul writes that "he emptied himself, by taking the form of a servant, being born in the likeness of men" (Phil. 2:7). Because Jesus was flesh and blood and walked the earth in the lands of Judea and Galilee, he would feel thirst (John 19:28) and grow weary (John 4:6). In addition to these physical manifestations of humanity, we would expect Jesus to experience a full range of human pain, human emotion, and human suffering. This indeed happened, according to the biblical accounts.

Second, *Jesus is sinless*. We know this truth from 2 Cor. 5:21 and Heb. 4:15: "For we do not have a high priest who is unable to sympathize with our weaknesses, but one who in every respect has been tempted as we are, yet without sin." Typically, and quite understandably, theologians discuss the sinlessness of Jesus in connection with Christology and especially atonement; a sinless sacrifice is essential for salvation. Rarely, however, does this theological truth arise in discussion of suffering and emotion.

From the sinlessness of Jesus we can know with certainty that any emotional expression of Jesus was a sinless emotional expression. If he had fear, anger, or sadness, we know that these were sinless fear, sinless anger, and sinless sadness. Corresponding to this, the implication is that it is possible for *us* to have sinless fear, anger, or sadness. That means you and I can feel anger without sinning, a truth Paul tells the Ephesian church when he warns them, "Be angry and yet do not sin" (Eph. 4:26 NASB).

But to say that Jesus was sinless is to make a negative statement, not a positive one. Thus we come to our third—and very important—consideration: *we must assert, positively, that Jesus is continuously virtuous.* His every thought, his every emotion, his every word, and his every action are in keeping with his Father's will—that is, God the Father himself becomes manifest in Jesus' acts (John 14:9). And this perfect obedience happens by way of his humanity. He lives the life we should live. The Father said of his Son, "You are my beloved Son; with you I am well pleased" (Luke 3:22). According to John, Jesus always does his Father's will (John 5:19; 6:38; 8:29). Jesus is our example not only of bad things to be avoided (sins) but also of good things to be imitated (virtue). Therefore, his every thought, his every emotion, his every action are wholly worthy of imitation. Paul said, "Be imitators of me, as I am of Christ" (1 Cor. 11:1).

But we can go beyond this and say that if there were times when Jesus was angry, then there must be times when we will be angry. If there were times when he was sad, then there must be times when we will be sad. That is, if Jesus is virtuous and worthy of imitation, then for us the display of Christlike emotions is not an option but a mandate.

And that brings us to the subject of our chapter: What painful emotions did Jesus experience? How did he express them? Why did he experience them? Space does not permit a complete coverage of all of Jesus' emotions. Moreover, others have already done that admirably well.[2] Since our topic is suffering, we will only sketch out the basic kinds of painful emotions our Lord experienced. We will look at compassion, anger, fear, and discontent.

THE COMPASSION OF JESUS
(MATT. 9:36; LUKE 7:13)

Compassion is a kind of suffering. It is a kind of suffering that is not primarily about my personal pain, but rather about the pain of another. In compassion one puts into practice the Golden Rule: "Whatever you wish that others would do to you, do also to them" (Matt. 7:12). The

Golden Rule requires a Spirit–guided moral imagination. With this moral imagination I visualize how I would feel if I were experiencing the pain or the trials that someone else is experiencing. Therefore Frederick Buechner is on the mark when he says, "Compassion is the sometimes fatal capacity for feeling what it's like to live inside somebody else's skin. It is the knowledge that there can never really be any peace and joy for me until there is peace and joy finally for you too."[3] Jesus, as love incarnate, was masterful at this.

It is exciting and convicting to note the language used by the gospel writers to describe Jesus' compassion. They employ a verb that is related to the noun for *inward parts* or *entrails* (*splanchnizomai*).[4] Regarding Matthew 9:36, R. T. France says that *splanchnizomai* is a strongly emotional Greek verb "which speaks of a warm, compassionate response to need. No single English term does justice to it: compassion, pity, sympathy, and fellow feeling all convey part of it, but 'his heart went out' perhaps represents more fully the emotional force of the underlying metaphor of a 'gut response.'"[5]

"Like Sheep without a Shepherd"

Such a response is what we find in Matthew 9:36: when Jesus saw the crowds, "he had compassion for them, because they were harassed and helpless, like sheep without a shepherd.'"

Without guidance from someone who cares for their welfare and knows their needs, the sheep are exposed to danger. They will starve, die of thirst, be exposed to the worst weather or terrain, and are prone to injury or disease. Jesus, as the Good Shepherd, knows this, and it pains him deeply. The shepherding that the crowds lack is moral, social, and spiritual leadership; this same sort of lack is seen in the refrain of Judges: "In those days there was no king in Israel. Everyone did what was right in his own eyes" (Judg. 21:25; cf. 17:6; 18:1; 19:1). It was the lack seen in God's rebuke through Ezekiel, when the prophet declares, "The word of the LORD came to me: 'Son of man, prophesy against the shepherds of Israel; prophesy, and say . . . Thus says the

Lord God: Ah, shepherds of Israel who have been feeding yourselves! Should not shepherds feed the sheep? You eat the fat, . . . but you do not feed the sheep'" (34:1–3; cf. Jer. 23:1–5).

Jesus feels the danger. He knows they are needy. He knows about the abusive leadership and the state people are left in when they experience such abuse. His compassion is a kind of suffering with them. But it goes beyond this; it is also a desire to relieve suffering that ushers in action to relieve it.[6]

Luke 7 is similar. There we find that Jesus went to a town called Nain along with his disciples and a great crowd. "As he drew near to the gate of the town, behold, a man who had died was being carried out, the only son of his mother, and she was a widow, and a considerable crowd from the town was with her. And when the Lord saw her, he had compassion on her and said to her, 'Do not weep'" (vv. 12–13). As a widow, her son is her hope for care in her old age. Without him, she has no one to supply her needs. This sad situation draws the Lord's compassion.

A Painful Compassion

The Old Testament gives precedent for such painful compassion. Joseph, one of Jacob's twelve sons, is second in command in Egypt when his brothers come down to buy food. As a test of them, he locks up Simeon, Jacob's second son, and sends the rest home to retrieve their youngest brother, Benjamin, the son of his father's old age. They return with Benjamin. Upon seeing his younger brother, "Joseph hurried out, for his compassion grew warm for his brother, and he sought a place to weep. And he entered his chamber and wept there" (Gen. 43:30). With this compassion probably came a mix of feelings. Certainly he was happy to see his brother. But pain is there as well, having been separated for two decades.

Another example comes from the prophet Hosea. Citing the Lord, the prophet says, "How can I give you up, O Ephraim? How can I hand you over, O Israel? How can I make you like Admah? How can I treat you like Zeboiim? My heart recoils within me; my compassion grows warm and tender" (Hos. 11:8). As with Joseph, so here with Yahweh, we meet a complex of feelings. Israel is long overdue for judgment, a judgment that God will indeed bring. But this is not simply anger; it is angry sorrow mixed with painful covenant love.

Finally, we come back to Jesus. As a man of compassion, he was a man familiar with pain and sorrow. Therefore, the Christian life, as a life that follows Jesus, is a life mixed with joy and pain.

THE *GRIEVING* ANGER OF JESUS (MARK 3:5)

Anger is a secondary emotion; it typically arises as a result of some other emotionally painful event, thought, or relationship.[7] When we look at anger, then, we will need to ask what lies behind it. This deeper look is especially important when we consider the anger of Jesus in Mark 3.

While in the synagogue on the Sabbath Jesus encounters a man with a withered hand. Mark writes, "And they watched Jesus, to see whether he would heal him on the Sabbath, so that they might accuse him" (v. 2). The watchers here are probably Pharisees, with whom Jesus has just had a controversy over the Sabbath (2:23–28). After commanding the man to come forward, Jesus asked, "Is it lawful on the Sabbath to do good or to do harm, to save life or to kill?" But he gets no response: "They were silent" (3:4). Then Jesus "looked around at them with anger, *grieved* at their hardness of heart, and said to the man, 'Stretch out your hand.' He stretched it out, and his hand was restored" (v. 5, emphasis added).

The Pain of Grief, Bringing Anger

Why was Jesus angry? It is an anger mixed with pain; it is anger that is redemptive. The logic works this way: First, he has love for the people and in this case especially for the disabled man. Second, the Pharisees display a hardness of heart that will not allow the doing of good (healing) on the Sabbath. Such a prohibition is clearly a distortion of God's purpose. Third, Jesus feels grief. The original language makes clear that their hardness of heart is the cause of Jesus' grief. Here we see the pain, the suffering of anger. But as we said, anger is secondary. The participle "grieved" is almost certainly causal: that is, anger in this particular instance follows from grief (and is not necessarily to be disjoined from it). From the pain of grief comes anger, the motivator to rectify the situation. Anger can be right at times. It depends on its underlying source.

But the cause of Jesus' anger while in the synagogue has a further component, the hardness of their heart. What is grievous about that? I take it that the issue is he sees the elders acting to oppress the needy. Jewish misinterpretation of the law has led to people being denied wholeness on the very day when it is most appropriate to enjoy it.[8]

To rephrase this: the anger of Jesus at the Pharisees is based, in part, on the love he has for the hurting and the oppressed. That is, it is not just anger at Pharisees. There is a relational web along with a set of perspectives—we might call these ethics, convictions, or beliefs—that should affect how we evaluate events.

A Recurring Anger

Furthermore, his anger is not confined to this event; we see Jesus demonstrate this kind of anger several times. Jesus was indignant that the disciples kept children from him (Mark 10:13–14). And it would be hard to believe that when he cleansed the temple, driving out the sellers and money changers, he was grinning or laughing the whole time (e.g., John 2:13–16). No, it was an angry action: controlled, righteous, but angry.

Commentator B. B. Warfield, writing in 1912, correctly argued that

> The emotions of indignation and anger belong therefore to the very self-expression of a moral being as such and cannot be lacking to him in the presence of wrong. We should know, accordingly, without instruction that Jesus, living in the conditions of this earthly life under the curse of sin, could not fail to be the subject of the whole series of angry emotions.[9]

THE FEAR OF JESUS (LUKE 22:39-46)

Fear and Jesus: this might seem like an odd combination. Indeed, there are some who assert that Jesus never experienced fear.[10] They have the opinion that fear—except for the fear of the Lord (e.g., Prov. 1:7; 2 Cor. 5:11)—is sinful. So, for example, on his blog post Denny Burk says, "In the Bible, doubt and fear are sins," and "doubt and fear have no place in those who are trusting in the promises of the God who resurrects from the dead, and they certainly never had any place in Jesus."[11]

Why Some Believe Having Fear Is Sinful

Why would someone adopt this perspective?[12] Typically they draw this conclusion using one or all of three arguments.

First, many define fear as the opposite of faith. In his book *Feelings and Faith*, Pastor Brian S. Borgman says that there is a good kind of fear "that helps preserve our lives." But later he adds,

> The Bible leaves no room for debate. The source of fear, worry, and anxiety is unbelief. The unbelief is specific, spelled out to us by Isaiah and Jesus. When we fail to believe that God is for us, will take care of us, has our future in his hands, and is with us right now, we cave in to fear, worry, or anxiety.[13]

But we should not accept the disjunction that says fear is the opposite of faith. Clearly, fear is an emotion; and just as clearly, faith is not an emotion. Fear might challenge our faith; but the opposite of faith is not fear. The opposite of faith is unbelief.

A second reason some argue that fear is sinful *is because fear seemingly ignores or doubts that God is sovereignly in control of the universe* and has our good in mind. After all, if Romans 8:28 is true, then we are guaranteed a good future. What is fearful about that? But this argument claims too much. For if God is sovereign, we could reach the similar conclusion that we should never be sad and never be angry. But clearly, as we saw above and in our chapter on redemptive anger, there were times when Jesus was angry and times when he was sad.

Also, this assertion that there can be no good reason for fear if a sovereign God controls everything seems to be based on the unstated principle that knowledge of a good future will, or should, take away negative emotions in the present. We will see in chapter 8 ("Leadership and Tears"), however, that this reasoning is also faulty. Jesus had such knowledge; Jesus always trusted his heavenly Father perfectly; and yet Jesus got sad and angry.

Third, a certain way of reading passages from the Old Testament might lead us to the conclusion that fear is sinful. The Bible says repeatedly, "Do not be afraid" (e.g., Josh. 10:25; Prov. 3:25; Jer. 1:8).[14] What should we make of such commands? Are we to conclude, for instance, that the command given to Jeremiah not to be afraid in his prophetic ministry is also a command prohibiting us from ever having the emotion of fear in any circumstance? Should we generalize the command and so conclude that fear—except for fear of the Lord—is always sinful?

The answer, of course, is no. It would be better for us to think of all the commands in Scripture against fear as context–specific and coupled to other concerns, attitudes, or actions. So in some instances, commands against fear are indirect commands to be obedient, especially when there are temptations to the contrary. Thus Joshua is commanded not to be afraid when he is taking over leadership in Israel—a frightening prospect indeed (Josh. 1:9)! He might be tempted to back away from this task, especially knowing how rebellious the nation has been (e.g., Deut. 9:7; 31:27). In other instances, commands against fear correct the reasonable but wrong view that pain, judgment, or death is near. When an angel appears, a fearful response is reasonable. Wrath might fall (e.g., Gen. 19:1–13; Num. 22:31; 2 Kings 19:35; 1 Chron. 21:15; Acts 12:23). But, for instance, in Luke the angel announces that he brings good news, and by implication not judgment (2:9–10). In other instances, commands against fear are indirect assurances of the Lord's provision, presence, or protection, especially when someone might doubt such provision. Jeremiah knows his own inadequacy (1:6) and the hard–heartedness of

Israel (5:23); thus the Lord reassures him: "Do not be afraid of them, for I am with you to deliver you, declares the LORD" (1:8).

Jesus' Rightful Dread

Now regarding the fear of Jesus, we turn to our primary passage: Luke 22:39–46. The setting is a garden in Gethsemane. Jesus is in painful emotional distress. Its source? We will see this distress comes from a certain dread—a type of fear—and that this dread is rational and virtuous.

Earlier in Luke Jesus had already predicted that he would go to Jerusalem and suffer mockery, abuse, and death (Luke 9:44; 17:25). Similarly he predicted his resurrection from the dead (Luke 9:22; 18:31–33). Yet as he enters the garden, he knows there is no going back. Judas will look for Jesus and his three closest disciples there. Jesus waits there, anticipating the arrest, abandonment, and brutality. As with the temptation by the devil in the wilderness, this is a time of darkness (22:53); being human, he will still face the temptation to escape or find another way.

The events at Gethsemane are also told by Matthew, Mark, and Luke, and all writers show Jesus clearly in distress. Matthew, for instance, reports that Jesus took aside Peter and the two sons of Zebedee, and "began to be sorrowful and troubled. Then he said to them, 'My soul is very sorrowful, even to death; remain here, and watch with me'" (Matt. 26:37–38). Mark's account is similar (14:32–42). Clearly Jesus is in emotional turmoil.

Luke's telling of the garden events is unique, however. Only seventeen of Luke's 114 words (Luke 22:39–46) match Mark's account (14:32–42),[15] and what Luke chooses to tell us highlights the Lord's distress. We will look, first, at Jesus' reference to the cup (found in Matthew, Mark, and Luke), and then at three elements that are unique to Luke: angelic aid, agony, and bloody sweat.

The Cup of Wrath

First, the cup. Luke reports that Jesus "withdrew from them about a stone's throw, and knelt down and prayed, saying, 'Father, if you are willing, remove this cup from me. Nevertheless, not my will, but yours, be done'" (Luke 22:41–42). In Scripture the term "cup" is often used as shorthand for encountering the wrath of God.[16] For instance:

> Wake yourself, wake yourself, stand up, O Jerusalem, you who have drunk from the hand of the LORD the cup of his wrath, who have drunk to the dregs the bowl, the cup of staggering. (Isa. 51:17)

> Thus the LORD, the God of Israel, said to me: "Take from my hand this cup of the wine of wrath, and make all the nations to whom I send you drink it." (Jer. 25:15)

> [The one who worships the beast] also will drink the wine of God's wrath, poured full strength into the cup of his anger, and he will be tormented with fire and sulfur in the presence of the holy angels and in the presence of the Lamb. (Rev. 14:10)

Thus the request of Jesus to escape the cup is a request to escape the wrath of God. There is great mystery and call to worship here! For the Son is the Lamb "who takes away the sin of the world!" (John 1:29), and "who was slain from the creation of the world"[17] (Rev. 13:8 NIV). He always does what pleases his Father (John 8:29). Thus he cannot fail to die as a sinless sacrifice. And yet the certainty of his obedient death does not take away the temptation to go the easy way; nor does this certainty make him a stoic as he faces wrath. Having from all eternity enjoyed triune fellowship and love, he has never before encountered the wrath of his Father.

In the garden he begins to get a glimpse of what he is to face; facing it now is pure dread. Scott Bader–Saye states it well:

> Gethsemane . . . marks the starting point of Jesus' road to the cross. Here we have the only time in the Gospels when Jesus is said to be afraid (*ekthambeō*). Yet he neither hides nor offers up the other to save himself. Unlike Adam and Eve he moves toward God in his fear; he seeks relief, but his prayer is not "save me at any cost." He subordinates his desire for safety—"remove this cup from me"—to his desire to be faithful—"not my will but yours be done" (Luke 22:42). Even

here, or especially here, Jesus lives out his own command to "love your enemies, do good to those who hate you, bless those who curse you" (Luke 6:47–48). Jesus continues to participate in the economy of blessing despite the fact that his own life is threatened by those who live the way of curse.[18]

The Angelic Visitor

Second, the angel. We read that "there appeared to him an angel from heaven, strengthening him" (22:43). Throughout his gospel Luke has highlighted the work of angels with as many references to them as Matthew and Mark combined. They announced the conception and birth of John to Zechariah (1:13) and of Jesus to Mary (1:31). They tell the good news to shepherds (2:9–11). Furthermore, only in Luke do we find that "there is joy before the angels of God over one sinner who repents" (15:10). Thus, as others among God's people have benefited from their service, so does our Lord; he is strengthened.

His Agony

Third, the agony. However, this strength does not lead to tranquility but to what appears to be greater struggle. Immediately after angelic aid we read that Jesus "being in an agony . . . prayed more earnestly" (v. 44). Only in Luke's telling—indeed only here in the New Testament—do we find "agony." This word could refer to an external struggle such as a military battle or an athletic contest. On the other hand, it could refer to an internal struggle such as apprehensiveness, anxiety, or anguish. Surely it is the latter of these here. Angelic aid does not make things easy for our Lord but enables him to be obedient even through more emotional turmoil.

The Turmoil that Leads to Bloody Sweat

Fourth, the bloody sweat. Only Luke mentions bloody sweat or *hemathidrosis* (also called *hematohidrosis*). It is "a condition in which sweat contains blood."[19] Commentators are divided over whether

Luke's statement is to be taken metaphorically or literally, with the majority taking it metaphorically. Hemathidrosis, however, is a rare but documented phenomenon.

> Hematohidrosis is a very rare condition in which a human being sweats blood. It may occur in an individual who is suffering from extreme levels of stress, for example, facing his or her [own] death. Around the sweat glands, there are multiple blood vessels in a net-like form, which constrict under the pressure of great stress. Then as the anxiety passes, the blood vessels dilate to the point of rupture. The blood goes into the sweat glands. As the sweat glands produce a lot of sweat, they push the blood to the surface, which come out as droplets of blood mixed with sweat.[20]

Bloody sweat is a further confirmation that Jesus is in turmoil. Taking the last steps of obedience toward arrest, brutality, and execution is not simple. It is dreadful; there is fear. Certainty of long-term victory—that is, the resurrection that he himself predicted—does not require nor guarantee tranquility. Yet, as we have noted, the emotions of Jesus in the garden cannot be classified as sinful or even substandard; they must be categorized as virtuous and worthy of imitation.

Confirmation is found in Hebrews 5:7–8: "In the days of his flesh, Jesus offered up prayers and supplications, with loud cries and tears, to him who was able to save him from death, and he was heard because of his reverence. Although he was a son, he learned obedience through what he suffered." Whether or not this is a specific reference to the emotions of Gethsemane is debated by commentators on Hebrews.[21] Close to the mark is David Allen, who asserts,

> It would be wrong . . . to say that Jesus' prayer could not have been motivated by fear. But what Jesus feared, or more accurately, dreaded, was not the torturous death on the cross, but that he would have laid upon him the sins of the whole world. . . . Jesus would face the judgment of God on our behalf; this knowledge, more than anything else, brought such an anguished cry that dark Gethsemane night.[22]

Jesus experienced godly fear. Other saints have as well, including Nehemiah before King Artaxerxes (Neh. 2:2) and Paul as he dealt with the Corinthians and their temptations to trust a false gospel (2 Cor. 11:3; see also Gal. 4:11).

THE DISCONTENT OF JESUS (MARK 7:34; MATT. 17:14–17)

Contentment is a valuable Christian virtue and is much needed in our age—an age filled with greed and the desire to gain more and more. In contrast, to be content with a thing or situation is to be at peace or satisfied with the thing or situation. When I am content with something, I do not seek to change it or replace it.

In the New Testament contentment entails being at peace with any financial situation (see Luke 3:14; 1 Tim. 6:6, 8; Heb. 13:5). But some say that contentment is required in every situation, not just financial situations. This perspective comes from a certain reading of Philippians 4:11 where Paul says, "I have learned in whatever situation I am to be content." Some read this verse as if contentment had to do with everything and every conceivable situation. Is that right? Should I be content that my neighbors are lost without Christ? Should I be content to live on a sinful planet? Should I be content to live with a sinful nature? The answer to these questions is No! Instead, like Paul, I should long for the salvation of others (Rom. 9:1–3; 10:1). I should long for the new heaven and the new earth so much that I could say with Paul that to live is Christ and to die is gain (Phil. 1:21). I should let the Holy Spirit work in me the groaning that eagerly awaits full adoption as a child of God and the final redemption of the body (Rom. 8:23).

And thus we can see why it is quite reasonable to speak of the discontent of Jesus. While he loves us as we are, he is not content to leave us as we are. There were times during his earthly ministry when he was frustrated and feeling painful longing for something better; that is, he displayed godly discontent. We will look at two examples.

When Jesus Sighed (Groaned)

Consider Jesus' response as he performs a miracle in the region of Decapolis (Mark 7:31–37). The crowd brings to him a deaf and mute man, begging Jesus to heal him. "And taking him aside from the crowd privately, he put his fingers into his ears, and after spitting touched his tongue. And looking up to heaven, he sighed and said to him, 'Ephphatha,' that is, 'Be opened'" (vv. 31–34). Our primary concern here is with the term "sighed," which would be better translated "groaned." What does a groan communicate? It would be helpful to look at some other uses of this word in Scripture. Consider its use in these five passages (all emphasis added):

Psalm 12:5. Early in the psalm David complains of the unrighteousness and evil that are so prevalent everywhere; he calls out for the Lord's intervention. God responds, "'Because the poor are plundered, because the needy *groan*, I will now arise,' says the LORD; 'I will place him in the safety for which he longs.'" Here the groaning—that is, the verbalized discontent—of the oppressed poor is welcomed, heard, and answered by the Lord.

Ezekiel 21:6. In the first few verses of the chapter the coming judgment of God is pictured as a drawn sword. How should Ezekiel respond to the news of coming judgment against Jerusalem? The Lord says this should be his response: "As for you, son of man, *groan*; with breaking heart and bitter grief, *groan* before their eyes." Although the coming judgment is deserved, Ezekiel is not to rejoice in it but to grieve over it.

Acts 7:34. In his defense speech, Stephen refers back to God's words to Moses in Exodus 6:5. The Lord says, "I have surely seen the affliction of my people who are in Egypt, and have heard their *groaning*, and I have come down to deliver them. And now come, I will send you to Egypt." Why would God's people be groaning? They want to be free. They are discontent with slavery and oppression.

2 Corinthians 5:2–4. Owing to conflicts and misunderstanding in the church at Corinth, Paul has to defend his apostolic ministry; he explains how he can have confidence even though he experiences much suffering and pain through his work. Confidence comes from a hopeful future, namely, the resurrection. When this earthly life is over, there will be new spiritual life and a glorified body (cf. Phil. 3:20). He says, "For in this tent we *groan*, longing to put on our heavenly dwelling, if indeed by putting it on we may not be found naked. For while we are still in this tent, we groan, being burdened—not that we would be unclothed, but that we would be further clothed, so that what is mortal may be swallowed up by life" (emphasis added). Again, why groaning? Why discontent? There are two reasons: first is current pain; second is future hope. This combination of the present and future leads to groaning.

Hebrews 13:17. This passage is different. The writer commands, "Obey your leaders and submit to them, for they are keeping watch over your souls, as those who will have to give an account. Let them do this with joy and not with *groaning*, for that would be of no advantage to you."

Groaning in Discontent

And now, we can see why in Mark 7 there is groaning. Jesus is not content with a world full of sickness; he is grieved to see people hurting in this way. His knowledge of the man's healed future does not take away his grief that suffering is happening in the present. His "sigh" reflects godly discontent with the current situation.[23]

Our second example of Jesus' discontent appears in Matthew 17:14–17. The Lord had previously given the disciples authority to heal and cast out demons (Matt. 10:1). But while he is on the Mount of Transfiguration with Peter, James, and John, a father brought his epileptic son to the other nine disciples for help; but "they could not heal him" (v. 16). How does the Lord respond? He says, "O faithless and twisted generation, how long am I to be with you? How long am I to bear with you? Bring him here to me" (v. 17). Why this outburst from Jesus?

The Lord twice asks, "How long?" We find this question often in laments of the Psalms as the writers express pain, longing, and frustration with their situation. For example, David expresses frustration over God's delay (13:1–2; cf. 35:17), Asaph appeals to God's reputation (80:3–4), and Asaph reminds God of their prayers and his relationship to them (74:10; cf. 79:5).

Closer to the language of Jesus, however, are examples of "how long?" used in rebuke:

Exodus 10:3. After repeated appeals to Pharaoh and his repeated hardness of heart, Moses and Aaron reprimand him, saying, "Thus says the LORD, the God of the Hebrews, 'How long will you refuse to humble yourself before me? Let my people go, that they may serve me.'"

1 Kings 18:21. At his confrontation with the prophets of Baal at Mount Carmel, Elijah said, "How long will you go limping between two different opinions? If the LORD is God, follow him; but if Baal, then follow him." And the people did not answer him a word.

Jeremiah 4:14. Israel had long toyed with idolatry (v. 1) and judgment was coming (v. 6). In his call to repentance the prophet says, "O Jerusalem, wash your heart from evil, that you may be saved. How long shall your wicked thoughts lodge within you?" (See also 13:27 and 31:22.)

Numbers 14:11. This response comes after the bad report about the land given by the spies (13:32). The people are discouraged and grumble against Moses and Aaron, saying, "Would that we had died in the land of Egypt! Or would that we had died in this wilderness! Why is the LORD bringing us into this land, to fall by the sword?" (vv. 2–3). They propose choosing a new leader and going back to Egypt (v. 4). In response the Lord said to Moses, "How long will this people despise me? And how long will they not believe in me, in spite of all the signs that I have done among them?" (v. 11).

The situation in Numbers is similar to Matthew 17. Just as the Lord had already promised to give the land to Israel, so also Jesus had already given the apostles authority to cast out demons (10:1). Furthermore the disciples had some success in it (Luke 10:17). But here they prove faithless. John Nolland rightly comments:

> Jesus' fierce words can be provoked only by the failure of the disciples. Here the disciples represent the present generation in its failure to respond to the ministry of Jesus, much as 'some of the scribes and Pharisees' do in Mt. 12:38–39. Whereas in 12:39 this generation is being likened by OT allusions to those sent into exile, here the allusion is to Dt. 32:5 (cf. v. 20).[24]

Jesus' words are indeed fierce. They are laced with understandable anger, the frustration clearly seen in the expression "how long?" And what lies behind the anger? We see his painful disappointment in the disciples, those closest to him, who should have known better.

These painful emotions of Jesus—compassion, anger, fear, and discontent—are congruent with the suffering of God that we saw in our last chapter. Since Yahweh is a covenant–keeping God who chooses to bind himself to his people, the God of the Old Testament suffers in and with his people. This does not change with incarnation. Our Lord Jesus is fully human. As a human he suffers, having the same sorts of painful emotions that we encounter. Warfield summarizes it well when he says that our Lord Jesus

> subjected himself to the conditions of our human life that he might save us from the evil that curses human life in its sinful manifestation. When we observe him exhibiting the movements of his human emotions, we are gazing on the very process of our salvation. . . . In his sorrows he was bearing our sorrows, and having passed through a human life like ours, he remains forever able to be touched with a feeling of our infirmities.[25]

AMID PAIN AND SUFFERING

1. Reflect on this statement: "Just as we consider ourselves obligated to imitate Jesus' positive emotions, such as love and joy, so also we should consider ourselves obligated to imitate his negative emotions, such as sadness, anger, and discontent."

2. Have you had a time when you were in painful emotional distress, distress that came in the form of dread? Was that dread rational and virtuous? Explain.

3. Do the fears of others make you uncomfortable? How do you typically respond to other believers who are afraid? Explain.

4. Does it surprise you that this chapter classifies anger as a kind of suffering? Tell why or why not.

5. Can you discern when your discontent is godly and when it is ungodly? Spend some time pondering Rom. 8:18–25. How does Paul's teaching help you in the discernment process?

CHAPTER 5

Longing to Lament

Returning to the Language of Suffering

BY ANDREW J. SCHMUTZER

In his essay "Singing the Meaning of the Psalms," W. Sibley Towner makes a sobering observation that is very true of contemporary faith:

Except for denominations committed to singing every psalm in chant, paraphrase, or hymn, contemporary hymnists and hymnals prefer to celebrate God as creator and thank God as liberator rather than to lament to the God who listens. . . . Yet, perhaps this is to be expected—singing about sin and suffering sounds like an oxymoron, especially in the communal context of a congregation. Perhaps this selection also says something about the theological climate in the mainstream churches in recent decades. Put in commercial terms, in the competitive denominational marketplace of the twenty–first century, *somber doesn't sell. We prefer to sin and repent, lament and die in silent privacy.*[1]

What Towner has observed reaches beyond mainstream churches and applies to far more than our musical tastes. *Towner has not only identified the danger of the marketed church, but our profound dis-ease with engaging suffering in corporate worship, ours or others.* In fact, every church attender today—and those who did attend—are keenly aware that expressions of deep personal pain, anger, and suffering are simply not welcome. Is a congregation that is filled with hurting people ever invited "to lament to the God who listens," as Towner puts it? Who among us has recently been invited into honest lament? Most probably don't even know what lament is.

HOW DOES THE CHURCH ENGAGE MISERY?

At one level our worship may be genuine, but it is also genuinely misleading. It appears that we are afraid of others' pain and so have lost our ear for grief. This lack of honest address for suffering means we also lack the vocabulary to engage misery. Are tearful whispers between friends in secluded church bathrooms really adequate to address our seasons of suffering? Are small groups the only place left to acknowledge pain and fear? Certainly not! Not when everyone knows that week after week, they are standing next to someone at church:

- who is angry with an "absent" God,
- who had another miscarriage,
- who just found out about their spouse's affair,
- who just lost a parent to cancer,
- who was raped in college,
- who was diagnosed with clinical depression,
- whose teen just attempted suicide,
- whose little sister struggles with anorexia,
- whose business just went under,
- whose sibling returned to alcohol rehab.

From earthquakes that tear cities apart, to civil wars that displace thousands to other lands, to Islamic warriors who behead Christians, this generation is "plugged into" catastrophes on a global scale. *Like every generation, Christ-followers today are longing to lament.* They crave an opportunity to draw a deeper meaning from the suffering that sweeps over the world. They long for Esther's lament, a lament that intervenes *for* others, near and far. This craving is more than justified. Scripture has speech for such profound suffering—it is called *lamentation*, and entire biblical books are rooted in this language.

If "somber doesn't sell," as Towner states, what are we losing by avoiding the biblical language of lament? What myths are we struggling with that have overwhelmingly limited worship to one primary emotional expression? The forces of marketing and appearance are stifling our need to cry out and voice our pain to God. People with hearts crippled by profound pain are forced to stand and clap week after week with little if any mention of the dark trials that fill their hearts. Is this a moral way of treating the hurting in our own midst? Wounded people among us "smell" a form of pretense that is as programmed and insincere as the canned laughter of sitcoms. They are correct. *Shunned grief is spiritual hypocrisy.*

REDISCOVERING LAMENT

Relearning the Language

From the beginning of Scripture, we find God in speech, and various forms of it: *declaring* as a Sovereign ("Let there be," Gen. 1:3), *conversing* as a partner ("It is not good," Gen. 2:18), *blessing* as a priest ("Be fruitful," Gen. 1:28), *questioning* as a parent ("Where are you?" Gen. 3:9), and *horrified* as a caring King ("What is this that you have done?" Gen. 3:13). From the very outset, the Creator is a *speaking* God. Appropriately, he is also a *hearing* God, attentive to the needs of people:

"I have surely *seen* the affliction . . . and have *heard* their cry. . . . I *know* their sufferings, and I have *come down* to deliver them. . . . The cry of the people of Israel *has come* to me." (Ex. 3:7–9, emphasis added)

Such passages clearly illustrate the attention and tenderness in the life of God. Notice how God's hearing and seeing match their groaning and crying. In fact, the first plea to God is a victim's blood "crying to me" (Gen. 4:10). And this cry of Abel echoes in the corporate lament of the martyrs, in the last book of Scripture: "O Sovereign Lord, holy and true, how long before you will judge and avenge . . . ?" (Rev. 6:10).

It is significant that God uses all kinds of speech acts, except monologue.[2] He remains an interactive God, always conversing. God does not edit the cries of people, allowing only certain kinds of pleas to get through. So rediscovering lament means we are called to join a faith of honest conversation with God. Israel's faith is a talking–faith.[3] When we look at the Psalter, we should not be surprised to find over 135 examples of things we can say to God—the Psalms teach us *how* to praise and lament.[4] We can identify four primary speech forms in the Psalter:

- *Praise.* We can proclaim to God: "You are great." We read, "O Lord, our Lord, how majestic is your name in all the earth!" (Ps. 8:1). Power and faithfulness are vital facts about God.
- *Thanks.* We can tell God: "Thank you!" We read, "I will extoll you, O Lord, for you have drawn me up" (Ps. 30:1). When God intervenes to help, it is natural to thank him. While praise psalms honor God for who he is and what he has done, thanksgiving psalms relate a personal story of how God has worked in our lives.
- *Lament.* We can cry out to God: "Help me!" So we read, "Hear my cry, O God, listen to my prayer" (Ps. 61:1). This language can even express intercession, as people identify with, pray for, and lament for others as well as themselves.
- *Trust.* We can admit to God: "I trust you." We read, "I will fear no evil, for you are with me" (Ps. 23:4). This is all about confidence that God does hear complaints, does protect, and does deliver.

Simply put, this repertoire of *praise–thanks* and *lament–trust* richly equips the believer as a partner in a full range of dialogue with their Creator who revealed himself through dialogue: "Let us make human beings" (Gen. 1:26 NLT).[5] *Humankind was made in dialogue, for dialogue* (cf. Gen. 2:23).[6]

One–third of the Psalter, about sixty–seven psalms, contains laments—about forty–two individual laments, sixteen corporate laments, and nine that use some lament. Nineteen of the individual lament psalms occur in Book One alone. These facts are important for the educational and catechesis–impact of the Old Testament. If the five books of Moses teach people how to live, the five books of the Psalter teach people how to worship. Lament is needed when one acknowledges that life does not match the aspirations of the Torah. Most of life is lived in the "painful and yawning gap between the liturgical affirmation of God's absolute sovereignty and the empirical reality of evil triumphant."[7] So worship must encompass both praise and pain, honestly brought to God.[8] In the Psalter, *the laments function as crisis–language*, appealing to God for the restoration of social status and the healing of body, heart, and community.[9]

For individuals, nations, and kings, lament is central to the message of the Old Testament, functioning between sin and mercy.[10] People cry out to God, and God himself grieves the judgments that must fall on his own people (cf. Hos. 11:8; Jer. 12:7–13). The disciples of our Lord must develop a taste for the words of our Lord. As Walter Brueggemann observes:

> The dialectic of lament (complaint) and praise (thanks), when appropriated in Christian tradition and transposed into Christological formulation permit the faithful church to utter the loss of Friday crucifixion in lament (Ps 22:1) and to voice the wonder of Sunday resurrection in exuberant doxology. . . . It is enough that the dialogic utterance of Israel (echoed by the church) walks fully and honestly into the reality of *abandonment* and walks boldly and buoyantly into the wonder of *restoration*.[11]

Suffering finds hope in the drama of lament and praise—crisis and resolve. As we will see, this is the very contour of a lament itself, a movement from protest to trust. *If the performance of praise exalts and affirms, the performance of lament names and transforms.* Without pain, praise is "thin" and halfhearted; but without praise, the pain seems fatal and unbearable.

The summons is to pray and preach both lament and praise. When both are taught, one invites the community of faith to remain in both joy and suffering.[12] It is the drama of pain in lament that extends the dialogue into all kinds of new situations. But pretense shortchanges hope.

Facing Our Facades

We must begin by facing some skewed notions we have about lament. Though Scripture is filled with powerful examples of lament (e.g., Psalm 13; 22), though stories do not shrink back from statements of deep suffering (like Job's), though characters have numerous examples of honest conversation with God (Moses, Numbers 14), and though the Psalter contains an entire literary genre dedicated to the use of lament, we seem to know less about this form of speech than ever before. There are some contemporary facades we must face, which are not just excluding the language of lament, but hurting people who long to cry out to God.

The Facade of Power

The person standing behind this facade declares, "All my necessary power comes through joyful worship." It is "High–powered" worship that helps one overcome personal despair, giving me the needed passion and strengthening my resolve.[13]

The result? *Lament is excluded* because expressions of pain and suffering do not communicate strength or empowerment. Instead, lament acknowledges personal weakness, sin, and even a God who did not intervene to stop the pain. Yet, worship that is Christian has a cruciform humility willing to enter into profound weakness, and still call it power (cf. 1 Cor. 1:27; 2 Cor. 12:10).

The Facade of Happiness

The person using this facade declares, "The Christian life is essentially about victory, which Jesus won on the cross for me." If victory is not central, then the Christian life will not be attractive to the lost and will be discouraging to other believers.

The result of this false front is that *lament is overwhelmingly ignored* because it does not fit the marketed expectation of "praise and worship." Yet lament is rooted in the believing community, and expressions of great pain can make others uncomfortable, especially when the worship is oriented to the unsaved. Lament allows for a fuller sense of hope. Living the Christian life does not remove deep seasons of suffering.

The Facade of Identity

The person using this facade declares, "I must show myself to be perfect, in order to show God that I really love him. The more enthusiastic, the more love I have for God. In fact, godliness is evident in my lack of grief, doubt, and complaint."

The result of accepting this facade? Lament is unacceptable, because it does not cater to the "positive vibe" and spontaneous individualism of popular faith. Lament runs counter to contemporary perfectionism, bringing an intensity to silence and weeping, as well as praise. Yet, what is corporate joy without corporate grief (cf. Rom. 12:15)? Lament is about honest process, social justice, and personal wholeness in collective transformation, not image–management, "victory" mantras, and the stiff upper lip.

The Facade of Sincerity

The person using this facade declares, "Obedience comes through my sincere desire and passion for God, which means I can become so passionate about God that I can actually avoid sin. My sincerity is really more important than truth itself."

The result? Lament is viewed as a "downer," since lament is the voice of pain, anger, and deep confusion over God's (in)action. This kind of candor is viewed as *negative* sincerity, and means something is clearly "wrong" in one's faith that is not mapped out and controlled. Lament calls out our preference for convenient emotion and sanitized interaction.

The Facade of Relevance

The person using this facade says, "God is fundamentally the Great-Need-Meeter. He wants me to be happy right now! So, my worship happens when I 'call down' God's insight to tackle the practical challenges I must face. God is most real to me when my faith works well."

The result? Lament is avoided because its honesty and introspection are not viewed as socially or emotionally cost-effective. An "App-for-that" culture is embarrassed by pain and offended by difficulty. But lament is about the raw truth of things that must be relationally faced, internally with God and externally with community. *Because popular faith views suffering as failure, people need permission to grieve.*

Responding to the Facades

For their part, Christian leaders and mentors must be able to lead others where they have also been if they hope to tear down these facades. They can read unedited stories, use lament psalms, model corporate grief, and name forms of collective suffering. In fact, all are necessary to turn these trends around. At one level, our discussion is really not about lament; it is about relearning the power of candid speech in conversation with God: to accept, craft, and enter into the language of suffering, socially and spiritually. As Nicholas Wolterstorff describes it:

> The lament, at its heart, is *giving voice to the suffering* that accompanies deep loss, whatever that loss may be. Lament is not *about* suffering. Lament is not *concerning* suffering. Lament does not count the stages [of grief] and try to identify the stage in which one finds oneself. *Lament is the language of suffering, the voicing of suffering.* Behind lament are tears over loss. Lament goes beyond the tears to voice the suffering.[14]

While the contemporary Christian is largely interested in what prayer *produces*, the biblical life of prayer is more concerned with the *tenacity of relationship* that is capable of summoning God's aid. For this reason, lament is a sharp "call of alarm" to a God who stands ready for his children. If prayer is interpersonal dialogue with God, then lament is a forceful communicative act that appeals for the intervention of the Cosmic Judge, in any number of ways, as we shall see.[15] First, we must take a closer look at how lament works.

GETTING TO KNOW THE LAMENT

The Character of Lament

In biblical studies, the lament refers to a type of psalm that makes up the largest category of the entire Psalter (primarily in Books One–Three). The great utility of lament is evident in its various subgenres of funeral dirge (e.g., 2 Sam. 3:33–34), city lament (e.g., Psalm 137), and the more common individual and communal lament. We will focus on the latter uses.

The common categories of psalms can be identified by their different displays of rich emotion. The lament was used when the worshiper was in great distress and God seemed distant. Also known as psalms of complaint, distress, or protest, laments can be broadly identified by their unique: (1) style, (2) structure, (3) content, and (4) mood.[16] While style and structure refer to elements used in sharp appeal to God, content and mood reflect the desperate condition, God's undeniable history, and the language used by the lamenter. Laments are commonly found in both individual "I"–types (e.g., Psalm 3) and communal "we"–types (e.g., Psalm 44). The vital role of laments is evident not only by their sheer quantity (one–third of the Psalter), but by their highly developed structure, their vibrant imagery, and the laments' ongoing life in the worship and instruction of God's people.

Several striking features of the lament must be noted. First, the language of the lament is vivid and assertive, and employs a wide spectrum of raw emotion.[17] In fact, the laments contain frequent pleas of desperation and outbursts of pained feeling. This somatic quality of language creates an emotional urgency and pathos that pulls the audience into the suffering.[18]

Second, the laments are not precise in their time frame, often switching tenses between "past" and "present." Laments do not capture the when of distress; rather, they highlight the *what* of personal suffering now felt throughout the psalmist's relational ecosystem. In the laments, a reader steps into the tense drama of human–divine dialogue, in all its candor (cf. Psalm 88). The psalmists use common imagery to capture uncommon suffering.[19] Following this portrait of pain can be a challenge for the reader since the language of lament is not carried by philosophical abstraction but theological themes of justice and suffering (Ps. 35:24).[20]

Third, there are no specific names or concrete charges that are mentioned. Even geographic locations are rare. *This has the effect of making the lament psalms forever relevant to new needs and situations*, right into our present day, e.g., "The LORD will keep your going out and your coming in from this time forth and forevermore" (Ps. 121:8).

Fourth, the lament always moves from expressions of pain to statements of trust. In the midst of their trying circumstances, laments climax in notes of confidence and celebration that God has acted or will act.[21] His proven history creates a confident future. In the communal laments, this might reflect the priest, who spoke a word of assurance to the psalmist.[22] But the individual laments reveal a transforming internal meditation on the part of the psalmist. As the lamenter considers the care, rule, character, and presence of God, this vital "theology comes crashing into human experience, and in that collision the life of faith is forged."[23] In fact, this arc of pain–to–praise reflects the macro–structure of the entire Psalter, beginning with lament (largely Books One–Three) and ending with hymns of praise (largely Books Four–Five). Before one can enter into the prize of praise, one must sit in the pain of laments. The doxology of Psalm 150 is the delight and joy of those deeply acquainted with grief.[24]

The Lament as Communicative Relationship

In the gift of relationship God has provided for people, prayer often is a primary element. Through prayer, humans and God can meaningfully interact with each other.[25] John Goldingay is correct when he writes, "The object of prayer is not to discover God's will in order to align oneself with it but to take part in determining God's will."[26]

In lament, "the worshiper becomes a participant with God," an agitator for a vital divine response.[27] It is in lament that humans report on the quality of life in this pilgrim journey.[28] The use of lament is evidence of a moral compass under strain, and God's need to rein in evil.

People enduring suffering often feel that God has "gone silent." The psalmists use metaphors of distance to describe God's nonresponsiveness, captured in phrases where God is far away (Pss. 22:1, 11, 19)[29] or needs to "turn" (Ps. 6:4) or "draw near" (Ps. 69:18). Closely related to spatial distance is God's *hiddenness*, evident in concern that God has hidden his face (Pss. 13:1; 17:15).[30] So, the lamenter can understandably be shaken by the silence of God: "You have seen, O LORD; be not silent. . . . O God, do not keep silence" (Pss. 35:22; 83:1; cf. 28:1; 109:1). Significantly, it is this silence of God—even prompting the lament—that allows the lamenter to have their full say.[31] God's silence is actually part of the larger process of communication.[32]

God may chastise people for their presumption, but not their raw honesty in lament. Lament draws on an existing relationship of commitment and loyalty to God. So questions of "how long" call out God's inactivity (Pss. 74:10; 94:3) and "why" questions come from people perplexed over God's lack of response (Pss. 22:1; 42:9). Clearly, God values words and tears far more than we do (Ps. 56:8), and like his accommodation to Hezekiah's plea for life, God can change his course of action when people cry out to him (2 Kings 20:1–11).[33] Because there is a tension here between God's sovereignty and human initiative, some texts have become lost to us: "*Take with you words* and return to the LORD; say to him, 'Take away all iniquity; accept what is good'" (Hos. 14:2a) or, more passionately from God's own mouth:

I was ready to respond, *but no one asked for help*. I was ready to be found, *but no one was looking for me*. I said, "Here I am, here I am!" to a nation *that did not call on my name*. (Isa. 65:1 NLT, emphasis added)

Such texts illustrate the relational life of God toward people, and the dynamic impact of human lament on the Cosmic Caring King.

The Lament as Meaning–Restoring

Some kinds of suffering are "language–shattering."[34] So it is important to understand how the lament works and why it is so common. In the words of Phil C. Zylla, "The Bible gives us permission to *say how bad things really are* and to move beyond silent acquiescence to articulate our pain. The disintegration of meaning that comes with suffering is slowly restored in the movement from silence to lament."[35] The lament is not an accountant's stoic report but an arousing exploration of broken relationship(s) that need healing. Lament begins the healing because its language "resists repression and overcomes denial."[36] When an injured party expresses their pain, there is a healing effect.

Since pain can smother speech, those in deep agony may actually find themselves socially isolated and functionally mute. "Mutism," claims Zylla, "is a state of inexpressibility. This leads to the sense of being cut off from community. All suffering is difficult to bear; suffering that is borne alone is excruciating and nearly impossible to express."[37] Put simply, lament restores the suffering person from mutism—"the harsh, empty chasm of wordless existence."[38] But when the normalized relationships of community are also lost, a further hindrance is added.

The very structure of lament brings shape to the formlessness of suffering.[39] Here, a unique contribution of lament begins to emerge: *because forms of affliction can paralyze speech and "steal" words, lament salvages the aching heart through intentional modes of speech*. Here are the core "stations" in most laments that help restore meaning for the lamenter:

- *Invocation*—the initial cry to God to take notice ("O Lord, how many . . . ?" [Ps. 3:1]). Or in rich expression, "O Sovereign Lord, what . . .

how" (Gen. 15:1–2, 7–8; cf. Hab. 1:2 NIV). The life of God remains open to honest cries for help.

- *Plea to God for Help*—a request, often in the imperative, for God to act ("Give ear . . . consider . . . give attention . . ." [Ps. 5:1, 2]).
- *Complaint*—focal point, a general description of the psalmist's suffering, revealing what has motivated the psalmist (e.g., an enemy, lamenter's sin, or God; "In arrogance the wicked hotly pursue the poor" [Ps. 10:2]).
- *Confession of Sin or an Assertion of Innocence*—confession in the context of sin, and assertion of innocence when no sin has been committed ("I acknowledge my sin to you"; "if there is wrong in my hands" [Pss. 32:5; 7:3]).
- *Curse of Enemies (Imprecation)*—seeking covenant vindication from their warrior God ("Repay them for their deeds and for their evil work" [Ps. 28:4 NIV, cf. 137:8–9]).

Several observations can be made about these curses. Consider the following characteristics of the lamenters who make imprecations within the Psalms:

1. Such lamenters are on the brink of despair. They are not powerful figures flexing their corporate muscles; rather, they are often powerless or poor, calling down the only agent that has their back.
2. They are never lying on their beds scheming of various ways to retaliate. Their darkest pain is poured out to God, not angels, idols, lawyers, or powerful spirits.
3. These lamenters are merely asking for divine *retribution* that corresponds to the nature of the offense they have suffered (cf. Ps. 54:3–5).
4. *These lamenters never take justice or vengeance into their own hands*—retribution remains with God alone (Deut. 32:35; Ps. 94:1; Rom. 12:19).[40] Unlike contemporary jihad, these lamenters beg God to act, not other people.[41]
5. There is a *ministry of presence* when the community simply hears the monstrous evil and raging of those so profoundly wronged. This is a formal speech tool for "siding with God" and victims of evil, against their perpetrators.[42]

Two final core "stations" exist in most laments:

- *Expression of Confidence in God's Response*—often a recital of God's proven record or trustworthy characteristics ("Behold, God is my helper; the Lord is the upholder of my life" [Ps. 54:4]).
- *Hymn or Blessing*—assurance of praise that will follow God's rescue ("I trust in the steadfast love of God . . . I will thank you forever, because you have done it [Ps. 52:8–9]).

The collective healing effect of these "speech–stations" is described well by Glenn Pemberton in his book *Hurting with God*:

> Lament is a structured, controlled language that by its methodical cadence helps restore a modicum of structure in times of disorientation. . . . Like the ritual actions of a wedding or funeral, these movements of lament enable us to negotiate the liminal space of pain with words that communicate to our God within a controlled setting. *In a way, lament itself begins to restore some sense of order in the midst of chaos.*[43]

PERFORMING THE LAMENT

In the ancient Near East, laments are *socially performed*. Bodily practices are highly charged with social meaning and value. In life's greatest seasons of joy and suffering, rituals speak as a form of enacted belief.[44] We can construct a good picture of how the ancients would lament:

> Schematically presented, the supplicant sets out an offering of various items, lifts the hands in a gesture of greeting, bows to the ground, rises up again, and then speaks the prayer (usually multiple times). All of this is intended to move the beseeched superior—whether human or divine—to be obligated to the supplicant and extend a helping hand.[45]

Of all Scripture it is only in the Psalter's laments that we find the voice of the people.[46] Here, they contend with God—because they are relationally committed to God. The greatest emotion is a gift, not a challenge, to the deepest relationships.

The Socioreligious Drama of Lament

There are four relational elements of the lament that should be observed: (1) the causes of distress, (2) the community, (3) the dramatic movement, and (4) divine royalty. Chart 1 helps to illustrate how the lament is performed within its *relational ecosystem* of faith. What emerges from the lamenter (personal plane) is always heard in community (social plane) before it ascends to God (spiritual plane). We will consider some of these elements.

Chart 1
Lamenting in the Relational Ecosystem

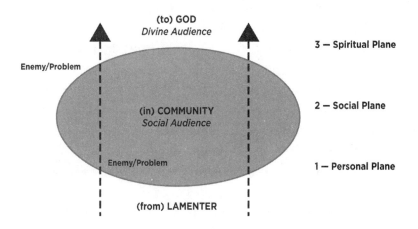

The Causes of Distress

In the laments, some "enemy" is the most common cause of distress, and rarely identified (vv. 7:13; 10:8–10).[47] Most often, the enemy is on the *outside* of the community, but there is some evidence that occasionally the enemy was part of the lamenter's own community (Pss. 41:9; 55:12–14, 20–21; cf. John 13:18).[48] For example, we find the stunning statement in Ps. 55: "If an enemy were insulting me, I could endure it; if a foe were rising against me, I could hide. But it is you, a man like myself, my companion, my close friend, with whom I once enjoyed sweet fellowship at the house of God, as we walked about among the worshipers" (vv. 12–14 NIV).

So while the lamenter addresses "enemies" [pl. noun] in 55:9 (cf. vv. 3b, 9, 15, 18, 23), it is clear that his betrayer [sing. noun] is from his own community (vv. 12–14; cf. vv. 3a, 20–21). This friend–turned–betrayer leads the lamenter to give a testimony–type recommendation to all assembled: "Cast your cares on the LORD and he will sustain you" (v. 22). Peter quotes this as an imperative of faith: "Cast all your anxiety on him because he cares for you" (1 Peter 5:7).[49] Lamenters did not dispatch their enemies by magic. "Faith is always also a threatened faith."[50] So the suffering endured by the lamenter is met with protests of their innocence.

There are two other causes of distress: self and God. *Self* refers to those psalms that contain personal confessions of sin, sometimes called Penitential Psalms (Pss. 32:3–5; 38:18; 39:11; 41:4; 51:2; 130:3). In these psalms, suffering brought on by personal sin has a stunning honesty and childlike appeal for God's forgiveness and restoration.

Within the classic Reformed tradition, the lament psalm has been wrongly minimized, with the focus placed almost entirely on the Penitential Psalm and the confession of sin.[51] Similarly, Augustine held that it was wrong to voice suffering, unless one is lamenting their own sin. And Calvin argued that it is misguided to cry out "Why," since believers already know.[52] After suffering the deaths of both his best friend and mother, Calvin concluded that his great grief was a sign that he had been guilty of too much worldly affection. For Calvin (and many today) profound grief is the sign of a sinful orientation. In the piety of many Christian traditions, the confession of sin has replaced lamenting over complex suffering.[53] But suffering comes in many forms, not just the forensic reality of guilt and sin.[54] As Horst D. Preuss notes, it is not just one aspect of the human person that suffers, but indeed, their entire being (Psalms 6, 22, 31, 63, 94).[55] Not all evil is chosen. From some expressions of biblical counseling to certain theodicies, this is not just a hermeneutic, it is a worldview whose anthropology lacks an adequate integration of the relational ecosystem. *Job's suffering will remain an embarrassment to "refined faith" unless we see his reactions as normal—his raging, protests, groaning, and straddling of confidence and despair.* Job is no reverent stoic. The entirety of Job's experience is carried over into the New Testament where he is held up as an example that we should imitate (James 5:11). *In truth, there is no lament outside the bounds of God's comfort, and no comfort that is not deepened by lament.*[56]

Finally, God himself can be a cause of distress (Pss. 22:2-3; 39:10).[57] On numerous occasions the lamenters call God out as the cause of unfair pain and suffering (Psalms 44, 88, 89). Moberly describes the divine cause as "most interesting theologically . . . psalms that see God as responsible for the painful situation and that do not end on a positive note . . . express[ing] the lament most fully and sharply."[58] For example, hear the complaint of the sons of Korah in Psalm 88:

> Why do you hide your face from me? . . . I suffer your terrors; I am helpless. Your wrath has swept over me; . . . you have caused my beloved and my friend to shun me; my companions have become darkness. (vv. 14-18)

The Community

Just as mourning was communal, not just individual, so the lamenter offered up his complaint within community.[59] Lament has a social audience that functions as a *listening community.* The social community hears the lament and is committed to determining a faithful response to the lament (e.g., opportunity for empathy, critique, and embodied aid).[60] The social community is the grieving community, "that circle of people among whom or against whom the one who laments stands with a complaint."[61] The social community that hears the lament has the obligation to become *discerning witnesses.* It is *how* Job's friends responded to Job's lament—lacking in discernment—that revealed their misguided critique and mistaken theology!

Within this relational ecosystem the laments are actually complaints, with enough time remaining to reverse the lamenter's problem. If the "problem" exists within the community and the lamenter's pleas have been neglected, then some sharp judgments may be leveled against them too. In other words, opportunity may exist for the community to respond appropriately, as well.[62] The appropriateness of any lament is initially evaluated by the social audience, and their empathy and insight uphold the lament and its cause before the divine audience.

The Dramatic Movement

The lament that begins with cries and a plea to God does not end there. In lament, sharp expressions of pain and injustice routinely culminate in some expression of confidence or trust. Either pole—a cry or statement of trust—seems feasible, but holding *both* cry and trust in the same exhale of worship would seem to fall somewhere between unnatural and cruel. This highlights a nurturing irony: *the lamenter not only engages the gritty depths of emotional pain at the beginning, but by the close reaches toward the heavens with intentional praise.* While pain finds full-throated statement, one cannot remain there. Like a pair of scissors, lament is comprised of two sharp edges we rarely see together. The pain of protest is no more unwelcome than the climax of trust is untimely. For one cannot weep on earth when one is not convinced that God's character is rightly praised in heaven. In lament, the pain is welcome and the praise is appropriate.

This dramatic movement of lament is both spiritually pedagogical and socially transforming. As John D. Witvliet correctly observes, "When practiced as an act of faith, lament can be a powerfully healing experience."[63] Lament captures a pain that *informs* but does not *define* the meaning of life.[64] Paradoxically, praise needs pain. Praise that makes sense echoes with the remembrance of suffering reversed. The current social trend views everyone as a victim. This capitalizes on the first part of lament, but without the crowning praise. Miller warns, "Both the lowly and the powerful will be tempted to conclude that the *status* is *quo*, that possibilities unseen are inauthentic and unlikely, that the world's power to define reality is ultimate and unchallenged."[65] The goal should be the social transformation.

Divine Royalty

When the lament passes through the social audience, with their critique and aid, it ultimately reaches the divine audience. It is no accident that the name YHWH appears most frequently in the Psalter—his name is cherished by lamenters and he "allows himself to be moved by them, even if on occasion they must cry out to him for a long time."[66] Like the cases brought before Israel's great kings for justice (2 Sam. 12:1–7; 1 Kings 3:16–28), so *the lament is ultimately placed before the cosmic King for his ultimate justice* (cf. Gen. 18:25). For the lamenter and their social community, God may be "my refuge" and "my light and my salvation" (Pss. 27:1; 31:4; 142:5), but God is foremost their King. The lamenter and community not only say "my God" and "my king" (Ps. 74:12; cf. 145:1), but even "my king and my God" (Pss. 5:2; 44:4; 68:24; and 84:3).[67]

From the social to the divine audience, lament was rooted in a rich relational ecosystem. Not surprisingly, "the human person is discussed primarily in the psalms in terms of his or her relationship to God."[68] Even the Davidic kings actually "sat on the throne of the LORD as king" (1 Chron. 29:23)! According to Mandolfo, "Nearly every lament can be characterized as a demand for justice."[69] *So in laments, a legal case is brought before divine royalty,* "for the LORD is a great God, and a great King above all gods" (Ps. 95:3).[70] Because there is no higher court, "it is an act of profound faith to entrust one's most precious hatreds to God, knowing they will be taken seriously."[71] There is no groveling before this King. Even lamenting one's sin becomes an act of worship. In the words of William P. Brown:

> The psalmist is a wounded speaker. . . . And therein lies the paradox: the very act of appeal to divine agency from a state of abject dependence actually heightens the power of human agency. The human

cry for help is itself a powerful affirmation of human dignity, [a dignity] violated yet destined for restoration. The cry of dereliction is not the cry of resignation or despair; it is the cry for vindication, the cry for justice. The bold language of the complaint, in short, rests on an intensely personal, trusting, and empowering relationship between God and the petitioner.[72]

Suffering makes the lamenters hunger for God, not to deconstruct him. He is "the Judge of all the earth" (Gen. 18:25), not an object of speculation. Even as the lamenter is steeped in crisis, Zimmerli explains:

There was no source to address from which help might come other than the one source: 'My help comes from Yahweh, who made heaven and earth' (Ps. 121:2) . . . Those other divine powers, whose existence is by no means denied on theological grounds . . . can only be [compared to Yahweh], who will call their actions to judgment (Ps. 82), or [mention these powers] in a spirit of superiority that mocks their impotence (Pss. 115:4–8; 135:15–18; cf. Acts 4:12).[73]

APPLYING THE LAMENT

Though it is starting to change, lament is still misunderstood in the life of the church. While the contemporary church has almost made a god out of "all-things-practical," we have yet to develop a taste for the practical realism of pain. Here, several implications need to be noted.

Our Prayers and Ritual Should Include Lament

First, if we are serious about justice, then *our prayer-dialogue with God must stretch to incorporate the audacious language of lament*, in print, prayer, and ritual. If words run out, "liturgy and ritual have the capacity to move beyond the word-form to the underlying reality of suffering—*entering the ineffable*."[74] Is there an index of laments a believer can find at church? Life under God is dialogue with God— both the messy and the majestic. The language of our new citizenship includes lament, because believers see suffering honestly, not just eschatologically.

Lament is no stage production. It is a natural "exhale of worship" when candor already exists in God's community, not merely when emergencies arise. That our experience of pain will be suspended one day, with the return of the King, does not mean we should airbrush suffering now. When suffering comes like a winter storm whiteout, then all surface definition disappears.[75] So our common pain must flower in collective patience. Coping with suffering and speaking to God about it is not an event to be logged but a discipline to be nourished in speech.[76] The Psalter offers a sanctuary of sighs and song.

The Church Should Invite Lament

Second, *we must start corporately* inviting *lament, not merely allowing it.* A holistic theological anthropology understands the created intersection of *physical pain, emotional anguish, social isolation,* and *spiritual weakness.*[77] Any one of these can be lamentable; but multi-layered suffering should be readily and regularly acknowledged within the social community of the redeemed. Too long have we carved up the human being, ignored evil systems, stigmatized certain suffering, and then placed value judgments on scars. Rather, "the articulation of affliction in lament must be nurtured and cultivated with an increasing capacity to bear up or to take on board all the complexity of *multivalent* suffering."[78]

Lament only occurs where there is community *solace,* not community information.[79] Our soulful pleas should naturally turn to our Wounded Lamb; our pleas should not come to church leadership, asking for permission to lament. We will lament when corporate honesty catches up with our personal pain.

We Should Welcome Painful Stories and Uncomfortable Questions

Third, if lament is going to be reclaimed, there must be a *shift from Christianity as an answering faith to one more willing to find mystery in painful stories and uncomfortable questions.*[80] We rarely find the answers we want in lament, but "where there is lament, there is life."[81] Lament is a precious reality–speech when meaning structures have collapsed.[82] But under mounting pressure to appease with "better answers"—amid a society intoxicated with the sovereign–self—there is little room left for pained questions from the inside. The church has few left who are willing to listen. Lament is risky because its pain and passion are unscripted. For complex suffering, faith is more than "aha!" answers, it is an intentional relationship of *unedited* dialogue. *Lament is a standing invitation to worship in pain, among the pained, not in spite of any pain.* And he who never sleeps (Psalm 121) will never be embarrassed by our tears, frailty, or questions.

Rather than dispensing answers, pastoral care reestablishes inner meanings by nurturing the expressions of anguish and disappointment.[83] Then one will not exalt in the "right answers" so much as in a God who hears rightly. The church can be a sanctuary in the midst of anguished cries. The danger is that the church will provide sanctuary only for Job's friends, but not for Job.[84] But genuine pastoral care combines hearing with knowing.[85] Church leaders must teach people to lament as an in–crisis response, rather than a post–crisis reflection. In fact, Christians must learn to worship in the midst of both lament and praise, as lament captures the moment. A theology of lament, according to Moberly, presents a "theological paradox: that lament and praise, sorrow and joy, belong together . . . praise rather makes explicit the context of faith and hope within which the lament is sounded."[86]

The Church Must Share in the Grief of Its People

Fourth, because the Western church tradition has replaced the corporate lament with individual confession of sin, the church has stripped out opportunity for the cries and groans of victims of many forms of violence.[87] Violence consists of multifaceted destruction, whether in abuse, battery, trafficking, terrorism, persecution, or genocide (e.g., Coptic Christians). The silence of the church—added to the existing trauma of such victims—makes the absence of lament multiply their suffering.[88] The church should listen to and assist those in pain and loss.

With growing attention given to theologies of peace, why is it such a sacrifice to help victims lament, those who have been broken through various forms of dehumanizing trauma? Individuals and communities who are enabled to tell their trauma story benefit from repeated truth-telling. Suffering people benefit from "being seen and heard" in the corporate setting. When external systems are combined with internal values that victimize people, there is multifaceted violence, and this clearly requires us to relearn the role of lament.

While confession is offender–oriented (i.e., forgiving the guilty), the sacrament of lament is victim–oriented, calling believers to share in the grief of others (Heb. 13:3). Lament exists for horrific experiences of suffering, not just conviction of sin. The communal–relational cry must be combined with the individual–legal confession. As Balentine writes,

> When the church takes seriously the practice of lament, it affirms that in a suffering world God is on the side of the victim and the castoffs (Ps. 113). If any word from God is to be spoken in the face of suffering, it must be articulated from the standpoint of the victim (Job), not the onlooker (Job's friends). . . . For victims, lament is the only sound that misery can make.[89]

The Church Must Recognize Lament as a Teaching Aid on Doubt

Fifth, lament is a powerful tutor to help people lean into the tension of faith and doubt. Because suffering can shake faith at its core, it is common to find a disparity between expectations and experience.[90] The scene of contemporary faith is increasingly strewn with the critical stories of believers–turned–atheist, in large part because faith is believed to be incompatible with the realities of real–world suffering. Faith and social–honesty are today believed to be at odds. Two options are available to relieve this tension.[91]

Option One: Christians double–down on their creedal trust and rationalistic affirmations about God to such a degree that they close their eyes to (i.e., deny) the awful reality of conflicting circumstances. These people say: "Really, everything's okay. This is what happens when you follow God." The danger here is that a greater degree of unreality will creep in, because their faith no longer opens their eyes, it has closed them. The consequences are all too common. This tension between expectation and experience will lead some to leave that faith community: "They're nice people, but naïve. They can't really face life!"

Option Two: Christians fixate on the painful circumstances, particularly innocent suffering, and abandon their faith. The extreme misery in life (e.g., terrorism, famine, economic inequity, sex trafficking, etc.) is simply too grotesque to make the faith tenable any longer. Humanistic education and exposure—defined by social activism and scientific insight—make their prior faith "irrelevant." The psalmic claim that "the LORD reigns" (Ps. 93:1) is now detested as imperialistic if not empty language that only trivializes the pain of "real life." They claim it is better to discard the faith and embrace disillusioned honesty rather than hang on to pious self–deception. The consequence is increasing difficulty finding adequate grounds for keeping any hope in life and resisting the toxicities of anger and despair.

The laments instruct us to sit in the painful contradictions of life, refuse easy rationalizations, and live with some unresolved conflict. In fact, one should neither abandon the faith nor deny painful and disappointing circumstances.

DOUBT AND FAITH, SIDE BY SIDE

Consider the following text:

> Remember your mercy, O LORD. . . . Remember not the sins of my youth. . . . Good and upright is the LORD; therefore he instructs sinners in the way. He leads the humble in what is right, and teaches the humble his way. All the paths of the LORD are steadfast love and

faithfulness, for those who keep his covenant and his testimonies.
(Ps. 25:6–10)

This text offers a great insight: complaint and reassurance, doubt and faith can be held in tension, functioning side by side.[92] Two voices offer two points of view: (1) The first–person voice (vv. 6–7) is the psalmist pleading with God to act justly, by his own standards. (2) The third–person voice (vv. 8–10) is a "teaching" voice that reassures the pleading psalmist of a core theological truth: "YHWH remains *steadfast (hesed)*, so do not worry" (cf. Ps. 44:26). The lesson is this: *faith without doubt is myopic, and doubt without faith is a slow slide into existential meaningless.*[93]

Samuel E. Balentine offers a profound reminder of the human spirit, in crisis:

> Perhaps the greatest irony of the biblical witness, and perhaps also its most impenetrable legacy of prayer, is that when one loses faith in God, it is precisely to God that one turns. . . . In the face of suffering our predecessors in faith risked standing side by side with the atheist, and discovered that they did not become atheists. *Their questions were the same, but their rebellion was different. . . . The revolt of the believer is not that of the renegade: the two do not speak in the name of the same anguish.*[94]

A *bruised faith*, emptied of nearness, can develop a taste for mystery that reason need not explain. Lament translates our *godforsakenness* to the only one who can truly absorb our darkest realities.[95] Moberly reminds us this is a faith issue, not an Old Testament issue:

> In general terms . . . there is no reason to suppose that the practice of lament is inappropriate in the context of NT faith. Lament is surely one of those vital areas where the witness of the NT must be seen to *presuppose and complement* that of the OT, and indeed to be potentially deficient without it.[96]

In particular, it is *personal vengeance* that the New Testament suspends, since God will ultimately issue a perfect justice (Rom. 12:18–19).[97]

Lament rightly used understands the correspondence between heart and word. The *sine qua non* of acceptable speech to the "great Shepherd of the sheep" (Heb. 13:20) is integrity between word and heart. As YHWH's words to humanity are pure words (Ps. 12:6), so his citizens must learn to speak in truth and honesty (Ps. 15:2; cf. Isa. 37:14–20; Jer. 15:18).[98]

As John Kessler explains:

> The theology of lament highlights divine accessibility—God's "otherness" does not deny the believer's access to God: "The LORD is near to all who call on him, to all who call on him in truth" (Ps.145:18). . . . All kinds of words may be spoken to Yahweh, even those that express the speaker's frustration, sorrow, and anguish regarding Yahweh's ordering of events in the world. Were Yahweh a weak or limited deity, one indifferent to the lot of humanity or the establishment of justice in the world, there would be no need to lament, question, or rail against God. . . . However, since divine accessibility implies true dialogue in the personal relationship, the speaker takes responsibility for the words spoken (cf. Job 38:1–3; Eccl. 5:1–3; Jer. 20:7a, 18).[99]

Lament names what only God can heal. Through prayer and intercession for others, God may be willing to alter the course of events and the way his purposes are implemented in human lives. A greater motivation for lament and intercession could hardly exist.[100]

As for me and my house, we will lament.

AMID PAIN AND SUFFERING

1. If laments function as crisis-language, what kind of guidance and access have you been given to cry out to God?

2. Which of the various facades have you witnessed most? What others could you add?

3. It was stated that in lament, the worshiper becomes a participant with God, agitating for God's action. Describe a current issue in your life in which you need to lament to God.

4. If suffering is language-shattering, then what are the implications for letting people speak about their pain in lament forms? Try writing out a lament for some suffering you are currently going through.

5. As it was discussed, explain how the very structure of lament can help restore a sense of order in the chaos of deep suffering.

CHAPTER 6

Be Angry and Do Not Sin

Suffering and Redemptive Anger

By Gerald W. Peterman

In a book on suffering, why include a chapter on anger? Is not anger less about *feeling* pain and more about *inflicting* pain? Further, how can anger be called redemptive?

These are good questions and they reflect a long history of seeing anger as only destructive, or worse, seeing anger as insanity.

Lucius Annaeus Seneca, a Roman stoic philosopher often known simply as Seneca, wrote in the first century that anger is

the most hideous and frenzied of all the emotions. For the other emotions have in them some element of peace and calm, while this one is wholly violent and has its being in an onrush of resentment, raging with a most inhuman lust for weapons, blood, and punishment, giving no thought to itself if only it can hurt another, hurling itself upon the very point of the dagger, and eager for revenge though it may drag down the avenger along with it. Certain wise men, therefore, have claimed that anger is temporary madness. For it is equally devoid of self–control, forgetful of decency, unmindful of ties, persistent and diligent in whatever it begins, closed to reason and counsel, excited by trifling causes, unfit to discern the right and true—the very counterpart of a ruin that is shattered in pieces where it overwhelms. But you have only to behold the aspect of those possessed by anger to know that they are insane.[1]

Similarly, from a Christian perspective, anger has long been classified as one of the seven deadly sins (cf. Prov. 6:16–19). Just how deadly has been detailed by Frederick Buechner in his classic *Wishful Thinking*:

Of the Seven Deadly Sins, anger is possibly the most fun. To lick your wounds, to smack your lips over grievances long past, to roll over your tongue the prospect of bitter confrontations still to come, to savor to the last toothsome morsel both the pain you are given and the pain you are giving back—in many ways it is a feast fit for a king. The chief drawback is that what you are wolfing down is yourself. The skeleton at the feast is you.[2]

If anger is only about insanity, bitter confrontations, spiteful revenge, or resentful alienation, it makes sense that we avoid anger at all costs. Yet often we do not know what to do with it, even when we are afraid of it growing intense and somebody getting hurt.

Or worse, perhaps we draw the conclusion that all anger is sin. So we fruitlessly try to never get angry or to hide it as best we can.[3]

Yet there is a better approach. The authors believe that it is important to understand what anger is, how it works, why God has given it to us, and how we are to express it. Although anger is sometimes viewed in a negative way, we hope to shortly clarify that insanity, bitterness, revenge, and alienation are not our only choices.

WHY ANGER IN A BOOK ON SUFFERING?

Let's ask again the question that opens this chapter: Why anger in a book on suffering? Let's recognize that anger is always a secondary emotion. It is a strong feeling of displeasure aroused by something one perceives to be morally wrong, personally painful, or threatening to the self or to something the individual considers valuable.[4] Thus, as we said before, anger reflects a suffering endured. The sufferer has been wronged or abused, or the sufferer has seen a loved one harmed unjustly. Alternatively, there might be a precious goal that is important to one's sense of self or one's sense of satisfaction in life, but the goal has been blocked.[5] All these causes of anger are first causes of emotional pain.

Stepping away from specific painful events, our anger can become generalized so that specific injuries or goals are no longer the issue. We have become generally angry: angry with life, frustrated with work, always short-tempered, or resentful of others. Furthermore, in instances where we try to express anger appropriately, we might find that it leads only to more pain and frustration: people will not listen to our attempts at reconciliation but only accuse us of dredging up the past, causing trouble, fault-finding, and the like. Then we find that reconciliation— another goal that is valuable to us—has been blocked. We are hurt yet again and so angry even more.

THE DESTRUCTIVE NATURE OF ANGER

We are well aware of many instances when anger is destructive, not redemptive. Cain was angry when his brother Abel's sacrifice was accepted but his was not. In anger he murdered his brother (Gen. 4:3–8). In their anger over the rape of their sister Dinah, Jacob's sons go to the extreme of slaughtering all the men in Shechem's city (34:1–4, 25–26). The eleven patriarchs were angered by their father Jacob's preferential treatment of Joseph and so hated their brother (37:4–5); in their anger they sold Joseph as a slave (37:28).

Destructive anger need not be about revenge or lashing out. Another sad result is alienation. In Esau's anger over having his birthright stolen, he threatens to kill Jacob (27:41). What results instead is the flight of Jacob and twenty years of alienation from his parents and brother.

In the New Testament, when magi from the east came looking for one born king of the Jews, Herod considered their arrival troubling (Matt. 2:3); even for such a cruel tyrant as Herod, his anger at least in part was about the pain of feeling threatened by another authority. In a deceptive request, Herod asked the wise men to tell him the location of this babe so that he might worship him too (2:8). But they did no such thing. "Then Herod, when he saw that he had been tricked by the wise men, became furious, and he sent and killed all the male children in Bethlehem and in all that region who were two years old or under, according to the time that he had ascertained from the wise men" (2:16).

HOW ANGER CAN BE REDEMPTIVE

But godlessness and cruelty are not the only motivations for anger; likewise pain, death, brutality, and alienation are not its only results. Instead, *anger may be motivated by love and its goal can be redemptive*: to rescue, to vindicate, to protect, or to restore.

The connection between love and anger might strike us as odd or unnatural. We might assume that love and anger are opposites or that anger is motivated by something that is unloving. But the opposite of love is not anger; it is indifference. If a wife is angry with her husband, that does not mean she has no love for him; her anger might be righteous jealousy. A parent who is angry with the child need not be motivated by lack of love but rather motivated by love to guide and correct the child. This is redemptive anger. Lester insightfully comments,

> Anger may arise, indeed *should* arise, within us as Christians *because* of our love, not *in contradiction* to our love. The more deeply we become committed to certain values, the more we may experience threat. Certain values matter to us because of our maturing commitments, and when they are violated by persons or institutions we are threatened and angry. . . . If we didn't love, we wouldn't be threatened. Here anger is *not opposed* to love, but is *in the service* of love.[6]

REDEMPTIVE ANGER IN SCRIPTURE

There are many examples of redemptive anger in Scripture. Here are four: Joseph, Nehemiah, Jesus, and Paul.

The Reconciling Anger of Joseph—Genesis 42–50

We do not need to rehearse in detail the pain that Joseph suffered because of his brothers—the hatred, the verbal abuse, the mockery, and finally his sale as a slave. After being sold and coming to Egypt, he suffered many years. When finally he saw his brothers again after two decades we might expect an immediate joyful and tearful reunion or immediate wrathful retaliation. Neither occurs. Instead we find Joseph speaking to his brothers harshly (Gen. 42:7); such harsh verbal treatment corresponds to the brothers' unwillingness to speak peaceably with him (37:4). Joseph demands to see the youngest—now favorite—son (42:20), in contrast to his brothers' previous action of shunning him when he was the favorite. "Joseph's brothers once sold him into slavery for financial gain (37:26–28)," notes Matthew Schlimm. "In an act of symmetrical retribution, Joseph strikes fear into their hearts by giving them silver that they do not deserve and should not rightfully possess."[7]

What is all this about? Joseph is angry about the pain they have put him through. But he is not thirsty for revenge. His anger is motivated by something else. He is taking them through an elaborate process by which he discerns that his brothers have changed. While he can forgive them unilaterally, only if they have changed can there be reconciliation. But if Joseph treats them harshly and tests them, does that mean that he did not love his brothers? On the contrary! Out of love for them and a desire to see their past resolved, he uses his anger of betrayal to guide his testing of them. This testing, however, was no easy task; it was painful in itself, as we see from Joseph's tears in the process (42:23–24; 43:30).

The Vindicating Anger of Nehemiah—Nehemiah 5:1–10

Here, under the governorship of Nehemiah, many Israelites have returned from exile in Babylon and are trying to reestablish themselves in Jerusalem. But there arises a complaint because poorer Jews are suffering economic exploitation at the hands of the wealthier Jews. At least one aspect of the exploitation was loans made at interest—a practice contrary to Mosaic Law (Ex. 22:25; Lev. 25:36–37). The poor were suffering economic hardship to the point of selling their children (Neh. 5:5).

What is Nehemiah's response? "I was very angry when I heard their outcry and these words" (v. 6). This is anger against injustice. The anger is founded on love for God's Word and love for God's people.[8] It is painful to see the one disobeyed and the other exploited. Nehemiah took action: "I took counsel with myself, and I brought charges against the nobles and the officials. I said to them, 'You are exacting interest, each from his brother.' And I held a great assembly against them" (v. 7).

Thankfully Nehemiah was angry, for the anger led to right action—redemptive action. This is how anger works; it motivates us to take action and bring about change. As commentator Charlie Summers notes,

> Nehemiah is concerned with the defense of the community against future enemies, and so wants to rebuild the wall around Jerusalem. He is also aware that the defense of the community clearly involves internal values. If the city is a place of exploitation and enslavement of the poor, then there is not much to defend—before God or the enemy. Ezra and Nehemiah continue the exodus theme that God intends the people to treat each other like kinfolk, like neighbors.[9]

The Weeping Anger of Jesus—John 11:33–38

John 11 provides a good example of a painful, grieving anger. In some ways, the passage is similar to Mark 3:5, which was treated in chapter 4 on the emotions of Jesus.

The story begins with a family that Jesus loved: sisters Mary and Martha and their brother Lazarus (11:5). Jesus hears that Lazarus is ill (v. 3). Because of his love, when Lazarus is sick Jesus delays until his friend's death, intending to raise him from the dead. But Jesus' purposes are misunderstood, as is common in the fourth gospel. When Jesus arrives in Bethany, the sisters only believe that Jesus could have saved Lazarus from death (vv. 21, 32); they do not believe that Jesus can raise him now that he is dead. Despite her earlier conversation with Jesus (vv. 21–27), Martha's objection to moving the stone (v. 39b) shows that she did not understand that he would raise Lazarus immediately. This lack of faith grieves Jesus. But his emotional reaction is not restricted to grief; it has anger as well.

Some translations (e.g., English Standard Version, New American Standard Bible, and New International Version) do not bring this out, however. The word we find translated as "deeply moved" (vv. 33, 38 ESV) is better translated "angered" or "outraged," as one finds in the Holman Christian Standard Bible: "He was angry in His spirit and deeply moved" (v. 33; see also NLT). The same word (*embrimaomai*) also occurs in Matt. 9:30 and is translated there as "sternly warned" (ESV). In Mark 14:5 it is translated "scolded" (ESV). Thus what we have outside the tomb of Lazarus is a mixture of anger and grief (cf. Mark 3:5; Luke 19:41–46); he has sympathy for Mary and Martha concerning the loss they have gone through, and he is angry over their evident lack of faith (cf. Num. 14:11–12).

Jesus wept here—or better, he "shed tears"[10]—but it is unlikely that the tears are about grief over the death of Lazarus since Lazarus will be alive in a few minutes. Rather, the grief has to do with a serious misunderstanding of this moment and its significance. When some bystanders see the tears, they rightly take them as a sign of love (v. 36a). Others, however, add a skeptical note and basically repeat the limited perspective of Mary and Martha: "Could not he who opened the eyes of the blind man also have kept this man from dying?" (v. 37). The lack of faith results in further anger on Jesus' part: "Then Jesus, angry in Himself again, came to the tomb" (v. 38 HCSB).

In what sense is Jesus' anger redemptive? The passage anticipates his own confrontation with death later in the book. Lazarus' death is to the glory of God (11:4); Jesus' death will be too, as has been indicated throughout John (e.g., 12:27–28; 13:31–33). When he faces death, the grave, and resurrection, it is no easy task, but one full of grief (John 12:27; 13:21; Matt. 26:38; Luke 22:44). To come face-to-face with death is not something one does in stoic calm; it is a battle. In this battle he is misunderstood. But in this battle he trusts, he loves, he grieves, he perseveres, and he lovingly rebukes all our unbelief: "Did I not tell you that if you believed you would see the glory of God?" (John 11:40).

The Indignation of Paul—2 Corinthians 11:29

After he planted the church in Corinth, false apostles came making trouble for Paul, opposing him and distorting his message. From Paul's description, they preached a false gospel (2 Cor. 11:4), were false apostles (11:13) and servants of Satan (11:15), and boasted of their connections, skills, and accomplishments (11:18). Paul finds such boasting absurd and even anti-Christian. Nevertheless he faces a choice: either he refuses to boast and so plays into his opponents' hands and is seen as inferior to them, or he boasts and thereby puts himself on their level. Neither option is appealing. In the end he feels compelled to "boast" as the opponents are doing (11:16); he feels forced to do it against his better judgment (12:11).

When he engages in boasting, however, he turns boasting on its head, and lists his imprisonments, deprivation, and beatings instead of his qualifications and accomplishments (11:22–28). The list includes incarceration, shipwreck, forced fasting, cold and exposure, and rejection by those who ought to love him. The crown of this long list of sufferings and pains is his anxiety for all the churches (using the noun form of the verb in Phil. 4:6). Finally, he ends with two rhetorical questions that demonstrate his concern for others: "Who is weak, and I am not weak? Who is made to fall, and I am not indignant?" (v. 29).

When Paul uses the term "fall" (*skandalizetai*) he is probably referring to the activity of the false apostles; their doctrines cause others to *fall into* sin or to *fall away* from the truth (see other uses of this word in Matt. 5:29; 26:31; Luke 7:23; 1 Cor. 8:13). When other Christians are misled in this way, Paul burns with anger (cf. 1 Cor. 7:9; Eph. 6:16). There are certainly other, more common words for anger or indignation,[11] but this one is in keeping with the graphic and visceral contents of the whole boasting sequence.

What is the result of Paul's anger? How can we see it as redemptive? The very letter itself is the result of his anger, filled as it is with sarcasm (2 Cor. 11:19; 12:13), deep emotion (1:8; 2:4; 7:4), and a distinctively Christian definition of gospel ministry (2:14–7:4) in contrast to the distorted definition brought by the false apostles. Paul's redemptive anger motivated him to plead with the Corinthians, using all his heart, mind, and soul to bring them back to the gospel.

RIGHTEOUS ANGER AND THE COMMAND TO BE ANGRY

In *Feelings and Faith*, Brian Borgman asserts, correctly, that there is a kind of righteous anger. He gives Jesus in Mark 3:5 as an example; and it is an excellent example. But despite his title, Borgman never talks about cultivating godly anger. In his chapter titled "Sinful Anger," he says there can be righteous anger. Nowhere, however, in that chapter or in any other part of the book does he talk about the need or the way to "cultivate" godly anger.[12]

But as the earlier examples in this chapter have shown, godly anger—that which seeks to change a sinful situation—is valuable. On the other hand, the previous examples were all descriptive, not prescriptive; we saw *examples* of godly anger but we did not find the moral *obligation* placed on God's people to be angry. Thus Eph. 4:26–27 is uniquely valuable, for it gives such an obligation. The command to be angry reads: "Be angry and do not sin; do not let the sun go down on your anger, and give no opportunity to the devil."

Some translations fail to bring out the command in the passage. Thus the *New International Version* (2011) translates, "'In your anger do not sin': Do not let the sun go down while you are still angry," and the *New Living Translation* says, "And 'don't sin by letting anger control you.' Don't let the sun go down while you are still angry." Both translations imply that anger is not commanded but is a possible condition for something else. But Paul here uses an imperative verb form. When he commands anger, it is not merely commanded in a conditional sense, as the thorough study of this passage by Daniel Wallace clearly shows. "Paul is placing a moral obligation on believers to be angry as the occasion requires." Furthermore, "if we fail to obey this injunction, not only will the enemy continue to make well-ploughed inroads into our churches" but we will be "suppressing our holy indignation."[13]

There is no contradiction between v. 26 ("be angry") and v. 31 ("Let all . . . anger . . . be put away from you"). As Wallace says,

> Vv. 26 and 31 clearly stand in tension. Just as it would be wrong—by appealing only to 26a—to say that all anger is a righteous duty laid on the believer at all times, so too it would be wrong—by appealing exclusively to v. 31—to say that all anger is wrong and utterly sinful at all times. Indeed, there are two internal clues which help to resolve the tension created by v. 31.[14]

Returning to Eph. 4:27, Paul commands his readers to "give no opportunity to the devil." The devil can gain an opportunity when there is no *redemptive* anger. There are a variety of possible ways this happens. First, the devil gains an opportunity if we fail to be angry and then take appropriate action to deal with sin, abuse, oppression, or apostasy. Second, one might be angry and yet not act. Appropriately, David is angered when he hears that Amnon raped his daughter Tamar (2 Sam. 13:21); but inappropriately the anger *leads to no action on his part*! His failure to act only outrages others within his family, causing more deaths and sexual violation. Third, one might become angry or show anger in a wrong way or to an inappropriate degree. We saw this with Cain and Abel (Gen. 4:3–8). Fourth, in contrast to Paul's exhortation to deal with anger promptly ("do not let the sun go down on your anger"), one might be angry over a long period.

THE TROUBLE WITH ANGER

Although the discussion here has been mainly positive about the value of anger, it is certainly true that there can be trouble with anger. We gave brief examples earlier.

What is the trouble with anger? It is the same trouble that we have with every other emotion: rather than arising from our love for others and from injustice, our anger often arises from our own pride, from our massively immature sense of being unsafe, or from a sinful desire for power and control.[15] We might experience it with wrong motivation or wrong causes. Even love could go wrong and do this: for Paul warns that love should not rejoice in unrighteousness but in truth (1 Cor. 13:6). We might direct our anger to the wrong objects. Similarly the apostle John warns us not to love (that is, *agapē*) the world (1 John 2:15). So while we might express our anger inappropriately, this can also happen with love as well. Thus the apostle John further warns, "Little children, let us not love in word or talk," for that is inappropriate expression; rather let us love "in deed and in truth" (3:18).

What is the trouble with anger? For those of us in positions of authority it can be especially problematic. The anger of a powerful person is always dangerous:

- When Potiphar heard his wife's (false) accusation against Joseph, "his anger was kindled" and he threw Joseph in prison (Gen. 39:19–20).
- Shadrach, Meshach, and Abednego refused to bow to Nebuchadnezzar's image. In a furious rage the king had them thrown in the furnace (Dan. 3:13–20).
- After Hanani rebuked King Asa, the king "was angry with the seer and put him in the stocks in prison, for he was in a rage with him because of this. And Asa inflicted cruelties upon some of the people at the same time" (2 Chron. 16:10).
- Saul persecuted Christians even to death because of his "raging fury against them" (Acts 26:11).

The anger of the powerful can be dangerous because of respect granted to their position and because of their influence over more people. We in ministry are in positions of the powerful: those in youth groups, congregations, and Sunday school classes will look to us for an example to be imitated. All these are especially vulnerable to being harmed by our anger.

PUTTING IT ALL TOGETHER

The Value of Anger

Even though all the caveats above are true, they should not blind us to the value of anger. Anger can be an appropriate response to evil and violence. It can provide the energy to take the necessary action against that wrongdoing. We doubt that the Civil Rights Movement could have occurred without plenty of anger against injustices witnessed. While it is true that most of it was nonviolent protest, nonetheless it was motivated by anger at oppression.[16] B. B. Warfield says perceptively,

> It would be impossible, therefore, for a moral being to stand in the presence of perceived wrong indifferent and unmoved. Precisely what we mean by a moral being is a being perceptive of the difference between right and wrong and reacting appropriately to right and wrong perceived as such. The emotions of indignation and anger belong therefore to the very self-expression of a moral being as such and cannot be lacking to him in the presence of wrong. We should know, accordingly, without instruction that Jesus, living in the conditions of this earthly life under the curse of sin, could not fail to be the subject of the whole series of angry emotions, and we are not surprised that even in the brief broken narratives of his life–experiences which have been given to us, there have been preserved records of the manifestation in word and act of not a few of them.[17]

Anger as an Essential Aspect of Being Human

We will not be rid of anger until the new heaven and the new earth.

As long as we live on a sinful planet, we must recognize that some anger cannot be avoided. It is part of being human. Although he is writing about anger in the book of Genesis, Schlimm's comments are apt:

> Anger is not something best left to psychologists for interpretation. One does not need Freud to understand how this emotion works. Rather, anger is a common feature of the fractured world and imperfect humanity that Genesis envisions. It is a permanent mark of the exiled from Eden. Anger cannot be avoided. It must be engaged, lest it ruin morality, community, and even life itself. Anger is thus not "merely a feeling." It is an ethical matter of the first degree.[18]

From the biblical references to anger in this chapter, we see that Scripture essentially views anger as normal or typical, without necessarily issuing a moral or theological judgment.[19] The anthropological backdrop sees a human being who feels compassion and shame, hatred and love. Anger is a natural response for those who have been wronged; consider the responses of many Old Testament individuals:

- Esau when he is swindled out of his birthright (Gen. 27:41–45)
- Jacob when he is blamed for Rachel's childlessness (Gen. 30:1–2)
- Laban when he is slighted (Gen. 31:35)
- Samson's hot anger after Delilah betrays him (Judg. 16:28)
- Saul's jealousy over the people doting on David (1 Sam. 18:8)
- Uzziah when priests confront him (2 Chron. 26:19)

Anger can be a powerful response to a sense that one has been personally devalued—human worth has been questioned.[20]

Anger most potently operates within the "relational ecosystem" (see chapter 2). Thus a backbiting tongue generates anger (Prov. 25:23); flowing from rejection is jealousy, bringing along slight and shame (Prov. 6:34). Joseph shows great wisdom and grace when he pleads with his brothers not to be angry *with themselves* (Gen. 45:5)—though they already dishonored themselves!

Anger as Part of Living Faith

If anger, worldview, and ethics are related—and they are, very closely—and if a significant part of biblical faith has to do with worldview and ethics, then anger will be a vital part of living faith. We do not have the option to live stoic lives; the God of the Old Testament is a God of steadfast love (Ex. 34:6) and also of great wrath (2 Chron. 34:21). Jesus our Lord is a man of deep compassion (Matt. 9:36) and also of anger and indignation (Mark 10:14). Anger as living faith can appear in at least the following ways:

First, anger *can be an invitation to conversation with God.* Thus the first anger in Scripture leads to a question from God (Gen. 4:8–9). The Lord does not reject Cain because of anger, but invites a relationship with him. Unfortunately, Cain apparently turned down this opportunity for dialogue with God; we should not.

A second way anger can be part of a living faith follows closely from this: *anger can be a window into one's own heart.* It can show you and me what is important to us. We do not become angry over things that mean nothing to us. If I am angry about a small scratch on my car but have no indignation over human trafficking, something has gone wrong with my perspective; I am walking by the flesh and not the Spirit.

Third, it is no accident that *Scripture gives us examples of righteous anger from biblical characters.* Earlier we considered the anger of Nehemiah, of Jesus, and of Paul. These examples are given to help us identify with the characters; but the examples do more. From these stories and examples we can see how life ought to be lived. They put flesh and blood on the command to imitate the faith of the godly (Heb. 13:7).

Furthermore, fourth, *Scripture's examples of righteous anger from biblical characters help us answer worldview and ethics questions,* another way anger can be part of a living faith. What is injustice? What is equity? What is oppression? How is life meant to be lived in community? These are valuable questions and rarely do we have enough personal life experience to answer them well. Scripture's guidance helps us learn the answers to these questions from the godly men and women who have gone before us.

The value of anger, properly expressed, should not be ignored. It is a God–given emotion to every man and woman, boy and girl, a powerful tool for change for ourselves and the world around us, and is meant to bring honor to God.

AMID PAIN AND SUFFERING

1. Give examples from your own life when anger has been destructive and when it has been redemptive. Explain how you can tell the difference.

2. Since "anger is always a secondary emotion," what do you find most typically is the first emotion behind your own anger? Reflect on your answer to the question. Would you say that the first emotion behind your own anger is painful?

3. Does it surprise you that Jesus was sometimes angry (e.g., Mark 3:5; 10:14)? If so, why? If not, why not?

4. Have you known someone with an anger problem? If so, keep the person's identity private and describe the situation.

5. Tell if you agree or disagree with this statement and explain why: "God gave us anger because it prepares us for action."[21]

CHAPTER 7

The Lord's Prayer

Suffering, Prayer, and Worldview

By Gerald W. Peterman

Why include the Lord's Prayer (Matt. 6:9–13; cf. Luke 11:2–4) in a book on suffering? That is a good question! The prayer has received extensive and insightful treatment many times over. These few verses are studied here because of the hints of disappointment, conflict, suffering, and evil seen in the prayer.

The prayer's worldview implies suffering or it touches—directly or indirectly—on suffering we encounter regularly. Looking at it this way is not to say that the prayer is negative or without hope; the opposite is true. Instead, highlighting the suffering behind these words helps us to see the hope and grace that shine through and present a glorious future.

"OUR FATHER IN HEAVEN"

The address "our Father" is only here in the Gospels. It is true that Jesus refers to his Father a few times (e.g., Matt. 11:27; 15:13; 16:17; 18:35).

Likewise Paul uses "our Father" quite a bit during the introductions to his letters (e.g., Rom. 1:7; 1 Cor. 1:3; 2 Cor. 1:2; Gal. 1:3; Phil. 1:2) and elsewhere (e.g., Phil. 4:20; 1 Thess. 3:11, 13). But none of these explicitly teaches us to address God as our Father. For that we must go to what Matthew tells us about the teaching of Jesus.[1]

Three things that we see in this prayer, namely the address "our Father," the concern that God act from heaven, and the longing that God's name be honored (the first petition of the Lord's Prayer), reflect broad concerns from the Old Testament but especially Isaiah 63–64. There we find the prophet praying to the Lord, saying,

> Look down from heaven and see, from your holy and beautiful habitation . . . For you are our Father, . . . our Redeemer from of old is your name. (63:15–16; cf. 64:8)

> Oh that you would rend the heavens and come down, that the mountains might quake at your presence—as when fire kindles brushwood and the fire causes water to boil—to make your name known to your adversaries, and that the nations might tremble at your presence! (64:1–2)

Similar themes are found in the prayer in Matthew 6. Our Father is asked to work from heaven on our behalf (v. 9). As he works he will honor his own name (v. 9). His work will bring his kingdom, and thus all other corrupt and oppressive kingdoms will be removed (v. 10).

Since Jesus invites us to call God "our Father," we need to ask: How is this Father viewed in Matthew? What sort of Father is he? The picture is rich and we will only scratch the surface. Among many others things that could be said, we note the following:

- *A Father who knows us.* "Do not be like them, for your Father knows what you need before you ask him" (6:8). As an omniscient Creator he is intimately familiar with us and all our needs. Likewise Jesus says the Gentiles seek after food, clothing, and shelter, "and your heavenly Father knows that you need them all" (6:32).

- *A Father sovereign over great and small.* Unlike how some in the ancient world viewed pagan gods, our Father is not distant and unconcerned with minor details. Rather, Jesus says, "Are not two sparrows sold for a penny? And not one of them will fall to the ground apart from your Father" (10:29), and "Look at the birds of the air: they neither sow nor reap nor gather into barns, and yet your heavenly Father feeds them" (6:26).

- *A Father who works in us.* Giving encouragement regarding the endurance of persecution, Jesus says, "When they deliver you over, do not be anxious how you are to speak or what you are to say, for what you are to say will be given to you in that hour. For it is not you who speak, but the Spirit of your Father speaking through you" (10:19–20). He does not despise us in our ignorance or weakness.

- *A Father who has compassion for the weak.* Jesus did not spend most of his time with the powerful and the wise, but with sinners, the weak, outcasts, and children. He rejoiced in such ministry, saying, "I thank you, Father, Lord of heaven and earth, that you have hidden these things from the wise and understanding and revealed them to little children" (11:25).

- *A Father who is generous.* This is a very common picture of God in Matthew and particularly appropriate when we talk of prayer. God our Father "makes his sun rise on the evil and on the good, and sends rain on the just and on the unjust" (5:45). We are happy to do acts of piety in secret since our Father who sees in secret will reward us (6:4, 18). Many parents know how to take care of children. But if we know how to give good gifts to our children, how much more will our "Father who is in heaven give good things to those who ask him!" (7:11).

Why spend time looking at how God is presented as Father in Matthew? One reason is so that having a clearer picture of what God our Father is like, we begin to see clearly that many earthly fathers are not like him or that often our experience of our own fathers is vastly different. Perhaps our father did not care to know us. Perhaps he was not in control; he was absent; he lacked compassion; and instead of being generous he was selfish. Therefore, the question arises: Can we address God in prayer saying "Our Father," or do we struggle to mouth the words? Alternatively, do we seek a more comfortable label for our heavenly Father and address him using simply "God," "King," or "Lord" because the word "Father" gets stuck in the darkness of our memory? The names "God," "Lord," and "King" are all are honorable and good. They do not, however, invite the kind of family intimacy that the term "Father" welcomes. For some of us, this family intimacy has been hard to achieve.

My parents divorced when I was about two years old. The first time I remember seeing my father I was eleven or twelve. He and my mother—after they had been divorced some ten years—took my sister and me to visit my grandparents. This was the first time I had seen them. After a few days there, my grandmother said it would be good if I could call my father "Dad." Even at that young age I could admit that it was a good idea; indeed it was something I longed for. On the other hand I simply could not bring myself to use the name "Dad." For me, speaking relationally and not biologically, there was no such person. The very thought of speaking the words was painful. Thankfully after years of growth and getting to know my own dad again through long conversations, calling God "Father" comes naturally and easily.

What will happen and is happening to our millions of children growing up in a divorce culture? What kind of damage is this doing?[2] Have we seen the worst of it yet?

"HALLOWED BE YOUR NAME"

Hallowed

We should admit that this first word, "hallowed," is not very helpful; it is archaic and almost meaningless. When do we use the word "hallowed" in our normal conversation? Perhaps the closest we come is a reference to Halloween (originally the holy evening before All Saints Day). The word, therefore, needs updating. And although many new translations have appeared in the last decade or so, one still finds "hallowed" in key Bible translations: ESV, NKJV, NASB, and NIV (2011). Other translations, however, are doing a better job and in them we find something like "may your name be honored" (NET), or "Your name be honored as holy" (HCSB), or "may your name be kept holy" (NLT).

Now we see right away that the "Lord's Prayer begins with three petitions for God himself."[3] Indeed, we cannot stress this enough: this prayer starts with the concerns of God, with the reputation of God, with God's plans for this world, with the big picture of all existence. It is about God's honor, God's goals, and God's moral requirements. Only when the concerns of God become our focus can we properly even ask for ourselves. How often we get this wrong! And this is another indicator of suffering in our world. Because of our own fear and weakness, our prayers often are wholly absorbed in our own worries and pain.

Now there is certainly no sin in running to God and crying out to him in trouble. The Psalms let us know that quite clearly. They cry out (e.g., Pss. 22:2; 27:7; 28:2; 30:8; 57:2; 77:1; 88:1; 130:1; 142:1). Nevertheless there is a fundamental distortion in a life whose model prayer, whose typical prayer, starts with the narrow, truncated concerns of the singular human life.

Your Name

What is in a name? In contrast to the ancient world, today's parents assign names with a very different kind of concern. Does the name sound good? Can the name be made into a mockery? Is it too common? Does it fit with the middle and last name? Will the grandparents like it? These considerations are quite contrary to the way naming happens in Scripture.[4]

The focus on the name in the Lord's Prayer reflects a very Jewish point of view, a view seen in both Testaments.[5] The name of the Lord is virtually equivalent to his will, person, and attributes. It is not enough to honor a "higher power" or a "divine being" in some sort of abstract way. "Referring to the name of God points to his specific personal identity as made known in his deeds and self–revelation."[6] From a biblical point of view, to know God's name is to know his works, his ways, and his character. The Lord tells Pharaoh, "But for this purpose I have raised you up, to show you my power, so that my name may be proclaimed in all the earth" (Ex. 9:16). This proclamation means much more than merely shouting out the label "Yahweh!" It means making known Yahweh's power and character.

Certainly in the Old Testament God is very concerned that his character be known, that his glory and honor be preserved—that is, that his name be glorified. So, for example:

> "You shall not profane my holy name, that I may be sanctified among the people of Israel. I am the LORD who sanctifies you." (Lev. 22:32)

> "For when he sees his children, the work of my hands, in his midst, they will sanctify my name; they will sanctify the Holy One of Jacob and will stand in awe of the God of Israel." (Isa. 29:23)

> "Now therefore what have I here," declares the LORD, "seeing that my people are taken away for nothing? Their rulers wail," declares the LORD, "and continually all the day my name is despised." (Isa. 52:5)

> "But I acted for the sake of my name, that it should not be profaned in the sight of the nations among whom they lived, in whose sight I made myself known to them in bringing them out of the land of Egypt." (Ezek. 20:9)

> "For from the rising of the sun to its setting my name will be great among the nations, and in every place incense will be offered to my name, and a pure offering. For my name will be great among the nation, says the LORD of hosts." (Mal. 1:11)

In all these instances, to sanctify the Lord's name or thank the Lord's name is the same as sanctifying or thanking the Lord himself. Alternatively, to despise the Lord's name is to treat the Lord himself with contempt. Thus the Lord's Prayer requests that God be known and that this knowledge would be viewed as holy, precious, and honorable.

But we cannot pray this prayer with truth and sincerity unless there is within us the longing to show God holy in our own lives, unless we desire to bring him glory through our good works (Matt. 5:16).

The prayer "may your name be honored" is vital for another reason. As Paul reminds us, "There may be so-called gods in heaven or on earth—as indeed there are many 'gods' and many 'lords'" (1 Cor. 8:5). We pray this prayer because there is a massive amount of dishonor in our world—a dishonor directly or indirectly to God. Here we are not thinking about people being angry with the God of Scripture. Old Testament saints did that and still honored God (e.g., Job 10; Ruth 1; Jonah 4). We are thinking rather of creating our own gods (Jer. 16:20) so that we can live as we want—gods of money and greed, gods of power, gods of sex, gods of self. The gods we create have no claim to be labeled Yahweh, and have no claim to be associated with his self-revelation and acts in history. The gods we create cannot claim to be Redeemers from Egyptian slavery and cannot claim to be the God and Father of our Lord Jesus Christ.[7] All these names—these labels that refer to his self-revelation and acts in history—belong only to one God.

If we are to pray this prayer in truth, it might involve the painful process of removing our idols and confessing that, as John Calvin said, "the human mind is, so to speak, a perpetual forge of idols."[8]

"YOUR KINGDOM COME"

The kingdom of God is a rich theme throughout Scripture and whole books are written about it.[9] So of necessity we will have to be very cursory.

Is Yahweh the King?

The request "your kingdom come" should bring a question to mind right away: Is Yahweh King or not? And we must answer by saying both yes and no. On the one hand, since Genesis 2, the Lord has been acting as King: establishing his land, giving his laws, establishing a people for himself, and asserting his rule over all.[10] Furthermore, in several places in the Old Testament we hear that "the LORD has established his throne in the heavens, and his kingdom rules over all" (Ps. 103:19; cf.

145:10–13). The confession of Ps. 103:19 also informs us that the Lord has people who honor and obey him; that is, they live as subjects of the King.

On the other hand, there are other kingdoms in this world, and since Genesis 3 God's kingdom has been contested. Israel's request for a king was a rejection of God's ruling over them as King (1 Sam. 8:7). Obadiah's prophecy of the return of Israel from exile promises that "saviors shall go up to Mount Zion to rule Mount Esau, and the kingdom shall be the Lord's" (Obad. 1:21). The use of the future tense here implies that at least the kingdom is not operating as it should. Furthermore, Jerusalem's rejection of the Messiah (Luke 19:41–44) is their rejection of the kingdom he offers.

Modern Challenges to God's Kingdom

Likewise, in our own age, there are many ways in which God's kingdom is contested: from the New Atheism, to New Age religion's rejection of the gospel, to professing Christians living in rebellion.

Of particular concern are brutal human kingdoms such as the following:

- President of Zimbabwe Robert Mugabe: During his rule this despot drove his nation from the prosperity it had after its independence from Britain in 1965 to its current desperate economic and political condition.[11]
- Islam Karimov, president of Uzbekistan: Under Karimov's rule there "is little to no religious or press freedom, with universities told not to train students in the realm of public issues. Brutal torture is seen as routine in the Uzbek judicial system, with Human Rights Watch expressing repeated concern over the accepted practices in Uzbek prisons."[12]
- Kim Jong-il, from 1994–2011 the Supreme Leader of North Korea: During his "16-year-long oppressive rule, he ensured that people remained trapped in poverty and prison camps. He invested heavily in the country's nuclear program, while showing no concern for the terrible famine."[13]

Many other examples could be named, including the post–Christian secularism of Western Europe, the brutal policies of Sudanese president Omar al Bashir, and our own daily disobedience to the King. Since the garden of Eden we have *all* rejected God's rule. Despite this, writers of Scripture assert God's kingdom remains universal and absolute. Its dominion is powerful and sovereign over all.

So we find both the assertion that God is King, sovereignly ruling, and the assertion that he is not King, for his rule—his kingdom—is contested. Therefore, with the pain of godly discontent in our hearts, we pray, "Your kingdom come!"

"YOUR WILL BE DONE, ON EARTH AS IT IS IN HEAVEN"

Your Will Be Done

We can think of God's will primarily in two ways. First, there is the revealed will of God or what we might call God's moral will. The moral will includes commands to love our neighbor (Lev. 19:18) and prohibitions against theft, adultery, and greed (Ex. 20:3–17). It is seen reflected in the fruit of the Spirit (Gal. 5:22–23) and other lists of Christian virtues (Phil. 4:8; Col. 3:12–13).

Second, there is the sovereign will of God, or what might be called God's secret will. Sometimes Scripture tells us what God's sovereign will is (at which time, of course, it ceases to be secret!); but many times it does not tell us. His sovereign will includes all those plans that he will accomplish by his wisdom and power regardless of the interference or resistance of men and angels. These two—the moral will and the sovereign will—can sometimes appear to be in conflict, at least from our limited human perspective. Thankfully we do not need to resolve that conflict here. It is the moral will of God that is the subject in Jesus' prayer.

Now we encounter a great failure of connection! There is a great disjunction, a great divorce between earth and heaven. In heaven the will of God is done; on earth it is done at times but often it is not done.

If we disobey the King regularly, then we fail to do his will. So the earth lags behind where it should be.

Our hearts are so corrupt that at times we can even think we are doing God's will when in fact we are not. Too often we hear of a husband and father who deserts his family and covenant partner for an adulterous lover. Yet all the while he makes the claim that he and the other woman are being blessed by God with a wonderful relationship, true love, great spiritual growth, and newfound Christian joy. Listening to reports like these is saddening, enraging, and confirming of the great need for us to pray, "Your will be done."

On Earth as It Is in Heaven

Sometimes this little phrase gets less attention than it deserves. It functions to describe *how* the will of God should be done. Jesus himself is quite aware that the will of God—obedience to a command—can be done in a way that is acceptable and in a way that is not acceptable. How is the will of God done in heaven? It is done freely, spontaneously, and joyfully. Do we find reluctant obedience? Do we find complaining when the will of God is carried out? Does it matter what heart motivation is behind the obedience? It does!

How we do the will of God is important because there is a wrongheaded approach to what God wants from us. This wrong view is an approach that says

> serving God is an issue of the body and not an issue of the heart. The love-is-action approach says, "God is looking for us to do something. It does not matter what emotion we have behind it." Jesus, however, spoke out strongly against such a perspective. For example, in Matthew 6:1–2 He said, "Beware of practicing your righteousness before other people in order to be seen by them, for then you will have no reward from your Father who is in heaven. Thus, when you give to the needy, sound no trumpet before you, as the hypocrites do in the synagogues and in the streets, that they may be praised by others. Truly, I say to you, they have received their reward."

According to Jesus, a good action (giving to the needy) with a wrong motivation (desire to be seen as godly) is not love. It's hypocrisy. We know that such actions are not godly actions because they receive no reward from God.[14]

But, again, this world lags behind. Often his will is not done here; or at times we have mere obedience for show. It is not the joyful obedience of heaven. It is not only others who fail to give heavenly obedience to God's will; on too many days our own hearts give only pharisaic obedience.

"GIVE US THIS DAY OUR DAILY BREAD"

At this point in the prayer there is a massive shift. We have gone from the concerns of the universe, namely that God's worldwide kingdom would come and that his will be done, and have moved to something so seemingly unimportant as whether we have something to eat today. But the abrupt shift is not accidental. Whether we admit it or not, we are totally dependent on God. We cannot make his kingdom come and we cannot make the world produce food. Just as we need him to be active so that his commands are carried out, so also we need him to work to feed us today. From start to finish this prayer is about my dependence. For those of us who like to think we are independent, self-sufficient, and hardworking, such dependence is insulting, if not maddening.

But we can push further than this. Just how dependent are we? And on whom are we dependent? As a Christian I might be comfortable with dependence on God or perhaps even dependence on other Christians. Yet here is something worth pondering. When we ask for bread, we ask for something that is both a creation of God and a creation of people. "In so asking we count on the fact that the Father in heaven is not only lord of nature and not only lord of the church but is lord of human economics as well," writes Schriver. "Not only that he may give the world good crops, but that he may give the world *bread*; that he may not camp on the perimeter of our marketing systems but may be present where bread is baked and its price fixed. In thus asking for bread, we are confessing our faith that God is more materialistic than men, for he is materialistic on a wider scale."[15]

We should slow down and notice that this is a prayer for food *before* we get it! Why is it that this request—asking for daily food—does not seem strange to us? It is only because we are so familiar with the prayer. We see right away that this is not thanking God for what has already been received—which we commonly do—but asking God for what is to come. The request displays a level of dependence unknown to most of us. "It is a lesson easily forgotten when wealth multiplies and absolute self-sufficiency is portrayed as a virtue."[16] Many of us live lives of abundant provision. We do not live from day to day; instead we are drunk on abundance.

"AND FORGIVE US OUR DEBTS, AS WE ALSO HAVE FORGIVEN OUR DEBTORS"

Several times the Gospels use debt as a metaphor for what we owe God; thus it can be an indirect reference to our sins. That is, when we fail to give him the obedience he deserves, we become a debtor to him (Matt. 18:27–34; Luke 7:41–42; 16:5). The prayer reminds us of what we often do not notice: how far short we fall in obedience to God. Therefore, just as we need daily food for physical thriving, so we need daily forgiveness for spiritual thriving; and if we truly grasp that daily forgiveness is needed, then we come face-to-face again with the painful fact that we often fail to do the will of God. Just as Scripture calls us to "rejoice . . . always" (Phil. 4:4)—that is, to make joy a habit of our lives—so in a sense we should "grieve always"; that is, daily we need the godly grief that leads to repentance (2 Cor. 7:8–10), confession of sin, and petition for forgiveness.

Forgiving as We Have Been Forgiven

What is even more challenging in this request is the basis for it. We ask for forgiveness since we have already forgiven others. This is a convicting prospect. What is more, shortly after the prayer Jesus will go on to say, "For if you forgive others their trespasses, your heavenly Father will also forgive you, but if you do not forgive others their trespasses, neither will your Father forgive your trespasses" (Matt. 6:14–15). What should we make of this? Bruner summarizes it well:

> We are not conscientiously to seek God's friendship where we have not honestly sought our wounded brother's or sister's. This reality sequence is an expression of honest faith and is not a difficult justification by works. The conscience that is able to ask for forgiveness without giving it is not a conscience living in faith.[17]

We dare not come to our heavenly Father asking for forgiveness when all the while we are refusing to give it to others. Such a stance in reality denies the prayer by insisting that it is others who *really* need forgiveness and I am holier than they are.

Two Myths about Forgiveness

At this point it would be helpful to mention several common myths about forgiveness, but we will restrict ourselves to two. The first myth says, "Forgiveness is the same as reconciliation." It is not. Many Christians falsely assume that the two are the same. Reconciliation is a good goal, but it requires the repentance of the guilty party. Forgiveness, on the other hand, can be one-sided. If we assume that forgiveness is the same as reconciliation, then after forgiveness we will think that everything is as it should be and we must act as if the sin and pain never happened. This brings us to the next myth.

The second myth says, "When I forgive, I must also forget." The Bible never says we must forget offenses. Furthermore, when the Bible speaks of God not remembering sins it is using a figure of speech that has to do with ceasing punishment, not a mental act of forgetting.[18] For

God to literally forget sins would cause him to cease being all–knowing. Regarding our forgetting sins, it might be at best foolish and at worst harmful to ourselves and others. For example, I can forgive a convicted child molester for his actions but I should not forget his past and then put him in charge of the church nursery.

"AND LEAD US NOT INTO TEMPTATION" (*peirasmos*[19])

On the one hand, we cannot help but think of what just appeared a few chapters back. "Then Jesus was led up by the Spirit into the wilderness to be tempted by the devil" (Matt. 4:1). In terms of the narrative of Matthew, the temptation just recently ended before Jesus began the Sermon on the Mount in which we find this prayer. On the other hand, we must insist that God does not tempt people to do evil (James 1:13). Nevertheless, we know that testing will come. God tested Abraham (Gen. 22:1); he will test us (1 Peter 4:12). Further, during the stress of Gethsemane, Jesus used language very similar to Matt. 6:13 when he told the eleven, "Watch and pray that you may not enter into temptation. The spirit indeed is willing, but the flesh is weak" (Matt. 26:41). Should we reach the conclusion that Jesus exhorts us to pray that our heavenly Father would not do what Scripture already says he will not do? Or does he exhort us to pray that we would not be tested even though the rest of Scripture tells us that testing is for our good and to be endured with patience and joy (James 1:2–3; Rom. 5:3; 1 Peter 1:6–7; 4:12–13)?

To attempt to resolve this tension would take us too far afield. Instead, we should make clear what is obvious:

- We are all vulnerable to temptation. To assume anything else is not only arrogant, it is dangerous.
- As the whole prayer has made clear, we are utterly dependent on God. Whether we are talking about temptation or testing, we know that we are helpless by ourselves.

- Admitting our own vulnerability and dependence is painfully difficult because, as we said earlier, we like to view ourselves as competent, in control, and independent.
- If the trial at Gethsemane caused the Son to say, "My soul is very sorrowful, even to death" (Matt. 26:38), then there will be times when testing or temptation will be painful for us as well.

"BUT DELIVER US FROM EVIL"

Before making specific comments about this request and suffering, we should note two issues of translation. First, the word would better be translated "save" or "rescue." It is true that the Greek word used here (*rhuomai*) can have the nuance "deliver."[20] But "the verb . . . expresses a rather strong intervention to rescue or to preserve someone or something from danger."[21] There is a specific danger mentioned here. Second, rather than "from evil" it would be better rendered "from the evil one" (see NET, NIV, and NLT). In the parable of the soils, the evil one comes and takes the seed away (Matt. 13:19). The evil one is further identified as the devil in Jesus' explanation of the parable (v. 38). Furthermore, as we mentioned earlier, the last reference to temptation had been personal—the devil tempted Jesus.[22]

The evil one threatens us and his ends are vicious. Although Scripture is quite clear on this point (e.g., Luke 22:3, 31; Acts 10:38; 2 Cor. 2:11; 11:3; Eph. 6:11; 1 Peter 5:8), we are bombarded with a contrary view. We live in a very impersonal culture, in an impersonal age, with materialistic voices shouting that the universe is impersonal. This materialistic worldview ascribes suffering to purposeless, impersonal forces. It is true that earthquakes and tornadoes have no personality; likewise, in our world many evil forces are structural (such as legalized gambling and implicit segregation). But we should not give in to the temptation to view evil as wholly abstract and impersonal.

Of course praying "rescue us from the evil one" does not put us in the position of being passive any more than praying "give us this day our daily bread" prohibits baking. As we have seen, each prayer implies action on our part. One aspect of our suffering is the need for constant vigilance, being ever watchful (1 Peter 5:8).

CONCLUSION

The new heaven and the new earth are our home. That future is secure because of trust in the Lord Jesus. Yet until its arrival, earth often lags far behind where it should be. And far too often so do we. Thus we groan (Rom. 8:22–23; 2 Cor. 5:2–4), painfully waiting for God our Father to act from heaven and bring his kingdom.

AMID PAIN AND SUFFERING

1. Have you ever before considered the Lord's Prayer as reflecting the evil and suffering in the world? Tell why or why not.

2. Does addressing God as "Father" come naturally for you or is it hard? Explain why.

3. Reflect on this statement: "If we ask whether Yahweh is King, we must say that the answer is both Yes and No."

4. Explain what role you think motivation plays in obedience to God. Does it surprise you that this chapter says, "On too many days our own hearts give only pharisaic obedience"? Tell why or why not.

5. Do you sometimes find that forgiving others is painfully difficult? If so, explain why.

CHAPTER 8

A Time to Weep

Leadership and Tears

By Gerald W. Peterman

The two parts of this chapter title go together. If you lead in matters of the gospel, sooner or later you will weep.

If there are no tears, we should begin to wonder if there is any leadership—at least leadership in a biblical sense. We are not talking about guiding a team of used–car salespeople, as important as that is. We are dealing with eternal realities. Spiritual leaders help people, dealing with painful damage, with innocent victims, and with violent abusers. When we speak of spiritual leadership, we are talking about parents training children, about pastors guiding a flock, about teachers seeking to transform believers into more mature disciples of our Lord Jesus Christ. We are talking about eternal realities.

With these eternal realities come present–day tears. Those tears flow from pain, disappointment, and frustration. A leader's weeping may come from rejection, hopelessness, and discouragement.

Such tears of leadership are voluntary; we take them on ourselves.

We do so because we choose to be invested in the lives of others; we choose to be emotionally engaged. Our suffering—that is, our emotional pain—is in a sense self-caused; if we remain distant, there is no pain. But to remain distant is not the call of gospel leadership, although it is a constant temptation. So while the tears of leadership are voluntary, they are truly a necessity. If spiritual leaders would become more godly, they will have many tears. That is the evidence of both the Old and New Testaments, as we shall soon see.

Of course, not all tears shed by leaders are godly tears. A particularly telling example in Scripture involves King Saul as he pursued David in the wilderness of Engedi, trying to kill David and thus end David's threat to Saul's dynasty (cf. 1 Sam. 20:31). Needing to take "a nature break," the king entered a cave, unaware David and his men were hiding deep within the same cave. David did not take this opportunity to kill his enemy, but secretly cut off the corner of Saul's robe (1 Sam. 24:1–4). After Saul left, "David also arose and went out of the cave, and called after Saul, 'My lord the king!' And when Saul looked behind him, David bowed with his face to the earth and paid homage" (v. 8). David then rebukes Saul's ill will, proclaims his own good intentions toward Saul, and calls on God to judge between them (vv. 9–15).

Saul's response included tears: "As soon as David had finished speaking these words to Saul, Saul said, 'Is this your voice, my son David?' And Saul lifted up his voice and wept. He said to David, 'You are more righteous than I, for you have repaid me good, whereas I have repaid you evil'" (vv. 16–17). The king's response sounds good, but from his subsequent actions and attitudes (e.g., 1 Sam. 26:1–2) we can see that he sheds these tears from self-pity and not from repentance.[1]

POSITIVE TEARS WITH NEGATIVE CAUSES

What are "positive tears"? They are tears that should be cried. That is, they are godly; they reflect love of people, grief over loss, and hatred of sin. We will not treat tears of joy. Such are quite rare in Scripture, although there are examples: Jacob and Esau have a tearful reunion (Gen. 33:4), as do Joseph and his brothers (45:15). Probably also the woman who wipes Jesus' feet with her tears and hair (Luke 7:37–38) was shedding tears of joy for forgiveness mixed with shame for her past actions.[2]

Ironically, positive tears may have a variety of negative causes. By negative we mean weeping that is incited by sin in its various manifestations: infidelity, betrayal, loss of loved ones through death, sexual abuse, social fragmentation, prejudice. Such tears may arise from abuse of power, arrogance, the crippling effects of disease or war, substance abuse, lack of love, violence, or deception. There are a seemingly infinite number of other possibilities—both small and great—that we may encounter on a daily basis. As with Lot in Sodom, we may also find that our righteous hearts are tormented by the lawless deeds we see day after day (2 Peter 2:8).

THE INTENTIONALITY OF LEADERSHIP AND TEARS

Please do not misunderstand. We are not talking about tears that flow without discernment. We can cry genuine heartfelt tears, yet they can flow with both wisdom and discretion. There is no contradiction here. To explore this, we go to Rom. 12:15: "Rejoice with those who rejoice, weep with those who weep."

This passage includes some key assumptions. First, the passage *presupposes* that we can see rejoicing and distinguish it from mourning, or vice versa. Second, the passage assumes that we are engaged enough in our time with people to know what the rejoicing or the mourning is about. Since the writer, the apostle Paul, says elsewhere (1 Cor. 13:6) that love does not rejoice with unrighteousness, we know that there are times not to rejoice with the rejoicing (e.g., when others are rejoicing over evil). Similarly, there can be times when we do not mourn with the mourning (when followers are mourning the death of an evil dictator).

But beyond its assumptions, the passage *commands* empathy.[3] It requires feeling with another, an emotional reaction that makes a connection with the other person. Such an emotional connection is part of love. Furthermore we should keep in mind that we do not empathize absentmindedly; empathy is not merely automatic like jerking one's hand off a hot stove. Rather, mature "empathy is metacognitive: One is aware of empathizing—that is, one feels distress but knows this is a response to another's misfortune, not one's own."[4]

As an expression of Christian love, empathy is a spiritual act. It is about walking by the Spirit (Gal. 5:16), not walking by our personality. Therefore, even the most stoic of us can learn this skill over time, at least to a degree. Lastly, we should not draw the conclusion that we are opening ourselves to emotional exhaustion; we do not empathize without limits. As with professional first responders or caregivers (e.g., firefighters, doctors, nurses, therapists, chaplains), we may need to carefully manage empathy lest it prevent or slow needed intervention.[5] Even Jesus needed time alone (Matt. 14:23; Luke 5:16) and grew weary (John 4:6).

BUT SHOULD LEADERS BE SAD AT ALL?

One might object to the approach we are taking and say, "But if God is sovereign, it is wrong for a leader to be sad.[6] Of all people, the leader should be the one who looks not to temporal circumstances but to the eternal promises of God and to his sovereign management. Are not such tears and sadness too focused on temporal successes and desires? Does such sadness by a spiritual leader indicate sin, selfishness, or immaturity?"

These questions are valuable and practical. But we suspect that they reflect an unstated assumption. As leaders we may be tempted to think that our faith must be bigger and better than the faith of our people. And if we *really* trust God, then we will never be fearful or sad. But this type of thinking reflects an overrealized eschatology, as if all the blessings of the new heaven and the new earth—no more death, mourning, crying, or pain (Rev. 21:4)—will come to us now if we just really believe God. But they will not come; we will have glimpses of them, indeed; yet they will not be fully realized in this life.

But if we wonder if leaders should be sad at all, the best response will come from looking at some biblical examples. To that we now turn.

BIBLICAL EXAMPLES OF SADNESS

Jeremiah

In Jeremiah's day the nation is in stubborn apostasy; the people of God have turned their backs on the Lord; for centuries their covenant faithlessness has been chronic (Jer. 2:20; 3:25; 22:21; see also Josh. 7:11; Judg. 2:20).[7] Jeremiah has the task of warning about judgment and of calling all to repentance; but the prospects of success are not good. Even from the mouth of the Lord himself Jeremiah is promised that the people will fight against the prophet (Jer. 1:19). How will this servant of God respond?

> Oh that my head were waters, and my eyes a fountain of tears, that I might weep day and night for the slain of the daughter of my people! Oh that I had in the desert a travelers' lodging place, that I might leave my people and go away from them! For they are all adulterers, a company of treacherous men. (9:1–2)

The passage brings up a series of questions. First, how can Jeremiah make such an extreme statement, virtually saying that he wishes he could cry all the time? The answer to the question actually came earlier, in chapter 8. The people, Jeremiah writes, have "turned away in perpetual backsliding" (v. 5); they have provoked the Lord with their idols (v. 19). Therefore the land and its people are devastated by conquerors (v. 10). So the prophet's joy is gone; his heart is sick (v. 18). The rebellion and resulting devastation of the people strikes Jeremiah deeply. He cannot contain his grief.

And why are the people devastated? We see the answer later in chapter 9. "They are all adulterers, a company of treacherous men . . . ; falsehood and not truth has grown strong in the land; for they proceed from evil to evil, and they do not know me, declares the Lord" (vv. 2b–3). In 9:2a, Thompson notes that Jeremiah, "disgusted at all he found in his people, sought to escape from the corruption and degradation he saw about him to some wilderness refuge. In that desire he was sharing the mind of Yahweh, who had turned aside from his people and would presently forsake the temple."[8]

A second question arises: Who exactly is speaking in these verses? Is it Jeremiah, or is it the Lord? There is no need to draw sharp distinctions. Jeremiah has not only absorbed the Lord's message, but also the Lord's passionate longing for his people. Thus, as the Lord is in pain for Judah, so is the prophet. "Jeremiah was never a dispassionate observer of his nation's suffering, but entered into the anguish of the people and suffered with them," Thompson adds. The grief mentioned here and the reference to the slain (9.1b) probably has to do with invasion of the land that happened in 598 BC. In any case, the prophets "were men torn asunder between God and the people, to both of whom they were bound with deep ties. This combination of love and anguish is nowhere seen more clearly than in Jeremiah."[9]

Does adopting the perspective of God mean that we will always be calm, tranquil, and undisturbed? Does a public display of such grief and discouragement betray the fact that we are not suited to ministry? We have heard this very assertion made forcefully by nationally known Christian leaders. But it is false. There is a time to weep (Eccl. 3:4) and sometimes we are in turmoil, not because we lack God's perspective, but because we do have God's perspective! We will return here when we look at Jesus' weeping over Jerusalem.

The prophet warns in Jer. 13:15–17:

> Hear and give ear; be not proud, for the LORD has spoken. Give glory to the LORD your God before he brings darkness, before your feet stumble on the twilight mountains, and while you look for light he turns it into gloom and makes it deep darkness. But if you will not

listen, my soul will weep in secret for your pride; my eyes will weep bitterly and run down with tears, because the LORD's flock has been taken captive.

Whereas in Jeremiah 9 the prophet might be speaking privately, here he speaks to the people whom he tries to rebuke. The prospects of their recalcitrance and hard–heartedness cause him deep pain. He knows that continued disobedience will lead to invasion from the north (4:6; 6:22), the brutality of war, and deportation to Babylon. He has a crushing grief over this prospect.[10] Although he admits that he will weep, he also admits that he cannot do the weeping publicly: "My soul will weep in secret for your pride" (v. 17). Alongside the grief of Jeremiah we might place that of Isaiah, who in 22:4–5 says, "Look away from me; let me weep bitter tears; do not labor to comfort me concerning the destruction of the daughter of my people. For the Lord GOD of hosts has a day of tumult and trampling and confusion in the valley of vision, a battering down of walls and a shouting to the mountains" (see also Lam. 3:45–51).

Many pastors know this grief. They have counseled, corrected, preached, and prayed. Though some listeners have responded positively, others will not heed correction; they will move headlong into self–destructive behavior or rejection of the gospel. While he has counseled, corrected, and preached with passion, he maintained his composure. But in the privacy of his own home or office, the pain has come out, weeping in secret over pride, rebellion, and hard–heartedness. These are the tears of leadership.

We return to the question: Should leaders be sad at all? Of all people, should not the leader be the one who looks not to temporal circumstances but to the eternal promises of God? We often hear Jer. 29:11 quoted: "For I know the plans I have for you, declares the LORD, plans for welfare and not for evil, to give you a future and a hope." Certainly this is a precious promise. But the future welfare and hope would not come in Jeremiah's day. In his day would come brutality and deportation.

Furthermore, the truth of Israel's future and hope did not take away Jeremiah's pain in the present. Similarly, other precious truths we might quote (e.g., Rom. 8:28) might not be intended to take away our suffering in the present.

Jesus

In the Gospels we find two instances where our Lord weeps, recorded in Luke 19 and John 11. We treated John 11 in our chapter on redemptive anger. Here, since it is much better suited to the topic of leaders and tears, we look at Luke 19.

> As he was drawing near—already on the way down the Mount of Olives—the whole multitude of his disciples began to rejoice and praise God with a loud voice for all the mighty works that they had seen, saying, "Blessed is the King who comes in the name of the Lord! Peace in heaven and glory in the highest!" And some of the Pharisees in the crowd said to him, "Teacher, rebuke your disciples." He answered, "I tell you, if these were silent, the very stones would cry out." And when he drew near and saw the city, he wept over it. (vv. 37–41)

All the other Gospels mention this triumphal entry (Matt. 21:1–11; Mark 11:1–10; John 12:12–19), but Luke's telling has unique features. Luke emphasizes the enthusiasm of the crowd. The words "rejoice," "praise God," "loud voice," "mighty works," "peace," and "glory" are all unique to Luke's telling of the entry. There is excitement, gladness, and shouting. All this heightens the contrast with Jesus' mood later in the story.

But not all is positive. Some of the Pharisees in the crowd find the excitement extreme, saying, "Teacher, rebuke your disciples" (v. 39). This draws a response from the Lord; the event is a time for enthusiastic joy and praise: "I tell you, if these were silent, the very stones would cry out" (v. 40). Praise is completely appropriate at this point. Creation is aware of Jesus, but the leaders are not! In his commentary on Luke,

Darrell Bock says: "That which is lifeless knows life when it sees it, even though that which is living does not. Luke portrays their rejection as a tragic, stinging indictment of their lack of judgment. Luke alone narrates this exchange."[11]

Now we find great contrast: the crowd is joyfully excited. But when Jesus sees the city he weeps over it. What triggers these tears? We should mention three closely related things:

First, many times before, Jesus has seen the beloved city, for Joseph and Mary brought him there on a yearly basis (Luke 2:41–42). But this is the last time he will see it before it rejects him, fulfilling the sorrowful proclamation the Lord made in Luke 13:34–35:

> O Jerusalem, Jerusalem, the city that kills the prophets and stones those who are sent to it! How often would I have gathered your children together as a hen gathers her brood under her wings, and you were not willing! Behold, your house is forsaken. And I tell you, you will not see me until you say, "Blessed is he who comes in the name of the Lord!"

Jerusalem represents the covenant people. As this city goes, so goes the people. If they reject, there is only hope for judgment.[12] And they will reject, for a small group of disciples praises Jesus during his entry into the city, but the leadership and the city as a whole are ignorant: "Would that you, even you, had known on this day the things that make for peace! But now they are hidden from your eyes" (19:42). The words are emotional; the indictment is fearful. The covenant people do not know that Shalom himself is entering their city.[13]

Second, thoughts about this coming judgment are a source of pain for Jesus. He describes it in graphic warfare terms and with images reminiscent of Old Testament warnings (Isa. 39:6; Hos. 9:7; Zech. 14:2): "For the days will come upon you, when your enemies will set up a barricade around you and surround you and hem you in on every side and tear you down to the ground, you and your children within you" (vv. 43–44a). Clearly Jesus has in mind Rome's destruction of Jerusalem in AD 70.[14]

Unlike the sinful rejoicing we might have when we see enemies suffer, Jesus is deeply hurt to foresee that people will undergo wrath for their sin. Certainly the wrath is deserved. And, of course, it is not as if Jesus will be a bystander in Jerusalem's destruction, for all judgment is given to the Son (John 5:22). But as the city's judge he is not only filled with anger, but the prospect of destruction a generation away brings him pain.

Sometimes we might think that knowing the future would help us to deal with it, would help us to be prepared for it emotionally, to escape the hurt of it. Sometimes we might be anxious to know God's will for our life because we worry that if we do not know it, we will go in some direction we ought not to go, something bad will happen, and we will be hurt. But omniscient knowledge of the future does not shield one from emotional pain. Even being certain of God's will for our life (as Jesus was), and following God's will for our life perfectly (as Jesus did), will not shield us from emotional pain. If it does, we might just be more spiritual than Jesus.

Third, and closely related, is the loss of relationship. The "Son of Man came to seek and to save the lost" (Luke 19:10). But, sadly, "he came to his own, and his own people did not receive him" (John 1:11). Jesus has lovingly pursued the city (that is, the nation). But in this love story the affection and longing have not been mutual. As with Yahweh in the book of Hosea, so here the Lord endures the pain of separation in the relationship.[15] This rejection by Jerusalem will mean his own torture. But he weeps over the pain that he sees is coming on hardened sinners, the very ones who will crucify him. Through the mouth of the OT prophets we have *read* about the grief and broken heart of God over the rebellion of his people (e.g., Hos. 11:8). But here we *see* the tears that stream on the face of God incarnate. We must admit with shame that our love pales in comparison.

We again return to the question: should the leader be sad at all? We might be tempted to think that such an emotional display might make us look out of control; it might make us look weak. But if such an emotional display makes Jesus look out of control or weak, then certainly we have misunderstood him. John Calvin, in one of his best moments, reminds us that Jesus

> both grieved and shed tears for his own and others' woes. Nor did he teach his disciples differently: 'Ye shall weep and lament, but the world shall rejoice,' (John 16:20). And lest anyone should regard this as vicious, he expressly declares, 'Blessed are they that mourn,' (Mt. 5:4). And no wonder. If all tears are condemned, what shall we think of our Lord himself, whose 'sweat was as it were great drops of blood falling down to the ground?' (Luke 22:44; Mt. 26:38). If every kind of fear is a mark of unbelief, what place shall we assign to the dread which, it is said, in no slight degree amazed him; if all sadness is condemned, how shall we justify him when he confesses, 'My soul is exceeding sorrowful, even unto death?'[16]

Paul

From Jesus we turn to Paul. Although he was the apostle of rejoicing (Phil. 4:4), we see just as many places in his letters that speak of his tears, pain, frustration, or grief (e.g., Rom. 9:2; 2 Cor. 2:4; Gal. 4:19; Phil. 3:18). Rather than the letters, however, we go to an example supplied to us by the book of Acts.

> Now from Miletus he sent to Ephesus and called the elders of the church to come to him. And when they came to him, he said to them: "You yourselves know how I lived among you the whole time from the first day that I set foot in Asia, serving the Lord with all humility and with tears and with trials that happened to me through the plots of the Jews; how I did not shrink from declaring to you anything that was profitable, and teaching you in public and from house to house, testifying both to Jews and to Greeks of repentance toward God and of faith in our Lord Jesus Christ. And now, behold, I am going to Jerusalem, constrained by the Spirit, not knowing what will happen to me there, except that the Holy Spirit testifies to me in every city that imprisonment and afflictions await me. But I do not account my life of any value nor as precious to myself, if only I may finish my

> course and the ministry that I received from the Lord Jesus, to testify
> to the gospel of the grace of God. . . . Be alert, remembering that for
> three years I did not cease night or day to admonish every one with
> tears. And now I commend you to God and to the word of his grace,
> which is able to build you up and to give you the inheritance among
> all those who are sanctified. (Acts 20:17–24, 31–32)

In Acts 20 Paul is on his way from Greece to Jerusalem, carrying
the collection he has taken up among the churches of Macedonia
and Achaia (Rom. 15:26–27). He stops by Miletus to give a farewell
speech to the Ephesian elders. To them he rehearses the ministry he
had during his three years with them (Acts 20:31), appealing to their
memory to verify his humility, his perseverance, and his passion to fulfill his commission to preach the gospel (v. 24): "But I do not account
my life of any value nor as precious to myself, if only I may finish my
course and the ministry that I received from the Lord Jesus, to testify
to the gospel of the grace of God." In his farewell speech we see Paul
refer back to his faithful fulfillment of leadership responsibilities, his
suffering because of Jewish opposition (cf. Acts 13:45; 14:2, 9; 17:5,
13; 18:6), and his attitude toward work and wealth.[17] Paul said that he
was departing Ephesus without regrets, leaving an example worthy of
imitation, and that with regard to money he was completely selfless. In
passing we notice what is absent: categories of success, results, numbers, and accomplishments.

First, tears were a mark of Paul's humble service; he probably uses
the term "tears" as an image (metonymy) for his whole experience of
pain, sadness, and crying. One hint as to the source of this sadness is his
reference to trials that happened to him through the plots of the Jews
(20:19b). Certainly opposition to the gospel by outsiders was common
for Paul (see Acts 23:12; 1 Thess. 2:15). Paul considers this opposition
(persecution) to be part of his commission (e.g., Acts 9:16; Eph. 3:13;
1 Thess. 3:3). Such opposition probably brought pain, for Paul himself
said that "I have great sorrow and unceasing anguish in my heart. For I
could wish that I myself were accursed and cut off from Christ for the

sake of my brothers, my kinsmen according to the flesh" (Rom. 9:2). Certainly there were times when this "unceasing anguish" for lost Jews could not be hidden but showed itself in weeping.[18]

Second, as Jesus anticipated Jerusalem's destruction, so Paul anticipates that to the Ephesian church will come abusive leadership and false teaching (Acts 20:29): "I know that after my departure fierce wolves will come in among you, not sparing the flock." Probably he means that he does not anticipate further pastoral oversight; without his guidance, trouble will come. Some of this trouble will come from outside: "savage wolves will come in" (see Ezek. 22:24–27; Zeph. 3:3; Matt. 7:15). Some of this trouble will come from inside (Acts 20:30): "from among your own selves will arise men speaking twisted things, to draw away the disciples after them." What is Paul's response to foreseeing these things? He says, "Therefore be alert, remembering that for three years I did not cease night or day to admonish everyone with tears" (v. 31). As with Jesus, he has grief in the present over anticipated (future) harm.

We can be deeply hurt by other Christian leaders, even if we would never describe them as "savage wolves." Last week my wife and I (Gerald) had dinner with a couple we have known for almost thirty years. Their son–in–law was a youth pastor for several years, suffering frustration, rejection, lack of trust, and generally being marginalized and demeaned by the elders—that is, the volunteer leadership. They, because of their immaturity, managed the ministry without his input. Over time the pain was too great; he left the local church for more fruitful work in another ministry.

To return to Paul, we highlight one last item: the whole speech to the elders is an implicit call to imitate him (cf. 1 Cor. 4:16; 2 Thess. 3:7–9). Based on what we know of Paul, this means they must not be emotionally remote (cf. 2 Cor. 6:11–12); must have joy at the appropriate times (cf. 1 Thess. 2:20); and must have appropriate sadness (cf. Phil. 3:17–18). A public display of emotional pain is not necessarily sinful (cf. Luke 19:41); likewise, a public display of emotional pain is not necessarily a reflection of inadequacy for ministry. If it was not such a sign in the life of Jesus, then it need not be in Paul's life nor in ours.

AMID PAIN AND SUFFERING

1. Give examples from your own life when your tears had a godly motivation and when they had an ungodly motivation. Explain how you can tell the difference.

2. Reflect on the following statement: "Our suffering—that is, our emotional pain—is self-caused; if we remain distant, there is no pain. But to remain distant is not the call of gospel leadership, although it is a constant temptation."

3. Does it surprise you that Jesus sometimes wept (e.g., John 11:35; Luke 19:41)? If so, why? If not, why not?

4. Reread Jeremiah 9:1-2. Does this language strike you as extreme? Why or why not?

5. Do we sometimes think that the more spiritual we become the less emotional pain we will have? On the basis of this chapter, do you believe this statement is actually helpful or accurate?

CHAPTER 9

Joseph's Tears

Suffering from Family Toxins

By Andrew J. Schmutzer

No pain may be as confusing and comprehensive as the relational pain of a fractured family. Current relationships can be permanently damaged and the ability to navigate future ones impaired. We are not talking about routine human conflict or seasons of life that follow every growing family. Rather, we are talking about destructive relationships that form the toxic family. The toxic family is more than a sad fact. It is a harsh reality to be mourned. When the formative becomes deforming and identity–making is identity–crushing, then what is nurturing has become deadly.

Our exploration will focus on the biblical character of Joseph and the painful experiences that not only formed his larger family but, in turn, brought great suffering into his own life (Genesis 37–50). We will close with an in–depth look at Joseph's forgiveness (Gen. 45:1–8; 50:15–21). Here, Joseph invites his brothers to view their lives with a fresh perspective. *What* Joseph does and says is a good lesson for us all. *How* Joseph responds puts before us a powerful ethical and spiritual challenge.

THE GENESIS OF "MESSED-UP" FAMILIES

Within the grand sweep of the Genesis text, there are three main "family sections." These focus on Abraham, Jacob, and Joseph, comprising about thirty-five chapters. These may even represent three *stages*, intentionally written to highlight different aspects of ancient family profiles. Each family is immersed in some form of conflict that creates tension on a spectrum of *alienation and reconciliation*.[1] Where God is very visible in Abraham's life, he falls silent in Joseph's life. In Abraham's family, there is conflict between two potential heirs (Isaac and Ishmael). God guides a functional resolution. The family portrait of Jacob zooms in closer, as Jacob is a participant in the conflict with Esau, another pair. The relationship ends in a social accommodation. In the third stage, Joseph is utterly immersed in conflict with his ten half brothers. God never speaks to Joseph, nor are the brothers reconciled. These sections focus on increasing detail and emotional vulnerability in each main character:

- the *parent–child relationship* in Abraham's life (highlighting barrenness against promise),
- the *sibling relationship* of Jacob and Esau and its many conflicting elements (highlighting selfishness against blessing),
- and the extended *brothers' relationship* in Joseph's experience within the larger family (highlighting human actions against God's provision), evident in how one navigates familial, political, and spiritual pressures.[2]

The book of Genesis goes into amazing detail about its families, but it slows down the most to explore ninety-three years in Joseph's life (spanning fourteen chapters). Integrating the *revealed* truth of Scripture (e.g., the creation in Genesis 1) with the *observed* truth of familial patterns in relationships brings a binocular vision to these biblical stories. Where revealed and observed truth merge, relationships emerge in their fullest form. For example, the lens of Family Systems

Theory is increasingly used to read these relationally freighted stories.[3] As Fretheim observes:

> One contemporary way of looking at chaps. 12–50 is through the lens of family systems theory and the manifestations of a dysfunctional family one sees throughout. *The various dimensions of family life belong within the sphere of God's concern.* God is at work in and through family problems and possibilities for purposes of reconciliation (50:20) . . . the high place given to the human role, from creation to Joseph, testifies to the depth of God's engagement with human beings as the instruments of God's purpose.[4]

In each scenario, God is neither disinterested nor "backed into a corner." By contrast, life on the human plane can appear hopeless if not ruined. In Joseph's story, for example, no brother interacts directly with God. "Instead, they confront God through each other," in a stunning mix of relational brokenness and spiritual crisis.[5] In each family section, the human and divine worlds are intricately woven together: barrenness would seem like cruel delay, but God intervenes through further acts of creation; blessing can be manipulated, but God is not confined by mortal schemes; human choices can be flippant and even evil, but God is both patient and innovative. *God works with each person, revealing his divine tenacity and creativity that overwhelms human scheming.* God is so relationally involved, he can employ famines, dreams, unloved wives, well encounters, lying husbands, arrogant rulers, and even a bout of wrestling—if his servant relates in that manner.

It is significant to see how God relates to people as unique persons, not as sterile copies of prior humans, "doomed" because of the fall. Only God can incorporate layers of human suffering and relational strife into his redemptive drama. In the end, one can no more escape the dire consequences of relational actions than one can miss the timely grace and love of a caring Creator.

PROFILE OF A TOXIC FAMILY

Before we explore this family account further, we must briefly consider the role and challenges to family health that avoid the potential slide toward toxicity. "We are all formed in a crucible called family," writes Susan Forward. This is obvious enough. But what creates a toxic family is not the reality of problems, but how these problems are addressed. Forward concludes that *toxic families fight the loss of control by increasing the chaos.*[6] The toxic home engages in some form(s) of violence. Sadly, toxic people are most comfortable when there is strife, McLemore concludes.[7] The environment of a toxic family is not safe and nurturing. In fact, as McLemore describes it, the relationship choice is either nourishing and joyful or toxic and harmful:

> Relationships can be wholesome (nourishing) or toxic (harmful). . . .
> There is nothing inherently noble about suffering at someone else's hands. We were made to relate joyfully to Him and other people, and it is difficult to do either if we are constantly feeling poisoned.[8]

All parents have broken places, but few grieve their brokenness. Nothing has a stronger influence on children than the unlived life of the parent—the parent's *uninspected pain.*[9] While the functional family resolves the pain and problems within their relational ecosystem, the toxic family, however, denies and redefines their problems. This creates an enormous reservoir of *original pain*, feelings that have not been allowed to be expressed, even going back generations. Children learn to identify only "family–authorized" feelings, and this creates deep relational wounds that can span generations.[10] Sadly, this social tutoring actually binds children to their dysfunctional home. While keeping a sense of balance and boundary is important in healthy families, it becomes a precarious high–wire act in the toxic family. Healthy families practice mutual respect, humility, honesty, listening, and forgiveness, and value the thriving of each person. Dysfunctional families, however, use self–promotion, shaming, favoritism, scapegoating, deceit, and recrimination.

In his book *Family Secrets*, John Bradshaw describes four "degrees of toxicity."[11] The first two levels, called *deadly* and *demoralizing*, are always toxic and need to be confronted and addressed. The third and fourth levels, known as *damaging* and *distressing*, are also destructive, and contextual variables need to be considered in handling them.

Ironically, as long as dysfunctional family members interact in predictable ways, the balance is not upset. This creates an illusion of love and stability—so long as everyone follows the "family rules."[12] But the real cost to relationships can be both devastating and lasting. In the toxic family, the members are not respected as persons but as *appendages* of a larger impersonal system. Members are pawns caught in power plays and hidden rip currents that are destructive. But "intimacy involves *mutuality*, a kind of give and take and bonding together, without either person sacrificing his or her individuality."[13]

By contrast, families worth modeling are honest and nurturing, not mysterious or addicted to unacknowledged cycles of chaos. In healthy families, moral boundaries are clear, goals are known, values are understood, communication is sincere, growth is celebrated, and love is never a performance!

THE TRIALS AND TRAUMA OF JOSEPH'S YOUNG LIFE

While we are aware that the families in the Bible are far from perfect—we both revel in and recoil from aspects of David's life—chances are that we are unaware of the extent of the relational "debris field" that really surrounds these families. Like the rings of a tree, biblical characters live within interlocking relationships. This is a similar relational ecosystem in which every person lives. Much like our stories, Joseph's life (Genesis 37–50) simply cannot be understood apart from his larger family. In the words of Thomas L. Brodie, Joseph's life "is not a special pearl, different from the rest of Genesis. . . . It is Genesis breaking into full bloom, *a blossoming that builds on all that precedes.*"[14] So, we should not be surprised that Joseph's "bio" is filled with many devastating events. Here are the major trials he faced early in his life.

- the death of his mother, Rachel (35:18–19)
- the object of his father's favoritism (37:3–4, 11)
- the scorn of his brothers' hatred (37:4, 8)
- denied family *shalom* and protection (37:4b)
- threatened with death by his brothers (37:18, 20)
- sold to Egypt as a slave by his brothers (37:27, 28)
- felt the loss of home and family "place" (37:28, 36)
- knew the disorientation of a foreign land and culture (37:36; 39:1)
- ongoing sexual propositions by his master's wife (39:7, 10)
- slander by his master's wife (39:14–15, 17–18)
- false charges of rape (39:14, 17)
- forgotten in prison for over two years (39:20; 41:1)

This is really an avalanche of catastrophes! Looking at these, we need to explore some dynamic realities of family life that defined Joseph. We will consider trauma in one's youth, transgenerational pain, and the loss of personal agency.

Trauma in Youth

First, except for his second imprisonment (41:1), Joseph experiences this flood of hardship largely during ages seventeen and eighteen (37:2). Who among us could stand up under such a torrent of traumatic events? One or two of these difficulties can permanently alter one's life. For Joseph, the traumas ranged from the brutalization and sale into slavery by his own brothers to the constant sexual harassment by a prominent woman, and then abandonment in prison on trumped-up charges of rape (39:12–20)! Such layers of trauma defy the imagination. Studies show, unfortunately, that people tend to respond to early forms of brutality with lifelong destructive tendencies. In her groundbreaking book, *Trauma and Recovery*, Judith L. Herman writes:

> Traumatic events overwhelm the ordinary systems of care that give people a sense of control, connection, and meaning. . . . Traumatic events are extraordinary, not because they occur rarely, but rather because they overwhelm the ordinary human adaptations to life. Unlike commonplace misfortunes, traumatic events generally involve threats to life or bodily integrity, or a close personal encounter with violence and death . . . certain identifiable experiences increase the likelihood of harm. . . . In each instance, the salient characteristic of the traumatic event is its power to inspire helplessness and terror.[15]

For Joseph, a full dozen devastating experiences (see the bulleted list above) occurred during his developmental years. Some conclude that Joseph was utterly driven by his own "demons," his traumatic memories, and is merely seeking revenge against his brothers.[16] With such a catalogue of traumatic events, Joseph has every reason to suffer from *unclaimed experiences*, that is, unprocessed pain accompanied by anger, self–pity, and various fears. In fact, with such experiences, it would be traumatic enough for Joseph just to realize that he survived![17] But as we shall see, Joseph would use his twenty–two year separation from his family to make some profound theological conclusions about his own story, God's activity, and the best way to reconnect with the "gang of ten" (his brothers who were present at his sale to passersby).

Significantly, Joseph weeps numerous times in the story (42:24; 43:30; 45:2; 46:29; 50:1, 17), but it never states that his ten brothers or his father ever cry. I believe this is evidence of *unclaimed suffering* on their part, mixed with years of denial and manipulation. Joseph eventually figures out what God is doing, but his brothers do not really get it. Ironically, in one of Joseph's darkest seasons, the text states four times that "the Lord was with Joseph" (39:2–3, 21, 23). Amid a slave's life moved around as chattel, sexual harassment, the horrible slander, then imprisonment, the Lord was there as well; yet I really wonder if Joseph felt God's presence or struggled with feelings of divine abandonment, much like the psalmists we revere (e.g., Ps. 88). Clearly, the presence of God does not mean the absence of trials or temptation!

Transgenerational Pain

Second, some of Joseph's toxic experiences are in fact *transgenerational* problems. That is, the problem and its related suffering actually began years before Joseph was around. Deep-seated family evils have a frightening momentum that does not conform to our modern culture's notions of individualism and self-direction. *Families recycle the toxic pains they are too embarrassed to name, too disoriented to understand, and too wounded to stop.* Outsiders, however, can see through the damaging dramas of adultery, "silent treatment," domestic violence, a critical spirit, sensuality, abuse, racism, and angry outbursts. They can find those transgenerational patterns of relating that have been woven into the relational fabric of an extended family. Forward reminds us, "Remember, your parents had parents too. A toxic family system is like a multicar pile-up on the freeway, causing damage generation after generation after generation. This system is not something that your parents invented; *it is the result of the accumulated feelings, rules, interactions, and beliefs that have been handed down from your ancestors.*"[18]

Family heirlooms are not the only things we inherit. We also receive a "moral compass," evident in our family's relational habits. While some basically use this reality as an excuse, declaring, "You can choose everything but your own family," relational profiles can also be laced with ancient poisons. Such sins are not passed down as some unit of legal guilt. Instead, these toxins are tied up in our beliefs, perspectives, routines, and social traditions. These toxins are complex ways of relating that we ourselves practice—even refine—and then extend to those closest to us, especially our children. *Our challenge is to accept what we did not start, face what we did not see, then grieve what we did not stop.* For example, both favoritism and deceit were entrenched in Joseph's extended family. Its effect on his life will be profound. Let's explore his two preceding patriarchs.

PLAYING FAVORITES:
JOSEPH'S GRANDFATHER AND FATHER

Joseph's Grandfather

Joseph's grandfather Isaac had long been blinded by his favoritism, loving the non–chosen Esau over Jacob (25:28). Even though God had given Isaac and Rebekah an oracle identifying Jacob as the next covenant steward (25:23), nevertheless, "Isaac loved Esau because he ate of his game, but Rebekah loved Jacob" (25:28). So what was Isaac's rationale? A food lust! Any father, driven by his senses, like Isaac, is going to make rather selfish decisions. Convention actually required Isaac to invite the entire family for the official blessing (cf. Genesis 48–50).[19] Isaac blessed the wrong person with the wrong *approach*. Understandably, Rebekah is incensed! But the profile of Isaac is of one who operates by taste (25:28) and touch (26:8 NIV). So it is poetic justice for his own self–centeredness that Isaac is deprived of sight (27:1), resorts to taste, touch, and smell, and ignores sound (27:21–27), when he is deceived (27:35).[20] The truth is, Jacob was the doted–on favorite of a dysfunctional family, himself! Lines get blurred now, because *favoritism needs deceit to survive.*

Their marital games are stunning: Isaac forces Esau to name the "Deceiver" (Jacob, 27:32–33), and Rebekah "brandishes a sense of utter revulsion" that her eldest (Esau, 27:46) has married into the Hittites.[21] Nameless favorites and social "end–arounds" drive their conversations. Blessing was performative, not "word–magic." As Thiselton points out, "To give the same blessing to Esau would be like saying 'I do' to a second bride"—which Jacob will also learn when he runs into Laban, an even more skilled deceiver (29:22–25).[22] Marriage is also a performative act and allows deceit to come full circle: like Isaac, Jacob would be plied with food and wine, deprived of sight in the darkness, baffled by clothing, and left with misleading touch!

Isaac and Rebekah used manipulation to promote their own "trophy–child." Within contemporary culture, "trophy–parenting" is epidemic among the affluent, and it still has the power to manufacture family favorites. Be warned. Children will repeat it! Sadly, the only time Isaac and Rebekah speak to each other in chapter 27 is at the close when she manipulates Isaac for Jacob's future marriage (27:41–46). The children have mastered their parents' deceit: Jacob began with a lie, calling himself the "firstborn" (27:19), but Esau uses "firstborn" status when, in fact, he has already sold off his legal rights (27:32). But at least Esau pronounces his own name! The truth is, favoritism can only exist where deceit and half-truths give it protection. *When families have severely bent their moral compass, then the basic skills of honesty and communication will be twisted.*

Joseph's Father

So it is no surprise that Jacob, Joseph's father, showed the same skewed love for Joseph that he had been tutored in. Small wonder we read, "Now Israel loved Joseph more than any other of his sons" (37:3). Or imagine how these statements from Jacob would sound to Joseph's brothers: "My son [Benjamin] shall not go down with you, for his brother is dead, and *he is the only one left*. . . . You know that *my wife bore me two sons*" (42:38; 44:27, emphasis added). Of course, Joseph and Benjamin were from the same wife, Rachel, whom Jacob clearly favored over Leah and his two female servants who also bore him sons (35:23–26). But the father who favored two of his sons also favored one of his wives. This language is stunningly cruel to his other children! Joseph is not entirely to blame for some of his tragic experiences.

Shockingly, much earlier Jacob had flaunted his special affection for Joseph by giving him a "royal robe" that elevated Joseph above his ten half brothers. David may have watched sheep as a young boy, but not Joseph (1 Sam. 16:11–12)![23] Yet Joseph became Jacob's special assistant at age seventeen (37:2, 13)! To make matters worse, Joseph talked about himself in a self-absorbed way—at his brothers' expense—describing his dreams rather egotistically (37:5–7).[24] As a result, the brothers hated Joseph both *before* and *after* his dreams (vv. 4, 8). A father's favoritism has matured into the brothers' jealousy and full-blown fury. But it happens again! "Wrapped in narcissistic wonder," Joseph insists on informing both his brothers and his father of their future bowing to his rule (37:9–11).[25] Why on earth would Jacob send his "royal son" on a three–day trip to check up on ten hate–filled brothers (37:12–14)? Why on earth would Joseph go—wearing his "royal robe" (37:23)? Neither favoritism nor teenage arrogance is capable of empathizing with others. In the end, the hateful brothers can rid themselves of Joseph, but they cannot dispel Jacob's preference for Joseph.

GOING BACK TO ABRAHAM

But family deceit also has a dark history. We could start with the way Abraham deceitfully "cuts a deal" with Pharaoh to save his own life— twice (12:10–13; 20:1–17)! Among other problems, this subjects Sarah to potential victimization. So we should not be surprised when his son Isaac—Joseph's grandfather—lies about his wife, Rebekah, in the same way (26:1–11)! In the end, the Egyptians, Philistines, and Canaanites will all field deceit from the patriarchs and their children (e.g., Genesis 38).[26] As we have seen, with his mother's aid (27:5–17) Jacob deceives his own father for Esau's blessing (27:12, 35). This brings a grudge, hatred, and murderous plans from Esau (27:41–45), who admits that Jacob deceived him, twice (27:36). Dodging hatred and murder, Jacob takes deceit with him into the next season of life.

Later, the narrator even states that "Jacob deceived Laban the Aramean" (30:20) when he fled, not that Jacob's manipulation left the reader doubting (cf. 31:26–27). For her part, Rachel steals Laban's household gods (31:19, 34). This same deceit is adeptly practiced by Jacob's sons (34:13), in their anger over their sister Dinah's rape (34:1–2) and Jacob's passivity. Jacob's sons abuse the covenant sign of circumcision (34:13–17), then they "took their swords and attacked the unsuspecting city, killing every male" (34:25). Women, children, and flocks were then plundered throughout the city (34:27–29). *These patterns of deceit and their consequences reach extensively into the fabric of a family* (though there is a serious family "cleansing" in chapter 35, when the foreign gods and amulets that the family had accumulated are destroyed [35:2–4]). With such history, we should not be surprised that the ten jealous brothers "dethrone" Joseph by tearing up the contract of their father's affection, Joseph's "royal robe" (37:23), dipping it in blood and then returning it to Jacob for the distraught father to identify. Through their actions we get a glimpse into the depth of their animosity toward both Jacob and his prince. The narrator has written a masterpiece:

- Now Jacob himself is deceived by a goat and clothing (cf. 27:9, 15).
- Now Jacob's own sons refuse to use truthful names (cf. 27:19).
- Now Jacob himself must "recognize" what Isaac did not (cf. 27:23).

JOSEPH'S LOSS OF AGENCY

A key outcome of such actions is Joseph's utter loss of agency. With so many people acting against Joseph, in physical hostility and social slander, his loss of personal choice (volition) and safety affect his response to this brutality. In Joseph's only "testimony" of his betrayal, he pleads with the cupbearer, saying, "Please do me the kindness to mention me to Pharaoh . . . for I was indeed stolen out of the land of the Hebrews" (40:14–15; or "forcibly carried off" NIV). Traded like a sack of grain, Joseph vividly describes his loss of personal agency and dignity. His own family did this! In the words of Clinton W. McLemore:

> Victimizers have no firm sense of boundaries and thus feel entitled to whatever they can take by force or persuasion. Right or wrong has little to do with it. People with this style care only about their own well-being and advantage and are quick to justify their ruthless and opportunistic actions. . . . Victimizers cannot afford the *luxury of loyalty or other emotional distractions.*[27]

In toxic families, manipulation and deceit drive family relations; no one freely chooses anything. All relating becomes contingent, a step to further control, an endless banter for power and affection. Love certainly is no motivator here! Whether it is Joseph's brothers who slaughtered the people of Shechem because their anger "required" it (34:25–29) or Joseph, as Jacob's "entitled" supervisor, who insists on recounting multiple dreams to an audience of siblings who hate him (37:5–11) or Jacob who rudely snubs his entire family's attempt at comfort in order to stay in suspended mourning for his prized son, Joseph (37:34–35)—no one takes responsibility for their actions in toxic families. No one uses memory to nurture others. No one apologizes. Toxic families starve each other of nurturing emotion. As McLemore writes, the toxic relater "is frightened by tenderness and weakness because both have become associated with vulnerability and pain."[28] Not surprisingly, *where there is no free agency in love, there is no intentional closure in conflict.*

The popular expression sounds like this: "I wouldn't have had to do this, but *you gave me no choice!*" In shame-based cultures and highly individualized societies, this social dynamic of shame—or "I'm offended" —means forgiveness is not an option, nor would one "lose face" in order to restore broken relationships. Placating the "offended" can assume the level of an art.

When Jacob sends waves of animals to Esau, 550 in all, Jacob attempts a form of social reconciliation by *restitution* of property—the blessing he stole from Esau (33:8–11). What has Jacob ever given to anyone? Similarly, when Joseph's brothers take their "gift" or "present" (מנחה) of choice fruits, balm, honey, gum, myrrh, pistachio nuts, almonds, and twice the silver, they are attempting to exonerate themselves of any underhanded actions and "smooth over" their relationship with Egypt's second most powerful leader (43:11–13, 26). Ideally, such actions can actually illustrate the power of restitution in relational healing and peace–making. But when human choices are selfish and vindictive, especially destructive and violent, then both the *horizontal* relationship with family and the *vertical* relationship with God are breached.[29] Significantly, wherever the language of "gift" is used in Genesis, the narrative is describing the possibility of fratricide

(Cain/Abel [4:3–5]; Jacob/Esau [32:1–21; 33:10]).[30] The consequences of a relational breach will naturally be felt throughout one's entire relational ecosystem. To break pattern and precedent, comprehensive damage needs comprehensive healing. As individuals are wounded over time, it similarly takes time to heal. Time was a gracious gift God gave to Joseph. He had over two decades to gather his head and heart before he saw his brothers who sold him. He spent ninety–three years in Egypt, and seventy–one years were next to his family.

It is quite baffling to consider how God works with such flawed and failing people. Where does human responsibility intersect with God's will? Does God just give Jacob and his family a "pass" on moral standards, blessing them regardless of their actions? It may appear that way. What we can say is that God is remarkably patient and undeservingly good! *But he also lets consequences take their due course.* As Goldingay reminds us, "The theological perspective Genesis offers readers is not a lesson in resolving conflict within families, but a promise that conflict is not the end of the world."[31]

Ironically, the organic continuum of sin is a stabilizing process in life that God guards. So it is significant to see how Joseph's brothers describe their accountability with God and compare that with how Joseph talks about God. Whether Joseph speaks with an aristocratic woman trying to seduce him or Pharaoh's cupbearer hoping for reemployment—Joseph always interjects God into the conversation (Gen. 39:9; 40:7–8).

JOSEPH'S FORGIVENESS (GEN. 45:1–8)

The power of forgiveness in Joseph's life is matched only by that power depicted by Jesus in the parable of the prodigal son (Luke 15:11–32). Psychologically, spiritually, and relationally, Joseph has suffered so much. The climax comes in Genesis 45, where we see Joseph's forgiveness in its beautiful yet costly form. As John Goldingay puts it, "Having suffered one way, he suffers another; for 'forgiveness itself is a form of suffering' because it involves giving up the right to justice."[32] By "giving up," Goldingay means passing on one's right to personally punish. This can be a tough pill, for sure! Forgiveness releases the guilty party into the hands of the better Judge, who has a timeless perspective. The "pull" of the New Testament to radical forgiveness is no sidestepping of justice (Matt. 6:14–15; 18:21–35). We must acknowledge the perspectives of both Scripture (the "map") and culture (the "ocean"), for forgiveness speaks into the darkest corners of life.

What Is Forgiveness?

Recognizing the high cost of forgiveness, some people cynically claim that "unforgiveness is the poison we swallow and wait for the other party to die." Such a view shows that some people see forgiveness as wimpy, counterproductive, and hardly the empowering option. They have it wrong, actually. Anger and bitterness have only a veneer of control. As Edmond Dantes begrudgingly admits in *The Count of Monte Cristo*, anger is all some people have left. This perspective reflects the *secularist's martyrdom*, in which one at least takes pride in their powerlessness![33] That is the point: for some, vengeance is preferable to healing. Ironically, even amid the growing politics of nonviolence, social protest may still be as cold and dehumanizing as the sword. Regardless, there is limited closure in protest, and certainly no healing. The dominant paradigm of social interaction today is to identify the party of power, and thus the dominated "other." The former is to be "unmasked," and the latter, pitied. While society is infatuated with *horizontal causation* (evident in excessive litigation), Scripture goes further and adds the *vertical interaction* with God. Both are realities. Sometimes healing is learning to live in the tension of "God's unpredictable choices."[34]

A Biblical Perspective

From a biblical perspective, *forgiveness relinquishes the right to personal vengeance, not the right to offense, outrage, or even legal action*. As Nicholas Wolterstorff explains, "To forgive is not to treat the act as not having been done but to enact the resolution *not to hold the act* against *the wrongdoer*" (cf. 2 Cor. 5:19).[35] Forgiveness is not condoning, excusing, minimizing, denying, rationalizing, or placating people and their evil actions. Instead, forgiveness removes self–in–revenge from the equation and places any retribution in God's hands (Gen. 50:19; Deut. 32:35; Rom. 12:19).

Joseph's forgiveness is a rare occurrence in the Old Testament, as biblical writers seldom attribute forgiveness to human beings. Nor in the Old Testament do the writers ever command someone to forgive another. But the Old Testament writers understood that a sin committed against a fellow human to also be a sin committed against God. The horizontal and vertical realms were not separated. By contrast, the New Testament focuses on the individual person, not on the national relationship with God.[36] In the New Testament, reconciliation is the evidence of forgiveness, available with both God and fellow humans (Rom. 5:10; Col. 3:12–15). That said, the emphasis falls on the God who forgives, in both Testaments. In the collective weight of Scripture, there is no distinction "*between the love of God who forgives and the love of neighbor who must be forgiven.*"[37] As revelation progresses, it becomes clear that human forgiveness is possible only because God has forgiven. God's practice of forgiving authorizes our obligation to forgive.[38] In this way, the followers of Christ must reflect his character (Col. 3:13). Forgiveness is not self–destruction.[39] Sometimes forgiveness is about halting evil, and that is called winning. *Some forms of evil are never understood; they are only "absorbed" through a vision and grace not our own.*

Receiving true forgiveness has both negative and positive effects. In forgiveness, there is both *freedom from* and *access to*. Negatively, it is *freedom from* bitterness, hatred, guilt, destructive acts, and punishment. Forgiveness involves an honest look at the damage one has suffered through the hurtful actions of another and, eventually, remembering that event differently. But positively, it is also *access to* peace, reestablished relationships, mutual affirmation, and a future with dignity.[40] For the offended, forgiveness relinquishes the attitudes of unforgiveness so that a new meaning can be nurtured from an old pain. In the highly relational contexts of vows, confession, and forgiveness, ritual can help express what words cannot. From weddings to funerals, births to burials, we ritualize what we want to remember. From planted trees to buried photos and burned clothes, forgiveness also takes ritual forms. As Frank H. Gorman explains it: "Rituals are thus means of holding back social confusion, indeterminacy, and chaos because they provide patterns for . . . maintaining order and constructive patterns for restoring that order when it has been lost."[41] Not surprisingly, some degree of ritual or formality will accompany Joseph's testing of his brothers and his forgiving of them.

Joseph's suffering has been acute largely because of the *terror of randomness*. For Joseph, forgiveness is the necessary corrective, not only for the resulting damages but also as a redemption from the irreversibility of his suffering.[42] There was a destructive randomness to Joseph's suffering, making him unable to undo what was done. For Joseph, both identifying the wounds and sifting for the truth are highly measured endeavors.

Whom has Joseph confided in? Familial wounds require familial healing. When others were misguided about his death or attempted rape, was anyone ever told the truth? Joseph's affliction has been unaided, isolating, and preserved in horrifying silence; the kind of silence that deprives victims of their personality and makes them into things.[43] Is he Joseph, viceroy of Egypt, "master dreamer," Rachel's eldest—or Jacob's errand–boy who never made it home?

JOSEPH TESTS HIS BROTHERS

Why Does Joseph Test His Brothers?

Joseph tests his brothers because he cannot entrust his true identity— a brother actually alive, emotionally affectionate, and a dynamic agent of God's work—to this "gang of ten" if their murderous hearts have not changed. McLemore explains why Joseph veils his own character as he searches for the heart–condition of his brothers: "Self-disclosure is therefore central to interpersonal relationships and hence to fellowship. Without sharing what is going on inside of us, there can be no true fellowship."[44] Joseph illustrates that *after deep betrayals, trust must be earned* and proven through genuine "life–fruit"!

So this is not payback. A revengeful person does not weep like Joseph (cf. 42:24; 43:30; 45:1–2). Repeating the scene of vulnerable tears three times proves Joseph is neither fickle nor vengeful. Joseph is portrayed as a feeling person, a whole person: he has the capacity for emotional intimacy, domestic engagement, administrative involvement, and spiritual sensitivity.[45] The writer draws from a new language–palette of emotional terms in the Joseph story: "anguish" (42:21 KJV), "distressed" (45:5), "quarrel" (45:24), and "grudge" (50:15 NIV). He feels for others and understands what God is doing. So the tears of Joseph reveal a holistic person "*acting against* his inclination," and so actually encountering further pain.[46] This is not Joseph's revenge, but the brothers' needful "cleansing," after twenty–two years of hiding a toxic family secret. Seeing God's hand in his dreams, administrative gifts, and international events, "Joseph is not acting for himself but *for the sake of his brothers*."[47] So I think Goldingay is correct:

> The way he deals with his brothers involves no revenge that parallels their betrayal of him . . . it is the way this 'wise' man sets about seeking to bring them to own their wrongdoing and to be open to reconciliation. He is not testing them in the sense he says (Gen 42:14–16), but he does want to discover whether there is any truth or trustworthiness (*ĕmet*) in them (Gen 42:16). And the test is effective, as it provokes Judah's self–sacrificing offer to become a servant.[48]

Joseph's testing gets at the root of vindictiveness that must be relationally explored, on a plane where the brothers operate. Joseph is not looking for truth in the abstract. Joseph needs to know if his brothers have any genuine love for their father and his full–brother, Benjamin.[49]

Joseph also has the grander program of God in full view, as we shall see
. . . as his brothers are asked to see.

Reenacting Scenes of His Treatment

One of the most fascinating elements of Joseph's testing of his
brothers is the way Joseph reenacts key scenes of his unethical treatment.[50] Ethically and theologically, these reenactments, rooted in the
many facets of Joseph's brutal experience (Genesis 37), verge on "symmetrical retribution."[51] For example, Joseph binds Simon in front of
them (42:16, 24)—the second son of Leah for the second son of Rachel
(Benjamin). This reenacts the spectacle of Joseph's sale (37:28). Joseph
turns other reenactments into healing tokens of his affection. For example, he gives new changes of clothes to brothers who stripped him
of his special coat (45:22).[52] Another healing reenactment is his gift of
three hundred pieces of silver to Benjamin (45:22). This silver blesses
Benjamin, rather than sells him. This silver is a gift, the final restoration for the sale of Rachel's eldest. And there are other reenactments
that restore relationships by calming fearful hearts.

In this way, scenarios of potential favoritism reenact their scheming; potential jealousy reenacts their betrayal, and potential violence
reenacts their hatred. As a ruse, Joseph is using an interpreter to talk
with them! If the brothers repeat any unethical actions or verbalize any
evil intentions, then Joseph has his answer—they've not changed! But
there are three particular tests that stand out.

1. *Test of Greed* (42:25). Will the brothers take more silver in exchange
   for another brother (Simeon)? No, but they are also unable to rid
   themselves of any silver.

2. *Test of Jealousy* (43:34). Will special attention given to Benjamin
   arouse the brothers' jealousy? No; in fact, Joseph's meal–fellowship
   grants them participation in his own life and they accept it.

3. *Test of Familial Loyalty* (44:2, 12). Will Joseph's surrogate (Benjamin)
   be discarded like Joseph, when put in harm's way? No, the brothers
   choose to extend loyalty when Benjamin is accused of theft. In grief,

all the brothers tear their clothes, expressing solidarity with Benjamin (cf. 37:34).

In each major test, some aspect of their relational accountability for Joseph, and their actual selfish action, is highlighted. Do the brothers grasp the depth of the crime they have committed? They sold Joseph into slavery, then lied about it for twenty–two years! Benjamin likely never knew the truth. Will the brothers repeat prior offenses, if given a chance? Are they even capable of remorse? Joseph has little reason to believe they have changed when ten brothers bow before him, but eleven was the number in both of his dreams! The harder question is this: *have they survived?*[53]

Each of the three major tests includes silver (42:25; 44:1–2, 17)! The silver shekels that initially sold Joseph into slavery—two pieces for each brother—they are now utterly helpless to return! If the brothers had picked up the pattern of *re–created* events Joseph was using, or just realized how current events replicated their past treatment of Joseph, they might have been horrified, not just terrified.[54] But they were not ready for these healing measures, and so did not "recognize" what Joseph was doing or even their own guilt, initially.

What the Brothers Say

What the brothers say reveals where their hearts are. Joseph asks them loaded questions, and they start divulging all kinds of details. Most telling is their use of plural pronouns ("we, us, our") that reveal their collective guilt and their struggle to make any reference to God. Their "heart condition" is revealed in the language they use. One readily sees the fear of recrimination and their belief that Joseph is dead. Yet, notice the rising presence of guilt and reference to God in their conversations.

In their collective speeches the ten brothers exhibit *sheer panic* (42:17–22, especially Reuben's reply, "Didn't I tell you not to sin against the boy? . . . Now we must give an accounting for his blood" [NIV]);

a terrified question (42:28); *disputing fear* (43:19–22); and a *desperate protest* to the steward sent by Joseph (44:6–9).

Finally, upon their return to Joseph's house (44:14) they display humility in their plea:

> How can we prove our innocence? God has uncovered your servants' guilt. . . . His brother [Joseph] is dead, and he [Benjamin] is the only one of his mother's sons left, and his father loves him. . . . Your servant my father said to us, "You know that my wife bore me two sons. . . . He has surely been torn to pieces." . . . Please let your servant remain here as my lord's slave in place of the boy. . . . Do not let me see the misery that would come upon my father. (44:16, 20, 27–28, 33–34 NIV)

This final speech by Judah gives full vent to their sense of guilt. *Their greatest act of freedom is their expression of guilt. Where there is no recognition of guilt, collective healing and reconciliation are impossible.* Here, they humanize themselves. Stunningly, Judah mentions "father" fourteen times, death six times, and "my father" six times! Clearly, the brothers do care for Jacob and Benjamin, having torn their clothes in grief at Benjamin's capture (cf. 44:13). The fourth son of Leah quotes Jacob's shocking comment that "my wife bore me two sons" (44:27) as the grounds for Benjamin's release! Of all the characters in Genesis, Judah has changed the most. *Judah cites his de-legitimization by Jacob as an argument for sparing Benjamin. Judah can finally admit Jacob's irrational love.* As Sternberg puts it, "Simply, Judah so feels for his father that he begs to sacrifice himself for a brother more loved than himself."[55] The son who suggested that Joseph be sold, now pleads for a living death as a slave, a worthy sacrifice for avoiding the inevitable death of his father. No little irony here! This self-sacrifice not only displays the character of kings, but his moving appeal utterly collapses Joseph's composure (45:1–2). The truth has emerged; now Joseph can, too.

JOSEPH'S FINAL "RELEASE" AND FORGIVENESS

Joseph Reveals His Identity (Gen. 45:1–3)

Judah has made the longest speech in Genesis before the viceroy of Egypt (44:18–34). Standing across from his brothers—their clothes torn (v. 13)—Joseph recognizes that his brothers' actions and words have finally lined up! The brothers have confessed their guilt, Jacob has released Benjamin, and Judah has offered himself as a slave. Now Joseph quickly dismisses all of his Egyptian administrators from the room. Revealing his identity concerns Joseph and his brothers, not the viceroy and his officials.

Now Zaphenath–Paneah (Joseph's Egyptian name given by Pharaoh; 41:45) relinquishes power (45:1b). Beyond insightful, Joseph forgives them *as a brother*, not as the second–in–command of Egypt. Joseph does not hide behind power. He has been longing for the transparency of brotherhood (43:30–31). Forgiveness requires Joseph's approachability, not a display of state authority. The courage to relinquish power is a hard lesson for the contemporary person, socialized for status and presentation; those who reach the top often try to cling to their station. Being "genuine" brings Joseph's third and climactic weeping (45:2). He reveals his identity, then tells of God's mission, and the scene closes with his weeping once more (vv. 4–15). His tears are uncontrollable and now flow freely in their presence (cf. 42:24; 43:30–31). This weeping is joyful and welcoming because forgiveness lifts the forgiver even more than the party forgiven.[56] This scene is filled with redeeming ritual, the *balm of forgiveness* is now given.

From self–revelation ("I am Joseph!") to a question ("Is my father still living?"), Joseph turns immediately to the well–being of his family. The disclosure of "Joseph" was more than revealing a name. It was a heart–stopping phrase![57] They are seized with the panic of those sensing their own doom (Ps. 45:5).[58] The brothers must admit that their attempt to eliminate Joseph over twenty years earlier not only failed, but it is Joseph, in fact, who is now talking to them—without an interpreter!

Joseph Proves His Identity (45:4–7)

To prove his identity and calm their fears, Joseph cites a fact only his brothers would know: I'm the one "you *sold* into Egypt!" (cf. 40:15). Notice the horizontal plane of searing honesty among the men (see chart 2). Even the terms are becoming more intimate. Previously, the narrator referred to "the men" (43:33; 9 times in chaps. 43–44), but now they are "his brothers" (45:1, 3, 4, 15, 24) and "Joseph's brothers" (v. 16).[59] Joseph has intentionally reaffirmed his identity within his family.[60] With their toxic family secret out, the brothers' new challenge is to now live their lives free from guilt. Can they view themselves apart from their past evil actions?

Chart 2
Joseph Forgives His Brothers

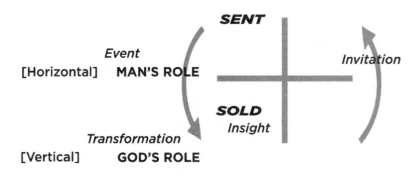

Immediately, *Joseph redirects their focus away from their sin to God's overriding design*: "Do not be distressed or angry . . . for God sent me before you to preserve life" (v. 5). They see Joseph in front of them. He wants his brothers to understand God's role in their evil. After a recap of the famine status (v. 6) and God's present activity (vv. 7–8), Joseph explains the extent of God's deliverance: it is international ("to preserve," v. 7a) and familial ("to save," 7b NIV). Joseph has been anticipating the migration of his entire family (cf. Ps. 105:17). He understands how God has interjected a whole new vertical reality ("sent") into his horizontal suffering ("sold"). Joseph's sweeping assertion is that the suffering he experienced served God's larger intentions.[61] Alter calls this "a luminous illustration of the Bible's double system of causation, human and divine," making suffering mysterious and healing majestic.[62] It is precisely by not collapsing "sent" or "sold" into each other that Joseph has made significant meaning of his suffering, even beyond his own lifetime.

Encouraging his brothers not to be "angry" shows stunning poise and psychological comfort on Joseph's part. His act of forgiveness (1) removes the weight of their guilt and (2) invites them to participate in God's ongoing work. We were informed earlier that "God was with Joseph" (Genesis 39); now we peer into the why.[63] This is Joseph's theological insight that he shares (see chart 2). It is as if he is saying: "I want you to join me in what God is currently doing!" For the brothers, facing a new man, as well as a new mission, is truly a monumental event. This is the brothers' challenge. Stepping into Joseph's new proposal is a fresh orientation to the future that just may release them from their toxic past. It is the brothers who have been in prison!

Let's be clear. Joseph is not ignoring his suffering (41:51–52) nor their evil (45:4b; 50:20). But he does choose to see God's bigger design for his family in lives preserved (45:5, 7; 50:20). Can the brothers accept the *challenge of transformation*: a life lived without anger and fear—a life living out the promises to Abraham? If the brothers can accept Joseph's *invitation to participate*, family reconciliation may also occur. Forgiveness has been extended by Joseph, but reconciliation requires both parties to come together. While Judah was preoccupied with death and the past (44:20, 28), Joseph has emphasized a future full of life (45:5–7). What Judah attempted through compensation, Joseph achieves through forgiveness—a forgiveness that gathers a very imperfect family. Watching Joseph's life so closely illustrates how forgiveness can be a gradual healing process that takes place simultaneously on three levels:

1. *Psychologically*, releasing negative cognitions about and emotions toward the offender,

2. *Spiritually*, accepting the reality of injury within a journey toward wholeness through the grace and insight God provides, and

3. *Relationally*, the reshaping of one's perception of the offender, resulting in release from related pain.

It is worth observing that the effort and skill that Rebekah, Jacob, and Rachel use to outmaneuver Isaac, Esau, and Laban are not accompanied by any clear sense of or reference to God's purposes.[64] By contrast, Joseph not only senses what God is doing, he genuinely tries to draw others into God's activity, constantly referencing the hand and freedom of God, regardless of whom he is speaking to. This text teaches us that *the sovereignty of God is not seen in what he prevents but in his majestic ability to take the broken pieces of our lives and make something beautiful from them.* In Goldingay's words, "the First Testament is not as interested in passing moral judgments on its characters as it is in seeing how God works out a purpose through them in their moral ambiguity . . . The stories also then implicitly summon people to be wiser than their fathers, and even than their mothers."[65]

ATTEMPTED RECONCILIATION

Fear in Reconciliation . . . Really? (50:15–21)

The story of Joseph's forgiveness does not end two years into the famine (45:6). Those brothers who had tried to slay Joseph found their very existence strangely dependent on that rejection.[66] Seventeen years later, triggered by Jacob's death, Joseph's brothers fear that the care they have received was merely prompted by Joseph's love for his father (Gen. 50:15–18). Maybe their limited recovery underscores the effects of toxic deception when it is left to run its course in a family for so long. Overwhelmed by currents of residual guilt, the brothers fabricate a letter in Jacob's name.[67] Laced with terms like "grudge" (NIV) and "pay us back" (v. 15; cf. 43:18), the letter is a device to speak for them, much as a bloody coat was forty years earlier (37:32–33)! Sadly, Jacob's ghost asks that Joseph forgive them for the harm and evil that they perpetrated against him (50:17). Maybe saddest of all, their ruse is not even in the name of *their* God, it is in the name of their father's God!

Joseph cries again (v. 17). These are not tears of joy. Joseph realizes that not only do the brothers fail to trust him, but deception still lives on in the family! Seventeen years earlier, Joseph attempted a legacy of family healing, when he extended forgiveness to them. Over twenty years of gracious provision cannot compete with their strained attachment to their now deceased father. As happens in the lifetimes of parents, some siblings will continue to make their father decisive in the relationship, even when he is dead.[68] The truth is: *they were never fully reconciled.*[69] The letter sent under the pretense of Jacob's wishes was really written in the ink of fear. Joseph's tears say as much as his words (vv. 19–20). Just because a family lives near each other does not mean they are reconciled.[70] Fear actually prefers to live with bullies, but forgiveness and grace can be strange neighbors to the fearful heart.

Joseph's forgiveness remains the singular healing overture that Jacob's family can muster. As Sacks wrote, this family struggle is also a nation's lesson:

> Joseph's forgiveness is the bridge between Genesis and Exodus. The first is about the children of Israel as a *family*, the second is about them as a *nation*. Central to both is the experience of slavery, first Joseph's, then the entire people. The message could not be clearer. Those who seek freedom must learn to forgive.[71]

However, Joseph refuses to engage in manipulation of any kind. As Wolterstorff explains, "Forgiveness is often granted in the hope, and sometimes the expectation, of reconciliation. But one can accept someone's apology for the wrong he did one, and forgive him for that wrong, while nonetheless holding out little if any hope for reconciliation."[72] This reality is hard to communicate because it lives so close to home.

The brothers want to view Joseph as God's proxy. But Joseph wants nothing of it—he understands true power as God's prerogative alone. With stunning theological understanding, *Joseph confines himself to his role as God's instrument* (v. 20). Joseph renounces punishment. Only God can properly match crimes to punishment (Lev. 19:18).[73] Therefore, they are "not to fear," a reassurance typically heard only from God's mouth.[74] A primal theme also reappears. "You intended evil" is correct (v. 17), but God consistently reconfigures harm for good.[75] This is also a theological summary of the "good–and–evil" that began in the Eden narrative (2:9). The entire book has shown that wicked human actions can be redeemed by God's goodness. Rolf P. Knierim applies core theology to Joseph's life:

> It is revealed that in this course the dynamic of evil has been over-taken by the dynamic of good; *Joseph yields his right and power to punish his brothers to the 'better' right and power already established through the complete reversal of the course of evil* ... he acknowledges the dynamic presence in a process which breaks the autonomous coherence of evil act and evil consequence by turning it into a process of goodness and which, therefore, represents the better justice. *Joseph accepts this better justice as the ethical basis for his own judgment of forgiveness.*[76]

Joseph's final reenactment comes when he "speaks kindly" to his fearful brothers. Consolation is given and forgiveness is reaffirmed.[77] This is a touching reversal for the brothers who, long ago, could not say a kind word (37:4).

MOVING BEYOND SUFFERING

Henri J. M. Nouwen has noted the healing and guiding work of the minister among family members. With keen insight, he observes:

The great vocation of the minister is to continuously make connections between the human story and the divine story. We have inherited a story which needs to be told in such a way that *the many painful wounds about which we hear day after day can be liberated from their isolation and revealed as part of God's relationship with us.* Healing means revealing that our human wounds are most intimately connected with the suffering of God himself. To be a living memory of Jesus Christ, therefore, means to reveal the connections between our small sufferings and the great story of God's suffering in Jesus Christ, between our little life and the great life of God with us.... *To heal, then, does not primarily mean to take pains away but to reveal that our pains are part of a greater pain, that our sorrows are part of a greater sorrow....* The challenge of ministry is to help people in very concrete situations to see and experience their story as part of God's ongoing redemptive work in the world. These insights and experiences heal precisely because they restore the broken connection between the world and God and *create a new unity in which memories that formerly seemed only destructive are now reclaimed as part of a redemptive event.*[78]

This statement by Nouwen seems more than appropriate after considering how Joseph forgives his family and points to God's mysterious involvement in their lives. This son of Jacob was truly able to "create a new unity in which memories that formerly seemed only destructive are now reclaimed as part of a redemptive event." This helps us realize that suffering by itself is not redemptive.

What is more memorable than Joseph's suffering is his forgiveness. It is only when suffering is connected to the larger redemptive narrative—beyond ourselves and beyond our strength—that insight comes, hope emerges, and relationships can mend.[79] Forgiving people have decided that they would rather live in a merciful world than in a fair one. Mercy does not abandon justice; it transcends it.[80]

FINAL OBSERVATIONS

Having considered various elements of the toxic family, we can make several observations in closing.

First, *there is "tough wisdom" needed in order to address the relational toxins in our families.* Which ones are yet to be acknowledged, understood, and removed? If we have not accepted the fact that God works through human weakness, we may be too fearful or offended to let God step into the messy relationships of our families. Chances are our own family toxins have been passed down and by now, other family members have felt their consequences. For the sake of our lives and coming generations, *we must understand the upstream issues that have shaped our downstream realities.* We must be willing to allow God to make decisive interventions into our families that cause a break in cycles of distress and relational disorder.[81] If necessary, we should seek the outside help we need to halt these family toxins and purge them from our marriages and families.

Second, *forgiveness places us at a crossroads.* We can choose to be enraged and cold or broken and hungering for deeper measures of God's grace. In truth, who among us has not contributed to the wounding of those closest to us? We are never the only wounded party. Mercy is needed, all around. God is actually more concerned about justice than we are! "It is the tension between God's justice and mercy that makes God so capable of dealing with wrongdoers. *God is able to punish people without destroying them, and to forgive people without indulging them.*"[82] Navigating this crossroads means we take our pain and look for the bigger design of God, not the more guilty party. Nor does finding healing mean we will understand everything that has occurred. Like Joseph, we may need to be satisfied in this life with "a sense of God's strange providence."[83] There are some kinds of evil that can destroy so much good. In such times, we remind ourselves that God does not simply abolish evil from life, but he does *contain* and *restrain* evil. This is part of the majestic surprise in God's healing work. He not only prevents evil from doing its worst, but as Joseph's story illustrates, God often uses the malice of other people to further his strange purposes.[84]

Third, *forgiveness is not the same as reconciliation*. It is high time we understand this. The nature of the offense (e.g., domestic violence, sexual abuse) and the lack of remorse or guilt really matter if one is interested in reconciliation. Forgiveness is a disposition that is rooted in an individual attitude, practicing forgiveness over time and across situations. The parties need not meet. Reconciliation, however, requires changes in both parties, not just in the offender. Several values must be present for reconciliation to occur:

- *Truth-telling*—"Uncovering" the facts must precede efforts at justice. Setting the record straight vindicates the innocent and honors wounds; it also helps avoid vengeance.

- *Justice*—Whether the form of justice is retributive (punitive expression), restorative (restores dignity), or structural (just practices), some social practices will need to be torn down and rebuilt. God's mercy and love must be allowed to embrace and surpass all parties involved.

- *Forgiveness*—As applied to reconciliation, there must be a giving up of anger and resentment. Forgiveness moves beyond resentment and tries to nurture shalom (kindness, safety, and harmony).

- *Peace*—Any reconciliation accomplished will always be an imperfect reconciliation. It also always takes more than one generation to achieve it. God's grace draws parties forward. Desperate optimism only lasts so long.[85]

Future attempts at reconciliation must also consider the realities of systemic evil, meaningful rituals within the faith community, the healing of memories, and the role of physical restitution to aid in healing.

Fourth, *we must learn to demonstrate greater skills of empathy* as we approach the brokenness in people's lives. Behind the "rough edges" of many people lie traumatizing experiences, layers of brokenness, and various coping mechanisms to lessen the pain. Like Joseph's experience, when trust has been betrayed, responsibility abandoned, and power abused, then lives can be deeply shattered. Ironically, it will take further relationships—lived in patience—to heal our broken lives and families. This requires "carrying–strength" on the part of the body of Christ in the form of quality teaching, quality support groups, honest naming of pain from the pulpit, disciplines of spiritual formation and healing, and the fresh fellowship of the spiritual family.

Fifth, even as we face some dark and difficult realities in our families, *we must remember that God remains active in our relationships.* There may even be various parties with different intentions—like Joseph's brothers and God himself. Many of the characters in the stories of our families are neither heroes nor villains, in which case we still need the reminder of a good God who is never pulled into an inferior outcome. Scripture testifies to both God's power and concern, design and dignity for our families. Honesty will place the abuse of power at the feet of reckless human agents. But faith will trace all good back to God (James 1:17).[86] Courage looks at both. There is a goal God is working toward. Our lives are not an endless series of events.[87] In the words of Jerry Sittser:

> He [Joseph] recognizes in the unfolding of his life that God is good in ways that he could not see earlier . . . our own tragedies can be a very bad chapter in a very good book. . . . I *choose to believe* that there is a bigger picture and that my loss is part of some wonderful story authored by God himself.[88]

AMID PAIN AND SUFFERING

1. In this chapter, the insights of Family Systems Theory were used, noting how all members of a family unit can be affected by individual actions, roles, etc. What do you feel are some challenges as well as insights of integrating the social sciences in the study of the Joseph story?

2. It was stated that "toxic families fight the loss of control by increasing the chaos." Explain some ways that you have witnessed this.

3. It was stated: "Where there is no recognition of guilt, collective healing and reconciliation are impossible." Give an illustration you have seen of this.

4. This chapter discussed *transgenerational pain*: "Families recycle the toxic pains they are too embarrassed to name, too disoriented to understand, and too wounded to stop." Looking back on your family life, how have you experienced this? What have you done to break such cycles?

5. In the diagram "Joseph Forgives His Brothers" and discussion of "sent" and "sold," what is most relevant to your life regarding forgiveness?

CHAPTER 10

Sexual Abuse

Suffering from a Host of Betrayals

By Andrew J. Schmutzer

Behind every occasion of sexual abuse is a destructive set of betrayals. In fact, when it comes to addressing sexual abuse, it is vital to realize that *story* always precedes symptoms. What often happens, however, is that the victim and their friends typically focus on the accessible symptoms and so miss the real "disease."

We begin with a definition of sexual abuse. Sexual abuse (SA) is any behavior that exploits a person for one's sexual gratification. Often therapists, pastors, and other advocates who counsel victims of SA deal with childhood sexual abuse, or CSA. The types of sexual exploitation of children may include force, intimidation, bribery, and abuse of power, such as using one's greater authority, knowledge, and age.

A distinction can be made between *contact* and *non-contact* SA. The former can include fondling, or forced vaginal, oral, or anal intercourse. But also traumatizing are non-contact types, such as exhibitionism, voyeurism, sexting, pornography, and obscene sexual phone calls. The suffering in SA stems from four key elements: (a) traumatic sexualization, (b) relational betrayal, (c) personal powerlessness, and (d) socioreligious stigmatization. Each one of these is really some form of betrayal.

AN INTEGRATIVE APPROACH TO UNDERSTANDING SEXUAL ABUSE

Adequately addressing SA is a complex undertaking.[1] Although some forms of suffering may have more stigmas attached, the complexity of SA makes it prone to oversimplification.[2] A biblical–theological study of sexual abuse is not common, either. Our study will use an *integrative* approach: a collaboration of social sciences, analysis of biblical texts, pastoral empathy, personal experience, and relational categories capable of addressing the "assault–factor" of sexual violation.[3] Similarly, the best stained–glass windows have many colors of glass, creating depth and contour. We are committed to the *revealed truth* of Scripture as well as the observed truth of empirical studies.[4] Where *revealed truth* and *observed truth* merge, then the complexity of the human condition is in fullest view—the "treasure in jars of clay" (2 Cor. 4:7).

In texts across Scripture, people are exhorted to scrutinize and investigate the natural aspects of life: "Go to the ant . . . *consider* her ways, and be wise" (Prov. 6:6), or "*Consider* the lilies of the field, how they grow; they neither toil nor spin" (Matt. 6:28b, italics added). We will consider Brad's story of abuse and then discuss it against the larger backdrop of SA.

BRAD'S STORY

Brad was raised in a good Christian home.[5] In fact, his parents traveled widely, leading marriage and family seminars. Life was normal enough until Brad was ten. Shelly, his babysitter, was his older cousin, a good friend of the family, and a regular volunteer with the youth at their church. Over the next three years, she sexually abused Brad in the swimming pool behind his house. At age eleven, Brad insisted on sleeping with the lights on and also struggled with bed–wetting. By age twelve, he regularly had nightmares and his schoolwork had dropped sharply. By age thirteen, he no longer wanted any friends over. He dropped out of sports because he claimed the locker room was "unsafe," and he was occasionally involved in fights at school.

Brad was sent to the school counselor after he gave a speech about war, and his illustration involved a box of small iron soldiers—all the soldiers had their arms sawed off. The school counselor recommended that Brad's parents take him to a psychologist, concerned about the aggressive behaviors that she was seeing. While Brad's parents were stunned by some of their son's actions, they believed their family was under spiritual attack because of their marriage ministry, so they took their son to their pastor instead. The pastor discussed Brad's struggle with pornography, how sinful this was, and told Brad's parents that this moral perversion may be the cause of Brad's anxiety. Brad was told that he could be healed from his lust and his relationship with Jesus, restored. Brad believed his problem with porn was responsible for bringing evil into the home and contributing to the struggle of his parents' marriage ministry.

When Brad finally saw a professional counselor at age fifteen—five years after the abuse began—he revealed that he had been sexually "tested" (Shelly's term) by his older female cousin, starting at age ten. But Brad did not see how his abuse related to anything else in his life, so he was surprised when the counselor diagnosed him with *severe depression*. Brad was filled with *self–loathing* and insisted on wearing shabby clothes.

Shelly was quietly dismissed from her leadership duties with the church youth, but no further investigation was done. However, some of her fellow youth leaders did try to get Shelly some help. On the advice of their pastor, Brad's parents chose not to press charges against Shelly. Additionally, they believed Christians should not use the secular court system. The adults agreed that this would cast a bad light on God's work at the church and their marriage ministry.

Brad was in therapy on and off throughout high school, feeling guilty that he could not find the "victory" his parents spoke of. Now in his early twenties, Brad avoids any intimacy in female relationships, refuses to go near swimming pools, and claims to be an agnostic. To the embarrassment of his parents, Brad remains angry and wants nothing to do with church, religious authorities, or God.

THE LARGER ISSUE OF ABUSE

Key Statistics

Brad's story highlights some key realities in sexual abuse. Brad's abuse began at age ten, which is close to the statistical average. Research shows that ten is the average age when girls are abused, and boys at age eleven. Overall, one in four girls and one in six boys—or at least one–fifth of all children—are sexually abused by the age of eighteen.[6] Anonymous surveys (e.g., Washington State Prison) show that between 75 and 95 percent of male inmates in prison were sexually abused. Yet because of social conditioning and stereotypes, it is widely agreed that males are far less likely to disclose their abuse than females.[7] *Delayed disclosure* in general leaves survivors talking, on average, twenty years after their abuse.[8]

As an older cousin, Shelly is a logical choice for a babysitter. As Brad's abuser, she is responsible for *interfamilial sexual abuse*, abuse among families. In about 93 percent of cases, the victim knows their abuser.[9] One recent study found that 43 percent of high school boys and young college men reported they had an unwanted sexual experience and of those, 95 percent stated that a female acquaintance was the aggressor.[10] That said, incest accounts for 70 percent of all SA.[11] "Stranger Danger" is a gross misconception in SA.

Shelly not only had access to Brad, but also many youth at her church. The long trips taken by Brad's parents left Brad socially isolated, emotionally vulnerable, and hungering for attention. Brad developed numbed emotions (known as "blunted affect"), in large part because he could not hate Shelly, who made him feel "special." But this is also betrayal. Abusers are often winsome people, placing themselves in social contexts that not only give them cover, but grant them access to other potential victims. (A classic example is former Penn State assistant football coach Jerry Sandusky.[12])

Common Trauma Signs of Victims

Brad showed the common signs of trauma that victims of abuse experience: *hyper-vigilance* (e.g., keeping lights on), *avoidance effort* (e.g., locker room seen as unsafe, baggy clothes, fear of swimming pools), some *post-traumatic stress disorder* (e.g., bed-wetting, self-hatred, object-mutilation), *distorted thinking and isolation* (e.g., fear of women, avoiding religious structures), and compulsivity in *sexualized behavior* (e.g., use of pornography).[13]

Sexual abuse during the developmental years can be extremely damaging, as evidenced by impairment in areas of social trust, relational intimacy, and the sense of personal agency.[14] In his preteen years, Brad was simply not capable of processing his sexual experiences. His feelings of personal helplessness and lack of professional assistance were urgently expressed by severing the arms of his toy soldiers, who functioned as symbols of needed protection and strength. In Brad's subtle protest, the soldiers' bodies—especially the arms—needed to look like his body felt, helpless and betrayed. Brad believes he should have been able to protect himself.

Inadequate Spiritual Response

His parents' conclusion that this was a satanic attack on the family was an unfortunate overstatement, one that delayed professional help that Brad needed as the victim. By appealing to a theodicy of *cosmic conflict*, cases of sexual exploitation and childhood betrayal "become remotely comprehensible . . . when attributed to a superhuman, supernatural, demonic source."[15] This spiritual response among some faith traditions is fueled by various dualisms: spiritual vs. material, temporal vs. eternal, and in–group vs. out–group. In sexual abuse, these dualisms function to dismiss complex embodied trauma that affects the entire relational ecosystem. Stunningly, among cases of SA, an estimated 88 percent are never reported to the authorities—a phenomenon far more common in insular faith communities than secular contexts.

Unfortunately, there are examples of church leaders learning of sexual abuse and not reporting it to the police—instead the abuse cases are handled as internal/spiritual issues.[16] This mentality is common among churches and some Christian institutions that hold to a separatist worldview and do not understand the need for specific policies.[17]

Basyle (Boz) Tchividjian, the executive director of Godly Response to Abuse in the Christian Environment (GRACE), is concerned about the culpability of evangelicals toward the abused. He wrote an open letter in 2014 to the church, signed by many supporters, that concluded:

> To all who have been abused, broken, deceived and ignored, we have failed you and our God. We repent for looking nothing like our Lord when we have silenced you, ignored you or moved away from you and then acted as if you were the problem. You are not the problem; you are the voice of our God calling his church to repentance and humility. Thank you for having the courage to speak truth. May . . . the day come when his church reflects the indescribable love and compassion of Jesus, even to the point of laying down our lives for his precious sheep.[18]

A Gateway to Pornography and Sexual Risk Taking

Brad's struggle with pornography illustrates how SA is really a "gateway experience." Neurologically, what is fired together is wired together. For example, two of every three adult rape victims were also sexually abused as children. Abuse destroys a victim's grasp of personal boundaries and the ability to "read" social encounters appropriately.

Abused teens are more likely to engage in sexual risk taking, putting them at greater risk for sexually transmitted diseases and HIV. Experiences of traumatic sexualization shape the developing brain and turn on powerful chemical appetites. Writing about the role of pornography in sexual exploitation, Christa Foster Crawford and Glenn Miles explain:

> 'Brain trails' are able to be initiated and 'paved' because of the plasticity of brain tissue. . . . Dr. Doidge notes that brain tissue involved with sexual preferences (i.e., what 'turns us on') is especially malleable. Thus outside stimuli—like pornographic images—that link previously unrelated things (e.g., physical torture and sexual arousal) can cause previously unrelated neurons within the brain to learn to 'fire' in tandem so that the next time around, physical torture actually does trigger sexual arousal in the brain. *This in–tandem firing of neurons creates 'links' or associations that result in powerful new brain pathways that remain even after the instigating outside stimuli are taken away.*[19]

Concerned family members and survivors themselves often fail to understand how the early sexualization and confusion of abuse can fuel later forms of sexual addiction.[20] These are explanations, not justifications. Unlike drugs, however, the effects of pornography are not metabolized out of the body. Ironically, Christians will talk about certain kinds of "acceptable" symptoms (e.g., pornography) when they are unable to sit in the pain of broken people, lack a holistic anthropology, or are just too horrified to face the far darker problems (e.g., parental incest, ritualistic abuse).[21]

Shelly confessed to one other youth leader that she felt some remorse about abusing Brad, but stated that she also had been abused by her own father and didn't know how to stop herself. This is how SA works: smoldering coals, unaddressed, keep the threat of fire alive until they can burst into flame again, given the right circumstances. This is the larger relational ecosystem of Brad's story, but no one took the time to piece it all together. Shelly herself was hyper–sexualized at a young age, but she knew she had to keep it hush-hush in her home and so never received any help or accountability. No formal background check was conducted on Shelly, since her family was well-known in the community. And perhaps no other secret is more deeply buried in families than abuse.

Theological Healing . . . What Are Survivors Finding?

Brad's abandonment of faith and God is very common among survivors and, in Brad's case, has a simple logic to it. Everybody involved—including his abuser—claimed to be "in" with God. Whenever SA occurs in a faith context, it also throws up a powerful stench of hypocrisy that can appear insurmountable for survivors. Now spiritual betrayal joins psychological, sexual, and social betrayals.

The sad truth is this: *In various ways, survivors will be "broken" for the rest of their lives.* Survivors' spiritual needs are least understood because research is biased against faith and the personal stories of survivors are so rarely heard anyway. This is also true in the church, where unanticipated experiences have created unwanted testimonies. There is profound pain to process before any "victory" is touted—by survivors, or their well-wishers. A chronic state of alert (i.e., *hypervigilance*) takes a toll on the victim's body with studies showing that sexually abused children are 10 to 15 percent more likely to suffer from cancer, heart disease, gastrointestinal problems, liver disease, and diabetes as adults.[22]

Mental illness is also brought on by SA. Jennifer E. Beste writes: "Common mental illnesses include dissociative identity disorder [DID], borderline personality disorder [BPD], major anxiety, and depressive episodes. These psychiatric illnesses often lead to chronic suicidality."[23] Such mental illness among survivors often results in an unfortunate sabotage of their relationships and even a socially cantankerous reputation. This is the nature of abuse-trauma, and exceptions only prove the rule.[24] So not surprisingly for Brad, he concludes that God is also complicit in his betrayal. The Christian leader or parent, who models God's presence, can also destroy this dynamic link for the survivor. Langberg makes an astute observation about the survivor's relationship to the *unseen* and the *seen*.

> *We look at the seen and learn about the unseen.* . . . This method of instruction is used throughout Scripture, including for our understanding of the character of God himself when God appears in the flesh (John 1:14). God explains himself to us through the temporal, the material, and the human. . . . What then are the lessons about the unseen when sexual abuse occurs? Think about hearing that God is a "refuge" or God is our "stronghold" (Ps. 46:1). . . . What does a child who is a victim of incest do with the idea of God as father (Gal. 4:6)? How does a traumatized and finite human mind reconcile the God of the Scriptures whom we worship and adore with the experience of sexual violence?[25]

In fact, I would argue that this fracture of faith is the saddest of outcomes for survivors, if they claimed any faith to begin with. *The need for theological healing is crucial and the most ignored aspect in the SA literature.* If God is retained for survivors, it's often a mystical "force" that remains, a detached and dethroned deity. How does a survivor submit their life to the Sovereign, Almighty God of heaven and earth, who did not step in to prevent their abuser from plundering their body? More than psychologically confused, survivors can be spiritually exasperated. If a survivor remains in the church, he or she might even view God as loving and powerful—but certainly not loving and powerful toward *them*. This is a profound disconnect that allows trauma story and loving deity to coexist. But combing one's personal story with a powerful deity can be beyond messy!

Anger at God for his betrayal of them is standard fallout for survivors from a faith context. Some biblical texts—like offering one's body "as a living sacrifice" (Rom. 12:1)—can become repulsive language. If not one sparrow falls without the Father's knowing (Matt. 10:29); if even the hairs on our head are numbered (Matt. 10:30); if the Father knows what we need before we even ask (Matt. 6:8)—yet not even one angel was sent (Ps. 91:11) to stop the violation—then the call for total surrender to God can feel like a vicious joke. However, this sense of divine betrayal is also due, in part, to populist Christian culture that is poised to accuse an "absentee deity" for allowing *any* personal suffering.

THE APPEAL OF SURROGATE ATTACHMENTS

Spiritually disillusioned, today's abuse victim is confronted with many diverse and even radical narratives, each claiming to be a better alternative to the "traditional" (always a negative word) God of the Bible.[26] For survivors, these narratives include: identity politics, recycled gender wars,[27] skewed proportionality arguments,[28] the New Atheism, angry memoirs,[29] secular therapy offices, rancorous blogging, and disgruntled support group leaders. However, what is the narrative the church has offered?—essentially a "sacred silence." The populist conviction is that religious systems are inherently flawed, especially those that smack of religion and patriarchy.[30] But this is little more than politics citing sociology.[31] In the absence of a transcendent foundation, only politics remains.[32]

Clearly, the need for a holistic address of *faith and trauma*—of the broken image bearer, not just the oppressed gender—has never been greater. What has happened to religious faith in universities, where classes on gender and diversity abound? Where is trauma addressed in our seminaries, while sin and salvation are constantly studied? The university lacks a robust faith and the seminary, a robust anthropology. From one end of the educational spectrum to the other, either God is protected and the victim ignored, or the victim takes center stage and God has to walk!

A SPIRITUAL ESTRANGEMENT

Abuse survivors are getting their cues from a spiritually conflicted society. Increasingly, it is some mystical form of spirituality. *Whenever survivors write off faith, their hope will be put in something else.* But toxic blogs and political platforms are not spiritually nourishing. For his gender, history, and teaching, God has been defriended, neutered, reprimanded, and reformed in order to serve the will of hostile masses who demand "gods" made in their image (cf. Rom. 1:18–32).

How are pastors and other Christian leaders trained to address the spiritual trauma of abuse? Many survivors who are steeped in perfectionism and hyper–vigilance may cling to some form of God, but the profound spiritual estrangement that now exists between their lived experience and God stifles any meaningful relationship. *The greatest area of needed recovery today is theological healing.*[33] What happens to faith, happens to community as well.

THE ABUSED IMAGE BEARER: SIFTING THROUGH THE DAMAGED REALMS OF PERSONHOOD

The Realms of Personhood

Having considered a spectrum of betrayals in SA, we saw how *observed truth* not only is powerfully displayed in layers of trauma, but must also be carefully read. Now we focus our attention on the *revealed truth* of Scripture. Various biblical texts not only highlight the Creator's design for sexuality, but also contain sober examples of how evil is expressed in the realities of SA. Looking at the theology of the image of God, we can now situate the suffering of SA within the distinct realms of personhood: the *physical, relational,* and *transcendent.* To explore this dynamic, these interrelated realms of personhood can be conceptualized in the following diagram.

These realms of personhood are individually definable, but they do not function in isolation. A person is a unity, comprised of physical, relational, and spiritual realities.

THE REALMS OF PERSONHOOD

Chart 3

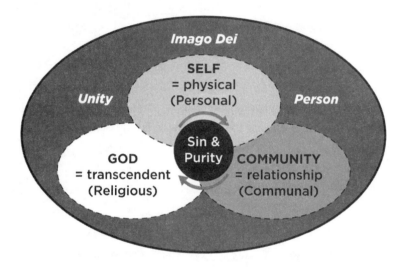

There is a wholeness required for the realms to properly function. The description of Samuel's maturity includes these same three: "Now the boy Samuel continued to grow both in stature and in favor with the LORD and also with man" (1 Sam. 2:26; cf. Luke 2:52). Clearly, these realms overlap (see diagram). These precincts of the person work together like the sections of a symphony—which means they are also mutually vulnerable to distortion. Therefore, sin and purity can affect all realms of life.

Positively, these realms are permeable, sharing vibrant *bonds* that enable dynamic interaction. But negatively, these are also protective *boundaries* that are vital to the health and integrity of these realms.[34] The physical or embodied realm can be plundered like a house; the social or communal realm can be silenced and shunned; and the spiritual or transcendent aspect can be poorly nurtured or utterly confused. Therefore, these boundaries are intended to maintain the holistic order of being human. As Christian Gostecnik explains: "Sexuality is and remains the arena where the most important relational configurations play out, and with all their power, point to a transcendence and sacredness of interpersonal and family system relationships."[35] Alistair McFadyen explains how sin can distort these relational configurations:

> Sin is hence, not so much free choice, as spiritual disorientation of the whole person at the most fundamental level of life–intentionality and desire. . . . In all our relations, we live out an active relation or misrelation to God; we enter the dynamic of worshipping God or other forces and realities. Sin is therefore living out an active misrelation to God. . . . Genuine transcendence, and so the grounds for genuine joy, are blocked.[36]

This may be a hard truth for some who think of sin and purity only in a "privatized" sense (e.g., "my sin/sexuality/salvation"). What Mc-Fadyen is describing is the dynamic interrelationship of the realms of personhood; the "numbing" and "spoiling" effect of sin that deforms on a spectrum. For survivors of SA, the distortion caused by abuse compromises relationships by contaminating individuals and severing communities, thus defiling the victim's proper orientation to God. Evil, and its shrapnel, can invade like a belligerent third party, and third parties are always wedge–shaped.[37]

Sexual abuse can damage every realm of the human person, tearing boundaries down and realms apart. But it is the *human–induced* trauma of SA that makes it uniquely devastating: person against person, psyche against self, leader against led, image bearer against image bearer. Such trauma "does not simply serve as record of the past but precisely registers the force of an experience that is not yet fully owned."[38] Because "trauma exists on a continuum," healing SA must address the marring that now runs throughout these realms.[39] Therefore, confronting an abuse survivor with their sin is analogous to chiding a soldier for losing a leg in an ambush. These responses are naïve, unethical, and further damaging.

We now turn our attention to creation theology (Gen. 1:26–28), targeting the related issues of gender, embodiment, and eschatology as they relate to a theology of sexual abuse and suffering. These are issues that have "gone off the rails" in various ways. Considering such issues helps restore some theological sanity in survivors' struggle to heal.

Gender and the Image of God

In Genesis 1:26–28, we find that sexuality operates in a holistic anthropology. God's speech is both creative and appointing, with the Creator's announcement, "Let us" (v. 26), culminating with his priestlike blessing, "Be fruitful" (v. 28). Genesis 1:26–28 can be structured as follows (my translation):

Announcement: "Let us make humankind (*'āḏām*) in our image/likeness" (v. 26a)

Purpose: "so that THEY may rule over (*rāḏā*): fish, birds, creepers" (v. 26b)

A So created (*waybārā*) God the human being (*hā'āḏām*, v. 27a)

Report: **B** in the image of God he created (*bārā*) him (v. 27b)

B' male (*zāḵār*) and female (*neqēḇâ*) he created (*bārā'*) THEM (v. 27c)

A' Then blessed (*waybārek*) God THEM and God said to THEM (v. 28a)

Blessing – Pt 1: "Be fruitful . . . subdue" (v. 28a)

Blessing – Pt 2: "rule over (*rāḏā*): fish, birds, creepers" (v. 28b)

This key passage shows that *'āḏām* refers to the broad category of human being—soon to be charged with an ethical mandate (v. 28)—not animal or some other creation. The human is special, implied in the shift from the impersonal, "Let there be" (v. 14), to the intimate,

"Let us make" (v. 26a). The Old Testament never uses *'āḏām* to distinguish man from woman.

In fact, the pronoun ("our" [2x], v. 26a) underscores a *theomorphic* perspective (i.e., having the form of God), as "our image" and "our likeness" fix their point of reference in God, not in "him" or "herself." God models our common humanity, not our gender specificity.[40]

As image bearers, their difference lies in sexual structure. Moving from the articular form ("*the* human being," v. 27a) to the collective singular ("him/it," v. 27b) narrows the "male" (*zāḵār*) and "female" (*neqēḇâ*, v. 27c) as two types of the same generic human being.[41] Significantly, the terms "male" (*zāḵār*) and "female" (*neqēḇâ*) refer to their capacity as sexual beings, thus making sexual potency the gravitational center of this passage (v. 27). Neither gender nor hierarchy is in view here. Not until we come to Gen. 2:23 and Adam's poetic celebration of woman do we find the terms "man" (*'îš*) and "woman" (*'îšâ*) used by God's agents. Only in 2:23 are *social* relationships evident—gender, as we tend to think of it.

God's vice–regents are custodians in an ethical trust: *endowment* for reproduction (blessing, part 1) and *commission* for governance (blessing, part 2). This is not a mission of power, but power for a divinely delegated and other–oriented mission. But aberrant expressions of sexuality do not build, they always deconstruct: a severance of reproduction from governance, a dismissal of society from self, a separation of ethics from "rights," or an elevation of personal choice over social obligation. But moored to the image of God, the biblical expression of sexuality operates within an ethical mission—*from* God and *for* others.

Sexuality may be personal, but it is never private. Sexuality is intended to live in a web of relationships that originate with the Creator who considerately observed, "It is not good that the man should be alone" (Gen. 2:18). Notice how God "allows himself to be affected, to be touched by each of his creatures. He adopts the community of creation as his own milieu."[42] Sexual intimacy is unique, a merging of blessed man and woman (Gen. 1:28), of a "male" and "female" who are structurally compatible with each other, possessing "the right degree of likeness and unlikeness to make the merger truly complementary" (see Gen. 2:23–24).[43] Significantly, when the Lord speaks to the human beings, he addresses them as persons, not genders (Gen. 1:26)—persons in a "community of need."[44] In fact, as Patrick D. Miller observes, "Once the declaration is made that it is as man and as woman that God has created human beings, *then the story speaks of them only in the plural.*"[45] Not surprisingly, healing a victim means restoring a community.

Our analysis shows that the difference in the sexed bodies of men and women actually grounds their intricate *interdependence.*[46] But contemporary identity politics are based on subject–object opposition. Ironically, this oppositional logic falls prey to its own protests of power and individualism, because it requires the *exclusion* of the other.[47] In other words, a theology of sexuality that facilitates healing and community for survivors is not found in *neutralizing* gender differences (i.e., "neither–one–nor–the–other"), nor in *synthesizing* gender (i.e., "not–the–one–and–the–other"), but as Miroslav Volf proposes, "affirming gender difference while at the same time positing one gender identity as always internal to the other" (i.e., "not–one–without–the–other"; cf. Gen. 2:18, 23–24).[48]

What helps heal victims of abuse are expressions of identity that consciously include difference and identity, rather than practicing exclusion through theories of opposition, dominance, political reductionisms, comparison of scars, or sanctioned stereotypes. These are *social atonements* that do not heal and even shun creation's design. But, as William P. Brown insightfully observes, "For every text in which creation is its context, the moral life of the community is a significant subtext."[49] Today, however, sexuality is overwhelmingly grounded in the politics of "self." Yet, how can a river be traced by ignoring its headstream? So, it is significant that Jesus specifically returns to creation—quoting Gen. 1:27 and 2:24—when he lays aside the accommodating legal practices of his day and, in their place, reasserts the theological foundation of sexual ethics in the design of creation (Matt. 19:4–6).

Moral ambiguity makes healing all the harder for survivors when their personal boundaries have already been disregarded. Ideologies of gender and liberation are not the biblical barometers of healing.

Embodiment and the Image of God

Notice that humankind was made *in* dialogue *for* dialogue—the man will not be heard speaking until there is woman, a corresponding being, to speak to (Gen. 2:23). In the flow of Gen. 1:26–28, the divine plural ("us") from the heavenly stage *initiates* a mission that the human plural ("them") *enacts* on the earthly stage. Bracketing this passage, God's speech is informative (v. 26) and investing (v. 28).[50] Rooted in the ancient historical and cultural setting, biblical theology sees God's angelic court in the plural "us" (cf. 1 Kings 22:19–22). What God announces to the angels (plural, v. 26a), he then "creates" by himself (singular, v. 27a). One similarly reads, "Whom shall I send, and who will go for us?" (Isa. 6:8).

The affirmation of the ontological Trinity emerges much later in revelatory history, and would be lost on the ancient audience of Genesis. Israel was passionate about their monotheistic God (Deut. 6:4) in a context of flamboyant polytheism (cf. Ex. 20:1–4; Josh. 24:14–16). In Gen. 1:26–28, humankind is cast as the terrestrial counterpart to God's heavenly entourage (cf. Psalm 148 with angels [vv. 1–7], followed by humankind [vv. 11–14]). "Glory and honor" are distinguishing characteristics shared by God with his vice-regents: "[You have] crowned him with glory and honor" (Ps. 8:5) means that royalty has been democratized to all of humankind, not one gender or an elite class of kings.

Only as a whole being is the Hebrew term "soul" (*nēpēš*) even appropriate in the theology of creation (Gen. 2:7). The Old Testament has no dualism of body/spirit (Ps. 103:1–2). In fact, *nēpēš* not only addresses the entire person (Pss. 42:6; 43:5), it can even refer to a corpse (Lev. 21:1; 22:4)! The Old Testament emphasizes the materialized aspects of human life: food, work, sleep, creativity, and sexuality are all enacted through embodied relationships.[51] They are God's good gifts.

It is on this dramatic stage that the image of God is lived out. So the image of God both *represents* for relationship and *resembles* God for missional task (cf. Gen. 2:15). One should realize that God always appears in human form when he and his aides come to earth (e.g., Genesis 18–19).[52] As God's under-kings, then, humankind was tasked with physical responsibilities from the very outset: "so that they may rule over" (vv. 26b; 28b; cf. 2:15 NIV); "You have made them rulers over the works of your hands" (Ps. 8:6 NIV).

These rich truths, however, highlight a sad contemporary problem—the *disembodied* victim. Here's the issue: if image is cognitive capacity, the *imago Dei* is *reason*; if worship is central, the image is *spiritual*; if the aesthetic is primary, then image is *creativity*; if image is Trinitarian, emotion–filled–relationship, then image is *relational*. The net result of all these different emphases is to locate the image of God in the *interior* of the person.[53] In other words, there is no warrant to address human embodiment or physical suffering in trauma. This is a grave misstep for a theology of sexuality, and disastrous if one hopes to understand physical violence that is sexual in nature.

The push to define "image–via–equality" (true as that may be), especially in recent Trinitarian theologies, has unfortunately resulted in minimizing corporality or ignoring the embodied realities of suffering entirely. A holistic theology of anthropology, that acknowledges differentiation and interdependency, brings a greater balance of internal and external realities of personhood. While gender identity is more fluid, it nonetheless "stands in marked contrast to the stable difference of sexed bodies."[54] People are gendered image bearers, not imaged genders (cf. Gen. 9:6). But protest politics fronts gender ideologies and disregards the moral compass of image. Yet, both representing via relationship and resembling via embodiment are vital to understanding key aspects of suffering and, in particular, the requisite healing needed in SA.

Those who would minister to the sexually traumatized must include the somatic referent in their definition of imaged personhood, corporality with equality, the treasure with its temple.[55] It is, after all, the body, not the soul, that is the temple of the Holy Spirit (1 Cor. 6:19–20). So whether through acts of compassion for others or violence against others, embodiment is communicated through performance, and in this way the *soma* is a social reality and requires community care and somatic modalities of healing.[56]

Eschatology and the Image Bearer

To be human is to be embodied in time and space, always relating to God and others.[57] The gift of sexuality has a "nested existence," both in this life and the next.[58] Thus addressing sexual abuse needs to consider what eschatology means, especially for embodied violence. To start with, a strong argument can be made that heaven for the believer will still be realized as a *gendered* reality, since gender is part of personhood. Mary will still look like Mary, and Thomas, like Thomas. While the role of sexuality may be different (cf. Matt. 22:30), Volf explains:

> Paul's claim that in Christ there is 'no longer male and female' entails no eschatological denial of gender dimorphism. What has been erased in Christ is not the sexed body, but some important culturally coded norms attached to sexed bodies. . . . The oneness in Christ is a community of people with sexed bodies and distinct gender identities, *not some abstract unity of pure spirits or de–gendered persons.*[59]

Considering those physically killed in Rev. 6:9—begging for vindication as they hide under the altar for protection—heaven may acknowledge differing kinds of earthly violence done to humans with colored robes or other special tokens (cf. Rev. 2:17). Regardless of the means, dehumanizing acts on earth may be acknowledged in heaven. The brutalized and suffering righteous have been crying out to God for justice since the blood of Abel soaked the ground (Gen. 4:10; cf. Joel 2:31; Isa. 34:4; Zech. 1:14–15).

Similarly, Green refers to life–after–death as "re–embodiment . . . provid[ing] the basis for relational and narrative continuity of the self."[60] Paul's description of being "with Christ" and "in Christ" elevates simple prepositions to profound relational realities (Phil. 1:23; 1 Thess. 4:16).[61] But this continuity of personhood may both frighten and liberate victims of SA. Whether "fleeing," dissociating, or anticipating, it can be hard to live in our bodies and also maintain hope. But in this life and the next, our relationship with God is realized through gendered expression, even if it is a heavenly version of our body. Thus, heaven as The Great Healing for victims is not a release from the material body into "nakedness." Just the opposite! Heaven is entrance into the "clothing" of a new soma—an unmolested body (2 Cor. 5:1–3, 8).[62]

It is significant to see how tightly Paul connects the Thessalonians' sexual ethics (1 Thess. 4:3–8) with Christian love (4:9–12) and their future hope (4:13–5:11). The fertility cults of their day were not their hope for a sure afterlife. Why should the Thessalonian Christians not participate in the sexual deviance of their culture? It is because Paul claims that Christians "are part of the eschatologically restored people of God," the fulfillment of Jer. 31:31–34, with God's law now written on their hearts.[63] Drawing on established texts of sexual conduct (Lev. 18:1–30; Ezek. 22:9b–11), Paul exhorts a largely Gentile audience to live a holy life (1 Thess. 4:7). This is our new reality and hope, because "as a corporate community, the bodies of Christians are no longer independent, autonomous entities" (cf. 1 Cor. 6:15).[64] Believers of any age know that their bodies are "a gift from God through which we can manifest our Christian discipleship and obedience to the Lordship of Christ *in the public, visible world.* Thereby accepting Christ as Lord becomes communicable and credible, which it would not be if it were merely an 'inner' or 'private' matter."[65]

The ground for sexual conduct "is their status as part of the eschatologically restored people of God predicted by the prophets."[66] So Paul warns that "no one should wrong or take advantage of a brother or sister" (1 Thess. 4:6a NIV). Evil forces in the world are always more powerful than isolated individuals, but fortunately, there is a new corporate solidarity in Christ.[67] The quality of Christian love, Frank Thielman states, signifies the eschatological work of God in our hearts.[68]

For the believer, the body is to be used to communicate what Christian service and futurity means.[69] Those who emphasize full healing from abuse in this life have likely not thought adequately about post-traumatic stress disorder, the theology of embodiment, or the continuity of personhood in the next life.

What kind of hope should be given to survivors? The matrix of personhood—of physical, social, and transcendent realities—not only makes healing complex, but should also guard against promising comprehensive healing across the realms of personhood. Marilyn McCord Adams offers a powerful reminder:

> The maker of all things has honored the human race by becoming a member of it, honored all who suffer horrendous evils by identifying with them through His passion and death. Still more amazing, God will be seen to have honored even the perpetrators of horrors by identifying with their condition, becoming ritually cursed through His death on a tree, taking His stand with the cursed to cancel the power of curse forever.[70]

SOME *BARRIERS* IN THE CHURCH THAT THWART HEALING FOR THE ABUSED

Of all places, our churches contain some significant barriers that are stifling healing from SA. These must be addressed if the local church is to be an active agent in healing abuse and turn around a tragic history of neglecting the abused in their midst.

The Barrier of "Sacred Silence"

The barrier of "sacred silence" must be exchanged for *timely honesty*. It is not about talking loudly or slowly, but honestly. Survivors have waited long enough for someone to speak out *for* them. Faith communities —regardless of their stripe—selectively discuss the ills they want to face. Ironically, this is accompanied by an avoidance of preaching and teaching of biblical passages that directly address rape, incest, and sexual betrayal! This barrier forces the frightened victim to "out" their story first because the leadership refuses to break the silence for them.

The Barrier of Minimization

The barrier of minimization must become *a hermeneutic of empathy*. Claiming that "all sin is the same" is a politically correct mantra that actually trivializes the complexity of evil in sexual abuse. Those who make such statements are unwilling to admit that *not all sin is equally devastating*. They minimize the consequences of SA.

For that matter, "not all evil is chosen. For, while evil can subtly seduce, it can also brutally enforce its will."[71] Such messages are particularly painful to hear when the non–abused tell the abused how they should feel and respond. Would civilians tell a returning soldier how to deal with their phantom limb?

The Barrier of Forgiveness

The barrier of mandated forgiveness must *prioritize the needs of the victim*. While it sounds spiritual, this call to forgive the abuser is a re–victimization for survivors that stems from not understanding the layers of trauma in sexual abuse. Additionally, this is the common mistake of equating forgiveness with reconciliation. It is time to let the needs of the abused set the agenda. A jewel thief can be forgiven, but should that person return to work for the store owner? For the abused, forgiveness is not an event to be logged, but a process to be nurtured.

Forgiveness only emerges as the "toxins" of trauma are slowly absorbed. The late Ray Anderson is correct: "In the end, reconciliation as well as forgiveness is a divine gift of grace that we receive bit by bit and grow into."[72]

The Barrier of "Victory" Theologies

The barrier of "victory" theologies that declare in Christ we overcome all and need not address the brokenness of our past must be exchanged for *a theology of brokenness*. Such theologies are not capable of addressing horrendous evil, such as the betrayals of incest or sex trafficking. In fact, victory theologies have little patience for healing as a *process*, blame far too much on the devil, and often search for some "silver bullet" to eliminate suffering.

Victory theologies commonly ignore or dismiss the candor of lament theology. Such theologies also lack adequate integration with the disciplines of psychology and medicine that also speak into the spectrum of abuse trauma. Behind "victory" theologies is often a mis-understanding of how SA lives on within the relational ecosystem. It's about care, not cure.

The Barrier of Isolated Suffering

The barrier of isolated suffering must be replaced with *collective grief*. The believer's new identity in Christ stems from their union with Christ that provides a new citizenship and a new corporate solidarity. The Christian community is morally preserving when it also learns to demonstrate a collective grief for its sexually broken brothers and sisters. Evil is always stronger than isolated individuals.[73]

To heal a survivor is to restore a community. Relationships in the believing community are to be characterized by a quality of love that signifies the eschatological work of God in their hearts—both the wounded and the grieving mark the new society of God.

CONCLUSIONS

A theology of sexual abuse is a sad tour through layers of betrayal, affecting the personal, relational, and spiritual realms of the survivor. In these very realms, a wonderful and God–designed sexuality can become distorted, further disturbing the unity of personhood, physical identity, and community shalom. Unfortunately, stories like Brad's are all around us, in families right next to us. When the breach in trust eats into multiple realms of a survivor's life, it makes people like Brad *incompetent trusters*,[74] people who do not know how to relate well to others. Distortions and fear cripple their relationships. When so many ligaments are severed, walking with a limp is to be expected. Brad may have to come back to his healing journey again and again, as he moves through the stages of life: dating, engagement, marriage, children, parenting, personal faith, and so on.

A Personal Word to Survivors

Let me talk directly to abuse survivors for a moment. Abuse is an issue people do not want to face till it hits their family or legally threatens their faith community, and even then some will not face it. Focus on your healing, not the politics of being a victim. Maybe you have realized this too: ten thousand car accidents and one thousand cancers are still a more welcomed topic than one abused child. Why? Diseases are contracted and one has a car accident, but abuse involves several "whos." Up to 20 percent of a congregation could have victims—and a staggering amount of them will remain silent, especially men.

Please do not affirm the silence. Find help. Talk to someone! Survivors like me can hear you. You do not have to be an exit-watcher the rest of your life.

Recommendations to the Church Family and Christian Organizations

A theology of sexual abuse reveals stunning "brokenness" where God intended wholeness within and between image bearers. The many kinds of suffering experienced by Jesus is a rich study that can help rehabilitate spiritually disillusioned victims. Whether friend, pastor, survivor, or spouse, we end with some closing recommendations.

Churches

Churches should allow the survivors to name and lament their abuse.[75] *Churches used to happy-worship must learn the value of naming in lament.* It's not about toning down joy, but amping up real-time expressions of pain—including survivors struggling to trust a seemingly distant God. Allow survivors to engage in redemptive naming, lamenting, and weeping. For example, in a special church service, survivors can speak of their stories in testimonies, written prayers, personal laments, or other significant expressions that allow survivors to describe their social and spiritual journey of healing. But one–sided worship that withholds the opportunity for these kinds of expressions forces the sexually broken to worship *in spite* of their pain rather than *in* their pain.

To disallow naming, lamenting, and weeping creates superficiality at all levels of community life. For one, it teaches that expressions of pain and penitence (by perpetrators and even victims) are unworthy of worship. But second, it does not call the larger faith community to shoulder *collective grief* on behalf of their sexually betrayed brothers and sisters.

Survivors

Survivors should tap into the strengths of the faith community. Learning to constructively engage with the faith community is a tall order for survivors, especially if they've bought into toxic narratives or were shunned by Christian leaders. Reengaging is a process. So, a personal message to survivors: learn to filter out the enraged voices that are hostile to the faith. Realize that you have your own issues to face as a survivor, and the church leaders are not perfect, either.

Pain and victimization may be the "lenses" you see through, but find some safe friends who have your back. Consider joining a support group, where you can air your feelings and receive empathetic advice. Incorporate meaningful rituals into your faith journey (e.g., journaling, writing prayers, seeing the Lord's Table as an expression of Jesus' "brokenness" alongside yours). Remember, what is not *transformed* can easily be *transferred* . . . to the next generation! Others may not have done the hard work of transforming their brokenness into gentleness, but you can break the cycle!

Biblical Counselors

Biblical counselors should prioritize comforting over confronting. Let the needs of the survivor set the agenda, not your timetable or desire to use the Bible with apologetic fervor. Survivors really need someone to believe them, so spend quality time *listening* to their story. Dial back the "for us versus against us" script. Some psychological tools are merely explaining complex relational behaviors Scripture doesn't address, not justifying those behaviors. Become more aware of how *triggers* work in the frightened lives of survivors. When the inexpressibility of trauma joins with the inexpressibility of God's nature, the crisis for a survivor of faith is acute and requires patience, not proof texts.[75] I knew a girl whose father would read Bible passages to her before molesting her—that's called a trigger! It's about healing, not "victory"; care, not cure.

Schools and Mission Organizations

Christian schools and mission agencies can elevate some wounded leaders within their organization. Wounded leaders can take empathy and insight to deeper levels. Such men and women are always horrified, but never surprised. Whether they share the same scars isn't the point; they can sympathize with the sexually abused because they've faced their own brokenness and then doubled down on vulnerability. Indeed, sometimes it takes wounds to heal wounds, but withholding wounded leaders (male or female) from leadership positions can leave the wounded survivors with no "safe" person to connect with their pain.

Therefore, recognize the skill sets and empathy of such recovered victims of SA in your institution and elevate them into key roles in teaching or administration. These leaders have learned to live out a cruciform brokenness that other victims—students and staff—need to see. Working with the sexually traumatized requires a leadership style of vulnerable partnership, certainly not Teflon power maneuvers. Prevention plans and written policies are essential, but when the wounded cry out for help, show them a wounded leader, ready to comfort.

So while cancer survivors have ribbons and soldiers have medals, neither ribbons nor rainbows, flags nor flowers will commemorate the thousands of abuse survivors in our families and churches. Survivors have no parade in their honor or recognized rituals of closure. We can help eliminate this kind of suffering. A life committed to healing is a platform worth standing on for the rest of your life.

AMID PAIN AND SUFFERING

1. What is it about Brad's story that angers you the most? Puzzles you? What would you tell Brad, if you could?

2. After reading this chapter, what do you believe are some dangerous myths about sexual abuse that are still out there?

3. If you have a friend who is a survivor (or are one yourself), what did their/your family do right in their attempt to help? What did they do wrong?

4. The chapter talked about how various "narratives" can initially seem helpful for hurting survivors, but may actually turn out to be "toxic" to their healing. How have you seen this play out? Why do you think the faith community struggles so much to be a safe place for victims?

5. What do you think are some constructive steps that can be used to help survivors struggling to believe in a loving, caring, and powerful God?

CHAPTER 11

Inner Darkness

The Unique Suffering of Mental Illness

By Gerald W. Peterman

The names can be fearsome and foreboding. *Attention deficit disorder. Anxiety disorder*, which can lead to anxiety attacks or panic attacks. *Bipolar disorder. Depression. Schizophrenia.* These are some of the leading kinds of mental illness.

Those suffering may need one or more kinds of treatments to manage or eliminate the specific illness, including medication and psychotherapy (counseling). For some severe forms, even a brief application of electric current may be recommended.[1] Formally known as electroconvulsive therapy, the electric current is briefly applied through the scalp to the brain while the patient is asleep under general anesthesia.

Mental illness presents a unique kind of suffering, a pain that affects not only the sufferer but those close to him or her. The sufferer, family, and friends enter a dark confusion, a confusion that asks many questions. *Where do we turn? How did this happen? Who's to blame? Is there hope?*

Common to sufferers and those close to them are feelings of shame, heavy and devastating. Society at large still attaches a stigma to mental illness, so sufferers and those who love them feel shame.[2] Similarly, there are often feelings of loneliness and rejection. One mother notes that the church, even pastors, contributes to the isolation. She reports that her "27 year old son, [who is] schizoaffective, is never called on by the pastor where he is a member because the pastor is not 'comfortable.' If Andy had cancer or any physical illness, I'm sure he'd be there. Also, my 'regular' friends just don't understand the devastation of mental illness."[3] Often there is despair, hopelessness, and depression. There is sometimes crippling fear and vulnerability.[4]

One of the unique features of suffering with mental illness is that some in church tell the sufferer that it is a sin problem. This makes mental illness doubly painful. Steve and Robyn Bloem indicate many in the Christian community "attribute mental illness to some spiritual or emotional defect in the ill person." They note how people often separate mental illnesses from other physical maladies:

> More understanding of medical science as it relates to the brain has filtered into our churches. But there remains a prevalent attitude among many leaders to "cordon off" mental illness. It is separated from other physical illnesses. Many of those who treat those with mental illness in the Christian community use their counseling experience and superficial biblical prooftexting to justify a position. Usually they attribute mental illness to some spiritual or emotional defect in the ill person. Some Christian counselors, psychiatrists, and psychologists confuse the issue because they apply a faulty hermeneutic to Scripture.[5]

DEFINING MENTAL ILLNESS

What is mental illness? We will use the following as a working definition:

> A mental disorder or mental illness is a psychological or behavioral pattern that occurs in an individual and is thought to cause distress

or disability that is not expected as part of normal development or culture. Mental disorders are generally defined by a combination of how a person feels, acts, thinks or perceives.[6]

Included under this definition would be well-known disorders such as depression, bipolar disorder, post-traumatic stress disorder, paranoid delusions, and schizophrenia. But by this definition eating disorders such as anorexia and bulimia, attention deficit hyperactivity disorder (or ADHD), and substance abuse/dependence (addiction) would be included in mental illness. Indeed, Matthew S. Stanford includes these in his book *Grace for the Afflicted: A Clinical and Biblical Perspective on Mental Illness.*[7]

There is debate as to whether mental illness is primarily about biology or behavior; so it is important to note that, on the one hand, this definition stresses behavior and emotion. The behavior is destructive to self, to others, or to relationships, and the emotions are painful. On the other hand, the definition does not specify anything about brain states or brain function. Probably most or even all mental illnesses or disorders occur with a biological influence.

Yet the biology and the behavior are not simply equivalent. We can give an illustration: suppose a man has a peanut allergy, but is never exposed to peanuts. Is he ill? If illness is pure biology (genetic predisposition), without reference to particular manifestations, then he is ill even without symptoms. If illness is manifestation of symptoms (or, in mental illness, if it is behavior), then illness for the man with a peanut allergy ranges from minor irritation to perhaps anaphylaxis and death.[8]

As with allergies, so also with mental illness: we expect that there can be severe and less severe cases. Since this is true, we should see mental health/illness on a spectrum without sharp dividing lines. We all have degrees of health and we all have degrees of illness. This is exactly the perspective we take when we are talking about the health of our body as opposed to the health of our mind. We have no problem assigning a relative health assessment to the body. Just as our body's muscles and functions deteriorate over time until death inevitably claims us, likewise with the mind we should not expect it to be perfectly healthy until Christ returns to establish a new heaven and new earth.

In his book *The Theology of Illness*, Jean–Claude Larchet has a similar view. He asserts,

> In this world perfect health never exists in absolute form; health is always a matter of partial and temporary equilibrium. We can even say that health in this present age is simply a matter of lesser illness. The very notion of ideal health is, in fact, beyond our comprehension, since it reflects no experience known to us in this life. In our present condition, 'health' is always in some sense 'illness' that has simply not appeared as such and/or is not significant enough to be identified as such.[9]

The exceptions to this would be extreme cases of brain trauma or some cases of schizophrenia that render people basically nonfunctional. But extreme cases are not our main subject. Our main subject is where most people live.

Our Road to a Biblical Theology of Mental Illness

There are a variety of approaches taken to mental illness; naturally we have our own approach. First, we will look at some false steps one might take when trying to establish a biblical theology of mental illness. As false steps, they often lead to more pain rather than to the healing we desire. Second, we will look at a few brief passages from both Testaments that speak of mental illness. In this section we will discover that Scripture does not treat this subject directly or extensively. So to help us we must cast the net wider. Third, we will look at Scripture's assumptions about other illnesses. We find plenty of material here. If there is a pattern, we would then be able to apply it to all illnesses. Fourth, we will attempt to integrate Scripture's teaching on mental illness and other illnesses with a biblical anthropology. That is, how does Scripture talk about the way we are put together, and how does that influence the way we think about mental illness? For instance, if one holds to sharp distinctions between body and soul (or body and spirit) one will tend to see mental illness as a spiritual problem and not a health problem.

Finally, we will attempt to integrate Scripture's teaching on mental illness and a biblical anthropology with our current multifactorial approach to other illnesses.

We will not specifically answer the question, "Why do mental illnesses exist?" Nevertheless, if the comments on anthropology are combined with a multifactorial approach to any illness, a purpose is implied. Although we could dispute some minor details, Larchet is close to the mark:

> The illness of the body reminds us of the illness of our entire fallen nature. The loss of health appears as the symbol and perceptible sign of the loss of paradisiacal life. . . . They teach a person the extent of their poverty, even their ontological nakedness (Gen 3:7), and remind him that he is dust (3:19).[10]

THREE FALSE STEPS IN THINKING ABOUT A MENTAL ILLNESS

A Parable

Before we move to mention specific false steps, consider the following parable about the hawk and the armadillo. One day a hawk was suffering from human–caused environmental changes that drove away much of his prey but brought diseases on the remaining mice, rabbits, and other small creatures. He is frustrated, weak, and discouraged.

He is approached by an armadillo who says, "Wow! You look terrible! What's going on? Can I help?" At this invitation, the hawk tells the story of what has been happening.

The armadillo offers to give a meal of insects in exchange for a feather. "I can dig lots of bugs out of the ground for you! And a few feathers would make a great addition to a bed that I'm making in my burrow," he says.

At first, the hawk takes a few meals just to get his strength back. After all, he can't hunt anymore because he's too weak from lack of food for the last few weeks. Then the meals–for–feathers plan is easy. It's a habit. Time passes.

Then one day the hawk says, "Well, it's time I get flying and look for mice." But he has no more feathers. He can't fly.

Who is responsible for the hawk's current immobility?[11] An overly simplistic approach says all the fault lies with the humans, or all lies with the hawk, or all lies with the armadillo. In fact, there are a variety of causes that have led to the hawk's current weakness.

False Step One: Drawing Sharp Distinctions between Weakness and Sin

We have a tendency to make sharp distinctions between weakness and sin. It's easy and we like easy. It avoids ambiguity. We don't like ambiguity, so we look for one simple cause. Black and white categories are easy to work with. Such easy and sharp categories make us feel in control (so we aren't afraid) and spiritual (so we aren't ashamed). Of course, the people on whom we impose these categories are shamed. But that doesn't bother us so much because we think they ought to be ashamed.

So, for example, some people might conclude that on the one hand colitis is a weakness, diabetes is a weakness, arthritis is a weakness, multiple sclerosis is a weakness, fatigue caused by mononucleosis is a weakness. On the other hand some people might conclude that seasonal affective disorder is a sin, depression is a sin, bipolar disorder is a sin, delusions are a sin, taking Wellbutrin or Prosac or Zoloft is a sin.

When we make these sharp distinctions, we are indulging a pagan worldview because it's convenient for some of our Christian subcultures. As chapter 2 has pointed out, the relational ecosystem of our world is not so simple. Genetic factors, family of origin factors, choices coming from weakness, choices arising from sin, trauma, and nonhuman environmental factors all work together in a web.

It is not that a complex approach—that is, an approach filled with gray areas, ambiguities, and intricate relationships—is better simply because it's complex. But nevertheless, would we come to Psalm 139:14—"I am fearfully and wonderfully made"—and use this passage to illustrate how intricately God has made us, both in mind and in body? If so, let us not use a convenient double standard.

False Step Two: Adopting a Hard Dualism

Hard dualism draws a sharp distinction between a human being's two parts or two aspects (thus "dualism"): body and soul (or spirit). This sharp distinction reminds one of the Marvel comic book character Iron Man. The character is industrialist/inventor Tony Stark, who creates a robot–like suit with a hard, impenetrable shell he can command. This suit, "the outer man," has no influence on the decisions of the inner man. Stark is its master and is known as Iron Man whenever he clads himself in the metallic suit.

Some people view human existence like this. We have an inner person (called "soul" or "spirit") that tells our outer person (the body) what to do. All the commands go one way, from soul to body, never from body to soul. The body might become sick from the environment—it picks up a virus—but the soul will become sick only through bad choices.

We call this view "hard" dualism because it draws such sharp distinctions between our two parts or aspects. Hard dualism is very common. Here are two examples.

First, Matthew S. Stanford, in *Grace for the Afflicted*, spends a few pages developing "a better understanding of how we were created, what effects the Fall has had on our physical bodies and minds, and who we are in Christ."[12] He says we are "the union of a physical body with an immaterial mind and spirit."[12] That is, *we have three parts: a body, a mind, and a spirit*. On the one hand, correctly, he asserts that "body and mind are intimately connected, each affecting the other."[13]

But then Stanford adds that the mind and the spirit are the two parts at work. He writes, "Our body, while we see it as our true identity, is little more than a container for our true essence, which is spirit (2 Cor. 5:1). It is in our spirit that we have opportunity to be in union with the very God of the universe (Proverbs 20:27; Romans 8:16)."[14]

Second, in their book, *Will Medicine Stop the Pain?*, Christian authors Fitzpatrick and Hendrickson assert a strong distinction exists between the inner and outer person (although they don't use these terms). The inner person makes choices. These choices are mediated to the body through the brain. "This inner person is the real you that God sees and interacts with (1 Sam. 16:7; Heb. 4:13). Your inner person is the source of the activity that can be measured in the brain, which is part of your outer person, your physical body."[15]

Why should we care about hard dualism? Strong dualistic thinking allows one Christian to rebuke another for depression, anxiety disorders, or bipolar disorder. The dualist will conclude that these problems are not bodily problems but rather soul problems or spiritual problems that must be addressed. We will return to dualism and its implications below.

False Step Three: Poor Definitions and Disjunctive Thinking

In *Broken Minds: Hope for Healing When You Feel Like You're "Losing It,"* Steve and Robyn Bloem speak a lot about "biological depression."[16] This label can be helpful to remind us that depression can have a physiological, or biological, element. But the label is unhelpful when it is used to draw sharp dividing lines between types of depression. Some people talk of biological depression as a disease. Then they can describe it as something that comes on them, like a cold or a virus. As we said above, certainly depression can have a physiological, a biological element. Far too many Christians are not willing to admit this plain truth. But if that is all we mean when we talk about "biological depression," then in that sense there is also biological joy, biological anger, and biological love. That is, all emotions have biological correlates. If they have a biological correlate, does that mean we are not responsible for our joy, anger, or love?

What some writers do is this: if the depression is "biological," they then force a strong disjunction between biology and choice, concluding that there is absolutely no responsibility to be assigned to those who are depressed. We could follow this false step, this disjunctive thinking, into other areas and conclude that if depression is simply a product of one's situation or environment—brought on by stressors in life—then the cause is neither biology nor one's choice. Likewise if the depression is brought on by poor thinking (choice), then there is no causative power that can be ascribed to biology and none that can be ascribed to situation.

THE SCRIPTURES ON MENTAL ILLNESS

Of course, Scripture should be a guide, yet the Bible does not address the topic of mental illness directly, and what it does say about mental confusion it does not delineate. The most important passages appear in Deuteronomy 28 and in a few New Testament passages.

The Old Testament

In a list of curses that will come because of disobedience to the covenant, Deut. 28:27–28 says, "The LORD will strike you with the boils of Egypt, and with tumors and scabs and itch, of which you cannot be healed. The LORD will strike you with madness and blindness and confusion of mind." Verses 32–34 continue, "Your sons and your daughters shall be given to another people, while your eyes look on and fail with longing for them all day long, but you shall be helpless. A nation that you have not known shall eat up the fruit of your ground and of all your labors, and you shall be only oppressed and crushed continually, so that you are driven mad by the sights that your eyes see."

In this first encounter with the concept of mental illness in the Old Testament we can derive two observations: First, both physical illness (boils, tumors, and scabs), and mental illness (madness and confusion of mind) can come as judgment from God. Second, as we know in our own age, war trauma can be a cause of, or a significant contributing factor in, mental illness.[17] In Deuteronomy, the mental and emotional trauma brought on by loss of beloved family, loss of fruitful labor, and loss of freedom can lead to mental illness (see also Jer. 25:16).

The New Testament

Two chapters of Matthew report Jesus' healing of those suffering from "epilepsy" (*epileptic[s]*, 4:24 and 17:15). The ancient world, however, had a specialized term for epilepsy (*epilēpsis*) and the word is not used in either passage. Matthew's term, used only by him in the New Testament, is better translated "subject to seizures" or "subject to fits," referring broadly to any sort of insane or irrational behavior.[18] In Matt. 4:24 the evangelist distinguishes between those "oppressed by demons, epileptics, and paralytics." In Mark 9:17 and 25, however, the parallel passage to Matt. 17:15, Jesus heals the boy by casting out a mute and deaf spirit.

In John 10, after Jesus describes his role as the Good Shepherd, there is a division among the listeners. Apparently, they find some of his claims and self-description incomprehensible. Thus in John 10:20, "Many of them said, 'He has a demon, and is insane; why listen to him?'" That is, some in the crowd find his words so odd that they must be ascribed to irrational thought or demonic activity.

Similar is Acts 26:24. Paul makes his defense before Festus, who, after hearing the apostle's words, says with a loud voice, "Paul, you are out of your mind; your great learning is driving you out of your mind" (see also Acts 12:15; 1 Cor. 14:23). Paul's actions and teaching, at least in the opinion of Festus, seem so odd that he must be losing his mind.

In 2 Cor. 11:23, Paul describes his suffering as an apostle, writing, "Are they servants of Christ? I am a better one—I am talking like a madman [*paraphroneō*]—with far greater labors, far more imprisonments, with countless beatings, and often near death." And in 2 Peter 2:16, Peter describes how the prophet Balaam "was rebuked for his own transgression: a speechless donkey spoke with human voice and restrained the prophet's madness."

Clearly neither Testament has a succinct summary of mental illness. For salvation by faith we have Eph. 2:8–9. That is simple, comprehensive, and clear. But we find no Eph. 2:8–9 for mental illness—or for that matter any illness. The Deuteronomy 28 passage does offer a precedent for mental illness provoked by trauma—physical, social, emotional (vv. 32–34). And John 10:20 tells us some people in the ancient world assumed mental illness can be provoked by demonic or satanic activity. Others assumed that mental illness could be provoked by using the mind improperly (Acts 26:24)—studying too much! It would be fallacious, however, to conclude that these are the only three "causes." Thus we need to find out more about illness.

SCRIPTURE'S ASSUMPTIONS ABOUT OTHER ILLNESSES

Because Scripture gives us no detailed discussion of mental illness, neither the causes nor the possible cures, where do we go in order that we might think biblically about the topic? We should look at how Scripture deals with other illnesses, particularly the causes and possible cures. This will give us a pattern of biblical thinking about all illness that we can then bring back to apply specifically to mental illness.

The Bible suggests several different components can come into play regarding illness. What follows is only a sketch of these.

There Can Be Divine Components

When the church was in its infancy, King Herod delivered an oration to the people who came to him from Tyre and Sidon. They praised his words as speech from a god and not a man. "Immediately an angel of the Lord struck him down, because he did not give God the glory, and he was eaten by worms and breathed his last" (Acts 12:23). Here we find that an illness with a mediate natural cause (worms) can have an ultimate divine cause (the Lord).

Similarly, in 1 Corinthians 11 Paul warned the church against taking Communion in an unworthy manner (v. 27). To eat the bread and drink the cup without discernment invites God's judgment. Such unworthy partaking is why many of the Corinthians were weak and ill and some had died (v. 30).

As a counterpart to this, it would be helpful to consider John 9:2–3. Here, upon encountering a man born blind, the disciples ask Jesus, "Rabbi, who sinned, this man or his parents, that he was born blind?" Jesus answered, "It was not that this man sinned, or his parents, but that the works of God might be displayed in him." From this interaction we can see that not all illness or disability is a result of human sin or divine judgment.

There Can Be Satanic/Demonic Components

The example of Job is well known. After his audience with God, "Satan went out from the presence of the LORD and struck Job with loathsome sores from the sole of his foot to the crown of his head" (Job 2:7). Although the Lord allows this suffering to occur, it is Satan who inflicts it directly.

Similar is Luke 13:16. On the Sabbath Jesus encountered a woman with a disability that for eighteen years made her bent over and unable to stand up straight. Jesus' healing of her drew the indignation of some who asserted that healing should not be performed on the Sabbath. Jesus, however, asserted that the Sabbath was a day for doing good and asked, "And ought not this woman, a daughter of Abraham whom Satan bound for eighteen years, be loosed from this bond on the Sabbath day?" (see also 2 Cor. 12:7).

There Can Be Personal Choice or Sin Components

Of course we know from personal experience that choices can influence health. We know that heavy drinking can cause liver damage; we know that smoking can cause lung and esophageal cancer. Scripture also gives hints of this recognition. So the psalmist writes, "There is no soundness in my flesh because of your indignation; there is no health in my bones because of my sin" (38:3).

Similarly, Paul advised Timothy, saying (1 Tim. 5:23), "No longer drink only water, but use a little wine for the sake of your stomach and your frequent ailments" (see also 1 Tim. 4:8). The implication is that the personal choice to drink a little wine will lead to better health and, conversely, abstinence to worse health.

There Can Be Impersonal or Environmental Components

Beyond those personal choices, some illnesses may arise from Satan's work or from divine retribution. But impersonal or environmental factors can be involved, such as bacterial or viral infections, parasites, allergies, or a host of other causes; the verses do not specify.

For example, in 2 Kings 13:14 we find simply that Elisha fell sick "with the illness of which he was to die." Similarly in Acts 9:36–37 we find "a disciple named Tabitha, which, translated, means Dorcas. She was full of good works and acts of charity. In those days she became ill and died." In both cases we find a righteous person; in neither case does the writer say that illness and death resulted from sins, from Satan's work, or from divine retribution.

Scripture can ascribe illness to a variety of causes. Since all these causes are possible, it is unwise, before further investigation is done, to automatically exclude one particular cause. It is likewise unwise, before further investigation is done, to always use one of these causes to wholly explain a certain kind of illness, as is done when people assert that mental illness is really a spiritual problem.

THE BIBLE AND ANTHROPOLOGY

At this point some may say that the above discussion of *other* illnesses in Scripture is true and helpful but has nothing to do with *mental* illness because *other* illnesses are about the body; they are physical. They may conclude that so-called *mental* illness is actually a *spiritual* issue; it's about the *soul*. Thus, when people have a spiritual problem, they can exhibit symptoms of mental illness such as depression, anxiety, and compulsions.

This approach is dependent on the dualistic thinking we mentioned above under "False Steps."

Does the Bible itself draw a sharp distinction between our two aspects? We take it that it does not. To answer this question well, however, would require a whole book, and indeed many whole volumes treat the question.[19] We will only be able to give a sketch here.

Monism and Dualism

Before we come to the biblical evidence, we look at typical answers to the question, "How are we made?" Two basic approaches are *monism* and *dualism*.

Monism (also called holism) holds that humans are a unity. The physical and the mental, the literal heart and the metaphorical heart (that is, the mind and will), operate as a combined whole. The different aspects of a person—the seen and the unseen aspects—operate as one in a dynamic give-and-take relationship. But these two aspects are not two independent substances, as if we have a physical body (made of one kind of substance) and an immaterial soul (made from a different kind of substance).

Dualism holds that we are indeed made up of two different substances: the physical body and the nonphysical soul or spirit. At this point we do not need to debate whether humans have a human soul in addition to and distinct from a human spirit. For the sake of our discussion, we simply differentiate between the material substance (body) and the immaterial substance or substances (soul/spirit).

Within the dualist perspective, one can hold to a hard dualism (illustrated above with the Iron Man character) and a soft dualism. The soft dualist asserts that, although the body and the soul are different substances, God has so bound them together that, first, their separation is unnatural, and second, they operate in the dynamic unity like monism, with each entity affecting the other.

Clues from Genesis

Genesis 1:26–27 is quite familiar. We find God creating man and woman in his image. The nature of this image is debated. We only note here that there is no explicit assertion that the image is some sort of nonphysical substance (such as a soul or spirit) with special capabilities. If the image of God has to do with relationship, with emotion, with relating to God, with self-reflection, with being moral and social, then the structure of our brain and the shape of our body make provision for all of those aspects of our humanity.

Further, Gen. 2:7 asserts that "the LORD God formed the man of dust from the ground and breathed into his nostrils the breath of life, and the man became a living creature." We note that it says God formed man from the dust, not that the Lord formed a body from the dust.[20] Although we should be careful with arguments from silence, they can be helpful for us to understand the significance of what is here—and what is not. Consider what is not here: We do not find a preexistent, immaterial person who is then cloaked in a body. We do not find God fusing two parts; rather, a man is fashioned and God makes him into a living creature by breathing life into him, that is, by making living and operative the image of himself that he had formed. This breath is not unique to covenant people but belongs to all the living (cf. Josh. 11:11, 14; Isa. 2:22). It belongs to animals as well; later in Genesis we see that during the flood, "Everything on the dry land in whose nostrils was the breath of life died" (Gen. 7:22).[21]

The Old Testament supports a monistic view of the person. We find a man formed of dust and enlivened. The creation account does not say a soul was added to another component. That is, using OT terms, it is not that Adam was given a soul. Rather, Adam was created and when God breathed into him Adam himself became a living *soul* (Hebrew, *nephesh*; LXX, *psychē*).[22]

Hints from the New Testament

When one moves from the Old to the New Testament there are small hints that the progress of revelation moves from monism to a soft dualism. Thus Jesus warns followers not to fear "those who kill the body but cannot kill the soul [*psychē*]. Rather fear him who can destroy both soul and body in hell" (Matt. 10:28). It might be, as John Nolland writes, "There is no better word with which to render [*psychē*] here than 'soul,' but it means more the essential person than an ontologically separable component of the person."[23] But certainly the passage could be taken dualistically. Thus Davies and Allison assert that *psychē* "is here the disembodied 'soul' which can survive bodily death and later be reunited with a resurrected body."[24]

In 2 Corinthians 5 Paul mentions the new redeemed body, writing, "We know that if the tent that is our earthly home is destroyed, we have a building from God, a house not made with hands, eternal in the heavens. For in this tent we groan, longing to put on our heavenly dwelling, if indeed by putting it on we may not be found naked" (vv. 1–3). A bodiless state is an unnatural state and is thus described as nakedness.

Later in the letter, referring to himself, Paul mentions "a man in Christ who fourteen years ago was caught up to the third heaven— whether in the body or out of the body I do not know, God knows. And I know that this man was caught up into paradise—whether in the body or out of the body I do not know, God knows—and he heard things that cannot be told, which man may not utter" (12:2–4). Although the apostle does not say so explicitly, the implication is that, from Paul's perspective, such travel and perception can happen without a body. Such a perspective is consistent only with some form of dualism.

We should note regarding these two passages from Paul, however, that the things that are potentially naked without a body are not called *souls* but *we*. When Paul traveled to the third heaven, he tells us that the *man* traveled, not that a soul traveled. To put it another way, the New Testament entertains the possibility of a disembodied self, but it does not call the self a soul (*psychē*).

Body, Soul, and Brain

While the biblical evidence does not clearly support a hard dualist approach, some may appeal to a common assumption about the relationship between mind and brain. The common view is developed using the analogy of a computer: we believe that our mind is the software while our brain is the hardware. We might think that our mind changes but our brain remains fixed.

But this view is faulty. Our brain changes throughout our life. "Unlike our modern computers, *the brain's software is its hardware.* We know from animal studies that early experience, and especially traumatic experience, alters the brain and body in measurable ways. Thus infant monkeys, who are repeatedly and traumatically separated from their mothers, suffer more or less permanent alterations in both blood chemistry and brain function."[25] Likewise in humans our brains are constantly being formed by our choices and habits.

One example of this formation comes from a study of brain scans of London taxi drivers. Scientists from University College of London performed the scans and found that the drivers had a larger hippocampus compared with other people. Significantly, the hippocampus is a region of the brain associated with spatial recognition and navigation. In addition, the researchers discovered that the more years the taxi driver was on the job, the larger the hippocampus.[26] The implication is that human choices (in this case driving) cause brain changes (in this case a larger hippocampus), and that the brain changes make certain choices easier (in this case driving). We see here a dynamic interplay between choices (soul) and our brain (body). Monism or soft dualism allows for this dynamic interplay; hard dualism does not.

Conclusion

People are a unity. Monism is the basic position. This is modified slightly in the New Testament, but we would not expect a wholesale abandonment of Old Testament anthropology. William Hasker concludes, "[B]oth dualism as it has traditionally been understood, and materialism in all its current versions, are inadequate as accounts of the human person."[27] Rather, there is a dynamic interplay between the two aspects of our person. Further, it is important to note that, even if we say humans have an immaterial soul, and that soul has a unique immaterial substance, and can exist apart from the body, we have not thereby proven that all mental illness is spiritual. It does not prove that the body cannot influence the mind.

MENTAL ILLNESS:
A MULTIFACTORIAL APPROACH

Most of us operate with a certain kind of medical model, at least when it comes to bodily illness. So, for example, we realize that heart problems could arise from a variety of factors. Until adequate testing is done, several potential factors are on the table.

First, *there might be genetic or gender components*. Some people may have genetically high cholesterol. Even with a very heart–friendly diet and plenty of exercise, total cholesterol numbers might still be 250–400. Also, it's well known that men are more susceptible to heart disease than women.

Second, *there might be personal choice components*. A poor diet can contribute to heart disease, as can smoking and lack of exercise. In addition, bulimia can lead to a number of cardiovascular problems, including imbalances in the electrolyte levels in the body.[28]

Third, *there can be environmental components*. Where we live can affect our access to good medical care and a proper diet, it can affect our heart health, and our income level can affect our ability to afford both medical care and a proper diet. Dr. Ted Schletter notes that even "the mineral content of drinking water can affect the heart by altering heart rate or rhythm, contractility and excitability of heart muscle."[29]

From this one example, we see that we do and should operate with a multifactorial approach when it comes to illness. In some cases of illness there might be one clear cause. But the best initial assumption should be that there are probably a variety of factors. Likewise with mental illness there is reason to assume a multiplicity of factors.

In addition, as we have seen, Scripture assumes that there could be many factors involved with other illnesses. Therefore, before sufficient investigation is done, it is unwise for us to assume that mental illness only has one cause. Larchet concurs. He speaks of a human being as having three dimensions: physical, psychic, and spiritual. He asserts,

> It is rare that all three dimensions are taken into consideration by those who have attempted to explain these problems, and, in examining the history of psychiatry (as usually understood), even those doing so have had great difficulty in integrating all three and usually end up splitting them apart while favoring one or the other.[30]

The brain's operation is more complex and unknown to us than the operation of any other organ of the body, and a person's thoughts and emotions have corresponding brain states. So we should conclude that mental illness is an amazingly complex phenomenon.

What sort of factors can be involved as contributing factors or causes of mental illness? Here is a mere sampling of possibilities:

Genetic Factors

As there are genetic factors in alcoholism, so there can be in mental illness. These are factors, not causes. That is, having a genetic predisposition does not guarantee that a person will engage in certain behavior. One example comes from the findings of two University of Wisconsin researchers. A study by Drs. Avshalom Caspi and Terrie Moffitt concluded that people with a variant of the serotonin transporter gene have double the risk of depression following life stresses in early adulthood.[31] On the other hand, having certain genetic dispositions does not guarantee the onset of depression. Some do not encounter sufficient life stress; others find ways to cope.

Prenatal Factors

Prenatal factors are not genetic factors; that is, they are not inherent to the person at conception. Yet they are not the fault of or the choice of the individual, either. Schizophrenia.com reports, "Recent studies have indicated that children . . . born to mothers who suffer from flu, viruses and other infections during the pregnancy are at significantly increased risk of schizophrenia—up to 700% higher than children who are not exposed to flu/viruses during the first 13 weeks of pregnancy."[32] It cited a 2004 Columbia University study that found 14 percent of schizophrenia cases seemed to have been caused by influenza during pregnancy.[33]

Likewise, flu, viruses, and other infections experienced during pregnancy do not make the mother at fault for the later onset of the child's mental illness. As with the other factors, experiencing certain prenatal factors does not guarantee the onset of illness.

Family–of–Origin Factors or Psychological Factors

During childhood and/or adolescence, several factors can contribute to developing mental illness. Severe psychological trauma, such as emotional, physical, or sexual abuse, can be a contributing factor. Other possibilities include an important early loss, such as the loss of a parent, being neglected as a child, and receiving poor training on how to relate to others.[34] On the other hand, experiencing some of these family or psychological factors does not guarantee the onset of illness.

Trauma Factors

Trauma factors can overlap with family–of–origin and psychological factors. Some things are obviously traumatic (e.g., being robbed and shot); in less extreme cases what constitutes trauma varies with the individual. As we saw earlier, Scripture gives us precedent for trauma factors contributing to mental illness (Deut. 38:34). Further, research does the same. Major depression can be associated with death of or divorce from a spouse, a dysfunctional family life, living in poverty, living with other chronic disease (either our own or that of a loved one), feelings of inadequacy, low self-esteem, loneliness, or changing jobs or schools.[35] On the other hand, experiencing some of these traumatic or stressful factors does not guarantee the onset of illness.

Spiritual and Demonic Factors[36]

To assert that there can be spiritual or demonic factors is not to say that these operate independently of any kind of physical elements, historical events, or family factors. Divine judgment came on Herod by way of worms (Acts 12:23). Rather, it is to say that the New Testament acknowledges a possible spiritual or demonic influence, so we would be ignorant (read "reductionistic") to exclude it altogether. It is also reductionistic to conclude that a spiritual or demonic factor has only a spiritual solution. That would be just as reductionistic as assuming that a body health problem can only be addressed with medication or surgery, nothing else.[37]

Responsible Choice Factors

The use of such street drugs as LSD, methamphetamine, and marijuana has "been linked with significantly increased probability of developing schizophrenia," according to schizophrenia.com. It points to more than thirty different scientific studies: "Experts estimate that between 8% and 13% of all schizophrenia cases are linked to marijuana/cannabis use during teen years."[38] In one study of Swedish soldiers, researchers found that "those who were heavy consumers of cannabis at age 18 were over 600% more likely to be diagnosed with schizophrenia over the next 15 years than those who did not take it."[39]

Further, our emotional and/or cognitive reaction to life's pain can establish a habit with us, that is, alter our brain structure. It is well known and documented that, for instance, certain lifestyle choices are associated with lack of depression. The online site WebMD, for instance, lists healthy sleep habits, eating a balanced diet, regular exercise, and cognitive behavioral therapy.[40] To this list we might add thankfulness and strong connections with a supportive community.

We should keep in mind, however, that these choices cannot cure depression nor guarantee that it will never happen. But there is a strong correlation between an elevated mood and regular aerobic exercise, periodic relaxation, strong relationships, and proper diet.

A RIGHT PERSPECTIVE
AND RIGHT RESPONSES

Christians become ill. If Christians are not immune to cancer, diabetes, heart disease, fibromyalgia, inflammatory bowel disease, and pneumonia, then we should not expect them to be immune to depression, bipolar disorder, obsessive compulsive disorder, and the like. The gospel proclaims that we are sinners (morally corrupted) and yet we can be saved from God's wrath by someone who is morally perfect: our Lord Jesus Christ. Therefore, we should not give the impression that one can have cancer and be a Christian but one cannot have mental illness and be a Christian. Rather, those with mental illness should be comforted by the fact that we can be saved from God's wrath by someone who is mentally perfect: our Lord Jesus Christ.

What should be our response to mental illness? As there are probably multiple contributing factors with a person, so there should be several responses. Psychiatry loses its soul if it prescribes only medication. Likewise Christianity loses its mind if it only ascribes mental illness to spiritual problems.[41] A full response involves doing all that can be done, using every treatment that could help. These steps might include medication, learning a new way of thinking, diet and exercise, formal counseling, learning to experience the love of Christ for those who suffer, service to others as a way of forgetting the pain (if only temporarily), and a broad prayer network from a supportive community.

WebMD.com is not far away from this when it says,

> Depression can be treated in various ways. Counseling, therapy, and antidepressant medicines may be used. Lifestyle changes, such as

getting more exercise, also may help. You can help yourself by getting support from family and friends, eating a balanced diet, avoiding alcohol, staying active, and getting enough sleep.[42]

Many mental health professionals are secular. They do not naturally bring in issues of faith nor do they normally see issues of faith as helpful for recovery. But as one Christian mental health professional writes, there is "more hope that the church would be open to developing policies and systems for supporting the mentally ill than [there is] hope in influencing the mental health professionals that paying attention to one's faith is an essential part of their healing and rehabilitation."[42]

Further, the Christian suffering from mental illness should have the best resources available. For not only are there doctors and counselors, but there is the Community of the Holy Spirit that treasures the weak as it treasures Jesus.

AMID PAIN AND SUFFERING

1. Present your own definition of mental illness. Explain it.

2. Have you known someone who suffered from mental illness? Share some of the story.

3. Have you heard the assertion, "Mental illness is really a spiritual problem"? Reflect on the assertion. Is it true, partly true, or completely false? What difference do you think it makes?

4. Reflect on the statement, "We should see mental health/illness on a spectrum without sharp dividing lines. We all have degrees of health and we all have degrees of illness."

5. In what ways are you currently taking charge of, or neglecting, your own mental health? Explain.

CHAPTER 12

Suffering and God's People

Community, Renewal, and Ethics

BY GERALD W. PETERMAN

W hat is the role of God's people regarding suffering? Too often suffering is framed as an individual issue disjoined from community concerns.

Such a perspective is harmful. No doubt the pain of my fracture or incision is uniquely mine. But while we acknowledge this individual element, we must also acknowledge that the more isolated an individual is, the more threat there is to suffering; indeed isolation leads to increased levels of pain both in body and emotion.[1] On the other hand, the closer one becomes to another person, the more he or she becomes vulnerable to being hurt. Further, while suffering will not end this side of the new heaven and the new earth, nevertheless, in our view, God's people have a three–part task regarding suffering: to help alleviate current suffering, to help facilitate godly suffering, and to help prevent future suffering. The rest of the chapter will discuss these.

Our chapter is divided into four sections. In section 1 we survey some portions of Mosaic law in order to show how they accomplished this three-part community task. Here we show that many of Scripture's commands have to do with the alleviation or prevention of suffering. In section 2, focusing mainly on the Old Testament, we show that much in narrative and poetry has to do with examples of suffering in godly ways. These examples teach us how to facilitate godly suffering, in ourselves and others. In contrast, in section 3 we give examples of how God's people, both ancient and modern, fail in their three-part task. Too often they suffer in ungodly ways, bring suffering on themselves, cause pain for others, or fail to prevent suffering. Finally, in section 4 we give some guidance as to how God's people might alleviate current suffering, help facilitate godly suffering, and help prevent future suffering.

1. SUFFERING ADDRESSED UNDER MOSAIC LAW

In Scripture, a majority of the commands—both those given explicitly and those given implicitly—have to do with alleviation or prevention of suffering. As such they presuppose the corrupted human nature and a fallen world that developed under the curse of Genesis 3. Among many examples, the following are exemplary.

Private Land Ownership

The law of Moses dictated that each tribe receive an allotment of land (Num. 26:53–55; 34:13–18). This property provided the working material needed to produce wealth such as crops, lumber, bricks, fodder, herds, milk, cheese, skins, wool, bone, baskets, rope, oil, wine, and the like. Thus Old Testament property laws were capitalistic in the sense that each tribe, each family, owned land, and the land was the means of production, dependent on the labor of the individual. This is bottom-up wealth creation and a way to ensure economic prosperity and so prevent the suffering of poverty and hunger. Top-down wealth creation (or charity) seldom works well and is at best a stopgap measure. In the end "what takes place in the community, on the street, in the home, is what will ultimately determine the sustainability of any development."[2]

Furthermore, in Lev. 25:23–24 the Lord says about the land that it "shall not be sold in perpetuity, for the land is mine. For you are strangers and sojourners with me. And in all the country you possess, you shall allow a redemption of the land." Again this is primarily about the economic security of the family. Wright correctly says,

> When the statement is interpreted in light of its immediate context in Lev. 25, it becomes clear that Yahweh's ownership of the land is affirmed to ensure the security of *individual families* by preventing permanent alienation from *their land*. It is not simply a grand statement of national belief about the national territory, but the theological sanction of an *internal* economic system of land tenure.[3]

Laws against Theft, Murder, and Adultery (Ex. 20:13–15)

It should go without saying that an individual suffers if she or a family member is the object of theft or murder. Such attacks are prohibited not only because they dishonor God and his image bearers but also because they bring pain on our fellow man. Likewise a breach of marriage vows is emotionally very painful and can lead to further breakdown in the family and to poverty.[4]

Laws against Idolatry (Ex. 20:3–5)

Besides the obvious importance of wholehearted covenant allegiance to the only God, laws against idolatry are intended to shield the people of God from the painful, hideous, and degrading self-destructive practices of the Canaanites. Among these we can include cult prostitution, bestiality, and sacrificing children to Molech (e.g., Deut. 23:17; Lev. 18:21–28; Ps. 106:38; Ezek. 20:31).

The Poor Tithe

The poor tithe is not to be confused with the Old Testament's two other tithes. First, according to Lev. 27:30–32 a tithe of everything—of grain, of fruit, and of flock—belongs to the Lord. Numbers 18:21–26 dictates, however, that the Lord gives that tithe to the Levites as their inheritance, since they have no property in the land. Second, Deuteronomy mentions the festival tithe. This tithe is not given to the Levites; it is taken to Jerusalem and consumed in a great feast (14:22–27). Third, there is the poor tithe, sometimes called the storehouse tithe.[5] Deuteronomy 14 says further that

> at the end of every three years you shall bring out all the tithe of your produce in the same year and lay it up within your towns. And the Levite, because he has no portion or inheritance with you, and the sojourner, the fatherless, and the widow, who are within your towns, shall come and eat and be filled, that the LORD your God may bless you in all the work of your hands that you do. (Deut. 14:28–29; cf. Mal. 3:10)

The Levite, the sojourner, the fatherless, and the widow are all people in threat of poverty and hunger. The poor tithe would either prevent their suffering or alleviate it or both. The law against full harvest works similarly (Lev. 19:9–10). It states that one must not harvest the whole crop of grain, grapes, or olives, but leave a portion for the poor and the sojourner. The commandment helps to alleviate suffering.

2. GODLY SUFFERING IN NARRATIVE AND POETRY

In addition to teaching us truths about God and his plans, narratives in the Bible are written to engage us by way of both positive emotion and negative emotion, that is, suffering. God has given us stories—not fantasy, but history. "Stories in every culture both depict and inspire emotion. . . . [W]e have reason to assume that widely admired depictions of emotions [such as we find in Scripture] tell us something important about the way people in a given society think about emotions."[6] The affective appeal is a way the writer gets our attention, draws us into what is happening in the story, and makes us ready to be hit by the message. Furthermore, the way admirable Bible characters feel in suffering, respond to suffering, and give voice to suffering teaches us how to do the same. This is the case with three Old Testament characters.

Hannah (1 Sam. 1:7–8)

As Bergen notes,

> Hannah was a woman of faith. In fact, Hannah is portrayed as the most pious woman in the Old Testament. Here she is shown going up to the Lord's house; no other woman in the Old Testament is mentioned doing this. In addition, Hannah is the only woman shown making and fulfilling a vow to the Lord; she is also the only woman who is specifically said to pray . . . ; her prayer is also among the longest recorded in the Old Testament.[7]

Therefore, when we see that she grieved her childlessness and wept bitterly before the Lord in prayer because of it, we should not conclude that this reaction and behavior were ungodly, immature, or even undesirable. Rather, agonizing prayer is a godly expression of suffering. We have the events of 1 Samuel 1 recorded for us so that we can learn to follow her example. Very similar are Naomi's comments after the tragic loss of her husband and two sons. Though she implicates God in the hardship (1:13), her expression of bitter grief and her vocalized feeling of emptiness are completely appropriate (1:15–17, 20–21).

Samuel (1 Sam. 15:35)

Samuel anointed Saul as Israel's first king, giving him clear signs and encouragement (10:2–7). Moreover, after Saul's disobedience he solemnly warned him of the consequences (13:13–14). Saul, however, proved to be fearful, selfish, and unrepentant. Later "Samuel grieved over Saul" (15:35) because Saul failed to carry out the Lord's command regarding the Amalekites (15:18–19). Tsumura notes, "Samuel grieved even over one with whom he probably had a rather rocky relation.

Here we can see a true pastor and prophet who did not rejoice in the wrong."[8]

Samuel's community, and ours, need to know of his godly grief. Leaders do not hide their pain from those they serve (see 2 Cor. 1:8). Similar is Paul's grief over the Corinthians. Although they are threatened by a false gospel (2 Cor. 11:4) and his relationship with the congregation is strained since some find fault with him (e.g., 1 Cor. 9:1–3; 2 Cor. 10:10–12; 12:11–13), he remains emotionally connected and transparent, saying, "I wrote to you out of much affliction and anguish of heart and with many tears, not to cause you pain but to let you know the abundant love that I have for you" (2 Cor. 2:4).

Heman (Ps. 88)

Hannah was in anguish over her infertility, but there was resolution; Samuel grieved over a leader's sin, but the leader was deposed and replaced with a man after God's own heart (1 Sam. 13:14). Psalm 88 is a bit different. As we saw in chapter 5, most lament psalms go from grief to joy (e.g., Pss. 13, 22, 60, 74). Not so with the psalmist Heman, however. "Afflicted and close to death from my youth up, I suffer your terrors; I am helpless," he writes in Ps. 88:15. He prays to God but no answer comes. Do things get better at the end? They do not; he concludes the psalm saying to God, "You have caused my beloved and my friend to shun me; my companions have become darkness" (v. 18). Regarding the psalmist's cries, Brueggemann wrote,

> Psalm 88 is an embarrassment to conventional faith. It is the cry of a believer (who sounds like Job) whose life has gone awry, who desperately seeks contact with Yahweh, but who is unable to evoke a response from God. This is indeed 'the dark night of the soul,' when the troubled person must be and must stay in the darkness of abandonment, utterly alone.[9]

The inclusion of Psalm 88 in Israel's hymnbook lets us know that God welcomes such an embittered cry from his suffering servants.

The cry is not rejected or despised. The cry is a healthy expression of suffering.

3. UNGODLY SUFFERING, ANCIENT AND MODERN

The community should strive to shield its people from suffering. Unfortunately, it sometimes does the opposite! That is, the community afflicts those it ought to help—whether knowingly, accidentally, or absentmindedly. We will look at biblical examples before turning to modern ones.

Biblical Examples

Rachel and Leah (Gen. 30:1–15)

We do not need to recount how it came about that through his father-in-law's deception Jacob is married to two sisters (Gen. 29:22–27). Leah is unloved but fertile; her sister Rachel is loved but childless (29:30–31). Though they suffer differently, they both have pain; the pain is quite understandable. Leah tries to gain her husband's affection (29:32); Rachel demands offspring from him (30:1), causing him to reply with the angry retort, "Am I in the place of God, who has withheld from you the fruit of the womb?" (30:2). As Westermann wrote, "To think that after the beautiful, gentle love story of 29:1–20 this angry exchange between the two is our first and only experience of their marriage! It is the suffering of a childless wife, of which we hear so much in the Old Testament (1 Sam. 1; Ps. 113),"[10] and the suffering of a fertile wife, a less common theme.

The wives compete for progeny through their female slaves (30:3–5, 9–10), thus spreading the pain, in which Jacob is complicit. We do not see community lament, mutual support, and contrite prayer; instead competition, blame, and faultfinding are rampant. Too often the same things happen now nearly three thousand years later.

Wilderness Grumbling (Num. 11, 13–14)

While the Psalms testify that God welcomes our painful prayers and laments (see chapter 5, "Longing to Lament"), the wilderness grumbling does not fit this pattern and instead is not a godly way to suffer. Whereas the Psalms give us complaints from the faithful who recall God's work in the past and expect God's work in the future (e.g., Ps. 22:5), wilderness complaining (grumbling) appears to be opposite. God is assumed to be unconcerned, to be unable to help, or even to have malicious intent. So, for example, the whole congregation grumbles in Num. 14:3, saying, "Why is the Lord bringing us into this land, to fall by the sword? Our wives and our little ones will become a prey. Would it not be better for us to go back to Egypt?" As a result, that whole generation died in the wilderness (Num. 14:21–23; Heb. 3:7–17).

Naboth's Vineyard and King Ahab (1 Kings 21:1–19)

Naboth's fine vineyard adjoined King Ahab's property. The king was envious and grieved that he did not own it. When Naboth refused to sell the land, "Ahab went into his house vexed and sullen because of what Naboth the Jezreelite had said to him" (21:4). Perhaps Ahab strikes us as selfish and infantile. Nevertheless, we should ask, "What should be done with such longings or such painful grief?" Whatever it is that should have been done was not done. Instead, Ahab's wife, Jezebel, conceived a plot to have Naboth unjustly executed for blasphemy (21:8–10). "And as soon as Ahab heard that Naboth was dead, Ahab arose to go down to the vineyard of Naboth the Jezreelite, to take possession of it" (21:16). Unfortunately such gross abuse of power is not rare (e.g., 2 Sam. 11:1–27; Ezek. 34:1–10).

Modern Examples

As with the biblical examples, there are many modern instances that could be described. Here we must be selective, giving a few different types. All the stories are true, although some details are changed to protect identities of the people involved.

Ignoring Signs of Trouble

I was involved with a small congregation being planted in central Florida. The founding pastor, before he started our congregation, was evaluated by the leadership of his previous church. He had struggles and they strongly encouraged him to get help for his depression. What should he have done with his pain? Whatever it was, he did not do it. Ignoring the advice he received, he left that church to plant our church. His depression worsened; he got involved in an adulterous affair known to the congregation, yet he continued in leadership and teaching. Finally he left the church, his wife, his children, and the faith. The one who should be a source of comfort became a source of pain. He ignored the warning signs, and even though neglecting himself might have sounded godly and sacrificial, our congregation was devastated and never recovered.

Abuse of Power

While at one level the above example might be included under the rubric "abuse of power," it is unfortunate that many more grievous examples exist. The type of power abusers we have in mind are pastors who typically belong to conservative churches, preach that one must be born again, and hold to the inerrancy of the Word of God. These leaders all have good theology and seemingly love ministry. Yet sadly among them we find those doing the following:

- Growing rich from the church's offerings, and leading an opulent lifestyle, while some in the congregation suffer in poverty or even malnutrition.
- Micromanaging the lives of people within the congregation so that they cannot change jobs, marry, put children into a school, or make a major purchase (e.g., car or home) without the pastor's permission.
- Feeding on the unhealthy dependence that members of the congregation have on him.
- Verbally abusing individuals in the congregation who do not meet certain "spiritual" standards.

- Sexually exploiting others in the congregation.
- Mocking other churches or denominations for their concern over social justice, their desire for sound doctrine, or their allowing Christians to think for themselves.

In his book *Churches that Abuse* Ronald M. Enroth summarizes:

> These leaders use guilt, fear, and intimidation to manipulate members and keep them in line. Followers are led to think that there is no other church quite like theirs and that God has singled them out for special purposes. Other, more traditional evangelical churches are put down. Subjective experience is emphasized and dissent is discouraged. Many areas of members' lives are subject to scrutiny. Rules and legalism abound. People who don't follow the rules or who threaten exposure are often dealt with harshly. Excommunication is common. For those who leave, the road back to normalcy is difficult.[11]

Unintentionally Afflicting the Hurting

One Christian man suffering with bipolar disorder and anxiety tells how he is often treated in his congregation. He is regularly told by brothers and sisters in Christ that his problem is not mental illness; they say that the problem is either demonic or spiritual. In both cases they put the fault on him; in their view, it is a sin problem. We have regularly heard of congregations foolishly stigmatizing mental illness in this way (see also chapter 11).[12]

Furthermore, because he struggles with anxiety, he is often pained by repeated statements from the pulpit to the effect that Christians must rejoice always and that all anxiety is a sin. The problem is compounded when teaching is further given that those who persist in sin (in this case anxiety) may not even be converted. On the one hand, all the comments the man hears are probably well intentioned; on the other hand, they are all hurtful.

"Following Our Heart," or Adultery

In an earlier chapter we mentioned the husband who, after twenty–

five years of marriage, was leaving his wife and children for some-one else. He and his adulterous lover were attending another church, posting on social media how they were having Bible studies together, and claiming to be "really drawing closer to God," spreading the news about their newfound "Christian joy."

This insidious distortion of longings and emotions has caused dev-astation not just for the three innocent people who were betrayed, but also for every onlooker who fails to see Christ's love for his church through a husband's love for his wife. As mentioned in chapter 2, such pain and betrayal is never isolated but inevitably has a ripple effect.

Leadership Betrayal

Against church policy, a volunteer youth leader—a young man of eighteen—drove home from a youth event two young women who were fifteen years of age. At this time he acted inappropriately toward them, and later was convicted of sexual assault. The damage went in many directions: loss of reputation for the church and the gospel, loss of trust that congregants can place in leadership, the young man's tainted future, the grief of the parents and the other leaders, and of course the victims who suffer the greatest pain of all.

In passing we might ask how the congregation should respond when a leader betrays a trust among those he leads. One appropriate response among several should be grief, just as Samuel grieved over Saul (1 Sam. 15:35) and Paul encouraged the Corinthians to grieve over the immoral man of 1 Cor. 5:1–2. This congregation, however, proved to be like so many. It has the unspoken belief that grief must be suffered or expressed individually or by family groups in private. It is rarely expressed within the church community. The faulty belief is that when a congregation gathers on a Sunday morning, it dare not be glum or sad; all must be joyful and upbeat. It does not confront the sin and express grief over the loss and betrayal.

4. GUIDANCE FOR THE TASK

A whole book could be written on how Christians should deal with suffering in their relationships. We will conclude this chapter with a few suggestions. Until we arrive at the new heaven and the new earth, all attempts to alleviate, facilitate, and prevent will be imperfect.

Alleviate Current Suffering

Admonish, Encourage, and Help (1 Thess. 5:14)

Near the end of his letter to the Thessalonians Paul summarizes some of their responsibility: "And we urge you, brothers, admonish the idle, encourage the fainthearted, help the weak, be patient with them all." Several insights can be drawn from this exhortation. We restrict ourselves to four comments.

First, discernment is required. Can we distinguish the one who is idle from the one who is weak? Can we distinguish these two from the one who is fainthearted? Paul's commands require such discernment from us; we must fine–tune our response to fit the condition of the one we want to help. If we are to be discerning, surely careful and gentle investigation will be required.[13]

Second, when giving this exhortation, Paul is certainly being representative, not exhaustive. Others in the congregation are suffering in other specific ways that he does not mention, and they need different kinds of help. How do we deal with the strong who hurt others? How do we counsel the discouraged? We need to respond to exhausted caregivers, bewildered parents, those dying with cancer, alienated siblings, the jobless, and betrayed spouses.

Third, and following closely from the above, each situation requires its own response, whether compassion or admonishment. Notice that Paul's instruction makes plain that not every one of these situations requires admonishment (that is, reprimand). Some responses must be gentle, others must be forceful. Nevertheless, we often fall into the error of approaching it as if every case involves reprimand. For instance, quoting Philippians 4, we sometimes tell the anxious that they should stop sinning and rejoice in the Lord always.[14] Such a response is more abuse than it is care and is a fulfillment of Ezek. 34:4: "The weak you have not strengthened, the sick you have not healed, the injured you have not bound up, the strayed you have not brought back, the lost you have not sought, and with force and harshness you have ruled them." Similarly Paul does not say that the weak need a sermon on being strong in the Lord. Rather, they need help.

Fourth, all cases Paul mentions have in mind the alleviation of suffering. When the idle begin to work, they relieve the burden from others. When the fainthearted are encouraged, they find hope to go on. When the weak are helped, their needs are met. When patience is exercised, all of these are moved toward perseverance or godliness with as much gentleness as possible. Paul's summary in 1 Thess. 5:14 is a different way of saying the command of Gal. 6:2: "Bear one another's burdens, and so fulfill the law of Christ." The burdens might be primarily emotional, or they could be primarily economic as in the next example.

Honor Widows (1 Tim. 5:3–10)

In the ancient world, as is too often still the case, a widow was economically and socially vulnerable. Therefore Paul instructs that true widows—those who have no family to help them—should be supported by the local congregation. We know that Paul does not mean widows in general, but those attached to Timothy's congregation because they are known for piety (5:5, 10).

But aid need not stop with widows; we help the weak (1 Thess. 5:14), feed the hungry (Matt. 25:35), and serve the sick (Matt. 25:36). We can include ministry to those in our congregation who are single mothers, or families with special needs, or those who are dying. Along these lines would come the exhortations from prophets to Israel's community when they instruct the people, "Learn to do good; seek justice, correct oppression; bring justice to the fatherless, plead the widow's cause" (Isa.1:17).

Contribute to the Needs of the Saints (Rom. 12:13a)

It is good to teach our people, in advance of an economic crisis, how to handle their finances. On the other hand, those already in trouble need help, not the latest DVD on how to manage your money. As Dr. Cassell puts it, "While the swimmer may be drowning because of failure of will, what is wanted at the moment is a life–preserver, not a psychological insight about willpower."[15] The needs Paul refers to are basic: food, clothing, and shelter.[16] One might supply these needs not by giving away but by bringing in, that is, by sharing one's home. Thus Paul adds that we should be eager to show hospitality (12:13b).

Economic sharing was very important to Paul and indeed in the entire Bible. Over the course of his ministry, he spent nearly two decades on the collection for Jerusalem (Rom. 15:26–27; 1 Cor. 16; 2 Cor. 8–9).[17] Not only was it aid helping to meet the needs of poor brothers and sisters; it was also fellowship offered to Jews from Gentiles, building a bond between these two branches of the church.

Facilitate Godly Suffering

In the previous section we hinted at how to help God's people suffer in godly ways. In addition, here are a few further comments.

Weeping with Those Who Weep (Rom. 12:15b)

Christian congregations should encourage those painful emotions that are appropriate to godly life on a sinful planet. That is, contrary to common belief, not all godly emotion is positive. Paul says that the Corinthians should have mourned when one of their own was engaged in immorality (1 Cor. 5:1–2). Therefore, at times mourning is godly suffering. So it follows that we must allow, encourage, and instruct people in giving voice to pain. Paul did not keep painful emotion to himself but voiced it readily. Consider these responses to the various churches he cared for:

For I wrote to you out of much affliction and anguish of heart and with many tears, not to cause you pain but to let you know the abundant love that I have for you. (2 Cor. 2:4)

My little children, for whom I am again in the anguish of childbirth until Christ is formed in you! (Gal. 4:19)

But God had mercy on him, and not only on him but on me also, lest I should have sorrow upon sorrow. (Phil. 2:27)

Therefore when we could bear it no longer, we were willing to be left behind at Athens alone. (1 Thess. 3:1)

But we cannot stop here. Paul does not say that we allow others to weep and that we are not allowed to ourselves. We must enter into weeping with others. We will take their pain on ourselves and have empathy, weeping with them. This empathy can be private or in small groups. It could also occur when the whole congregation is assembled. From the absence of such community sorrow in our day, it is almost as if congregations are saying, "Christian rejoicing can be a group activity but Christian mourning must be an individual activity." Where would they get this idea?

Suffering without Vengeance (Rom. 12:17)

On the one hand, I am allowed to protect myself from painful or destructive relationships. When Jesus sent out the Twelve to preach and heal, he said, "When they persecute you in one town, flee to the next" (Matt. 10:23). On the other hand, persecution, hatred, and rejection will come (e.g., John 15:18); and we must leave the vengeance to God. Paul says, "Repay no one evil for evil, but give thought to do what is honorable in the sight of all" (Rom. 12:17).

A Good Death (Luke 22:39–44; Heb. 9:27)

Unless the Lord returns first, each one of us will die. We should prepare ourselves to die well. Understandably, a good death is not a topic much discussed from the pulpit. One godly woman I know who is suffering with cancer observed that Christians neither know how to die well nor how to talk about death. While she was very ill, her Christian friends could only pray that she would be healed. They could not pray that she would die well. How should we think about dying well?

First, we should reject the common view that says death is just a natural part of life; it is not. Death has entered into the world through sin (Rom. 5:12). Paul further says that death is an enemy (1 Cor. 15:26). Nevertheless, as we said before, unless we are alive at Christ's return (the rapture), we will die. While we seek to remain as healthy as possible as long as possible, "it is appointed for man to die once" (Heb. 9:27). We cannot avoid it. Thus dying well involves many elements, not the least of which is acknowledging that I am a sinner on a sinful planet.

Second, there is no need to endure as much pain as possible. We can ask to avoid suffering, as Jesus asked that the cup might pass from him (Matt. 26:39). We can share our pain with others, as Jesus expressed his sorrow to the three disciples with him in the garden (Mark 14:33–34).

Third, we might find that we can understand suffering in life as a way to form our character (Rom. 5:3–5; James 1:2–4), but we might have a very hard time concluding that our suffering in death has any meaning or significance. To help us here we can draw on the insight of Christopher P. Vogt in his article on "A Christian Model of Dying Well." He draws "upon the passion narrative of Luke's gospel to describe the shape of Christian patience, compassion, and hope in the context of dying."[18] He asks "whether Jesus' death can be a model of dying well for contemporary Christians" and concludes Christ is our perfect model.

One of Vogt's primary concerns is our having the patience of Jesus. As he defines it, patience is, in part, the willingness to faithfully endure in suffering knowing that it is God's will and that he will work in and through it. As such, patience is tied to belief in God's providence. Vogt writes,

> The model of patience that I have described runs counter to two currents that are prevalent in Contemporary American culture and

Christianity as it is sometimes expressed in the United States. Patience in imitation of Jesus is countercultural in the sense that it calls into question the contemporary emphasis on independence and self-reliance as a source of dignity and worth. It points to the possibility of value in allowing oneself to be acted upon—to putting one's own destiny and care into the hands of others.[19]

Where will we find the patience needed to give up our sense of autonomy and entrust ourselves to God at the end of life? One thing is certain, such patience cannot simply be switched on as we come to die. "Instead, in order to be capable of dying patiently, it is necessary to practice patience as it has been described here throughout life," Vogt argues. "One must seek out the opportunity to grow in patience by nurturing a sense of Providence or of being called by God to a service that might entail suffering or sacrifice."[20]

At the end of life Jesus did not boldly claim heaven, nor was he giddy knowing that bright light and the angelic choir were just around the corner. But he continued in obedience to God's plan (Matt. 27:39–43), showed compassion for others as he was dying (John 19:26–27), and entrusted himself to his heavenly Father (Luke 23:46).

Prevent Future Suffering

What we have said thus far about alleviating current suffering and encouraging godly suffering can in many ways be applied to the prevention of future suffering. We will not run over that ground again. Here we focus on certain proactive elements of church policy and of good teaching that protect God's people or ready them for all of life.

Ready Ourselves for Joy and for Tears

Our lives are seldom wholly one or wholly the other. Typically we find that God gives enough gladness to make life bearable or even enjoyable, and enough pain, sorrow, and trial to remind us that we are just passing through. The new earth will be our real home; this cursed planet, even with its immense beauty, will pass. D. A. Carson reminds us that we sometimes absentmindedly but wrongly expect a happily–ever–after sort of life:

> Much mental suffering is tied to our false expectations. We so link our hopes and joys and future to a new job, to a promotion, to certain kinds of success, to prosperity, that when they fail to materialize we are utterly crushed. But quiet confidence in God alone breeds stability and delight amid "all the changing scenes of life."[21]

We must pursue, and help others pursue, a healthful lifestyle especially as regards our thinking and feeling about hardship. One does not need as much instruction on how to deal with victories and joys. One needs instruction on how to develop a mindset about hardship, to persevere in difficulty, to live with pain, to recover from rejection and betrayal, and to respond to persecution.

This last type of suffering—persecution—is particularly challenging for those living in the comfortable West. Nevertheless, signs indicate that more challenging days are ahead. Those days will be like many that our brothers and sisters throughout the world have already encountered. We recommend regular engagement with The Voice of the Martyrs[22] or reading works such as Paul Marshall's book *Persecuted: The Global Assault on Christians* (Nelson, 2013).

Teach and Train the Younger (Titus 2:3–6)

Hopefully those with decades of experience following Christ have learned, through their own hardship, how to live in wise ways that avoid unnecessary suffering. Surely this is one of the aspects Paul had in mind in his exhortation to Titus when he wrote that "older women likewise are . . . to teach what is good, and so train the young women to love their husbands and children" (2:3–4). A wise and experienced wife knows how hard it can be to love a husband! Likewise, the children, while a source of great joy, can wear one out. Further, Paul says: "Likewise, urge the younger men to be self–controlled" (2:6). As we can both attest, lack of control can certainly bring great pain into life—into marriage, family, friendships, and community.

Be alert and on guard. While giving parting words to the elders of the Ephesian church, Paul gives this warning:

> Pay careful attention to yourselves and to all the flock, in which the Holy Spirit has made you overseers, to care for the church of God, which he obtained with his own blood. I know that after my departure fierce wolves will come in among you, not sparing the flock; and from among your own selves will arise men speaking twisted things, to draw away the disciples after them. Therefore be alert, remembering that for three years I did not cease night or day to admonish everyone with tears. (Acts 20:28–31)

If leadership could go wrong in the first century, it can go wrong today. It is the better part of discretion, therefore, to put church policies in place that are designed to protect individuals in the congregation, especially those who are the objects of ministry. For example, how would your local church respond to these practical questions:

- What is the best policy regarding background checks for leaders or for nursery workers? Recall Shelly in chapter 10. She had her own history of sexual abuse before she started babysitting and working with the youth group.

- What are the requirements for handling the offering? When Paul was giving direction about the collection for Jerusalem, he was concerned for "what is honorable not only in the Lord's sight but also in the sight of man" (2 Cor. 8:21). Our financial policy must be above reproach, helping exonerate or hold accountable those who handle money.

- How is money from the benevolence fund distributed? Strict policies do not imply that the congregation is unwilling to help; on the contrary, Paul was concerned that widows be supported by the congregation but he gave strict guidelines regarding who should be put on the list (1 Tim. 5:9–14).

CONCLUSION

Suffering is inevitably an issue of both individual and community. Unfortunately, at times individuals bring pain to communities and vice versa, doing so sometimes intentionally, sometimes accidentally, and sometimes absentmindedly. Nevertheless, God's people have a three-part task regarding suffering: to help alleviate current suffering, to help facilitate godly suffering, and to help prevent future suffering.

AMID PAIN AND SUFFERING

1. Read Psalm 88. Have you experienced something that feels similar to what Heman was going through? Can you call out to God the way Heman did? Tell why or why not.

2. It's almost as if congregations are saying, "Christian rejoicing can be a group activity but Christian mourning must be an individual activity." Have you noticed this? Where would they get this?

3. We say above that "the way admirable Bible characters feel in suffering, respond to suffering, and give voice to suffering teaches us how to do the same." Do you agree or disagree? Tell why.

4. Reflect on the following statement: "God gives enough gladness to make life bearable or even enjoyable, and enough pain, sorrow, and trial to remind us that we are just passing through."

5. In your view, what would a good death look like?

CHAPTER 13

Longing for Home

The Metanarrative Renewed

BY GERALD W. PETERMAN AND ANDREW J. SCHMUTZER

In our current metanarrative—the overarching narrative of human life for those of Christian faith—we find two opposing qualities existing side by side; indeed, they are sometimes mixed together. First, there is death and those things that go along with it, such as suffering, sin, frustration, betrayal, violence, corruption, and groaning. Second, there are blessings of the gospel: new life, redemption, the indwelling Spirit, adoption, hope, life in God's community, and ongoing transformation.

Truly, the Christian life means to exist between two worlds: the old world of sin, alienation, and death and the new world of righteousness, holiness, and life.

Life in the present age is not wholly darkness and pain, devoid of joy, bereft of love, or absent of care. By God's common grace we can see much beauty and enjoy our Creator's earth. In addition, elements of the new have been *inaugurated*, uniquely evident in the community of the redeemed, and so are beginning to invade the old. But the old has not vanished, and the new is not wholly come.[1] Thus we have groaning, which contains both of these elements: the desire to get away from sin and death and the longing to enjoy fully the life that awaits us.

This overlap of joy and sorrow, death and life can be illustrated in a selection of passages and theological themes from the Old and New Testaments.

JOY AND SORROW, DEATH AND LIFE IN THE OLD TESTAMENT

Within the metanarrative of Scripture, the Old Testament reveals God relating to his creation through much *plot complication*. As the drama of redemption leans into the New Testament, many themes converge in *plot resolution*. Because the redemptive climax of Christ is tied so deeply to history's earlier stages, there are powerful characters in this drama who require a closer look.

God's Redemptive Agents

One of the most stunning characteristics one finds in the flow of redemptive history is that *God always uses human agents to carry his plan forward*. It would seem that the desperate needs of humanity and the precious antidote of the divine message would cause God to use more guaranteed instruments to advance his plan. But Scripture expends great energy in the development and transformation of the agents themselves. Though these agents remain frail, flawed, and even obstinate, God always channels his work through his image bearers. Relationship remains primary, whether God's agents summon divine discipline or healing. For their part, the agents are never perfect before they are chosen. The God that sends spies and prophets in the Old Testament sends disciples and witnesses in the New, under the same missional impulse and ethical concern.

God does not guide in detached ways. Instead, redemptive history follows the arc of: *Creation → Devastation → Restoration*, consistently employing human agents who partner with God in his redemptive drama, moving it to the next stage. Quite often, the relational anguish they suffer stretches the imagination itself.

From the very beginning, the cosmic King has been working toward the restoration of his *entire* cosmos, not just the "salvation of souls."[2] Beginning with the royal under-kings of creation—"God blessed them.And God said to them" (Gen. 1:28a)—humankind was intended to mediate the blessing of God to the entire world. The Presence of God was always intended to be richly *mediated*, not "immediate," which means "without mediation."[3] To extend the glory of God is, indeed, a daunting mission. Beginning in heaven, the royal presence moved out through his royal ambassadors. These royal under-kings he made "a little lower than the heavenly beings and crowned . . . with glory and honor" (Ps. 8:5), intending the entire world to be filled with the intensity of God's glorious presence.[4]

Job and the Redemptive Antidote

Though Job is not a classical prophet, few characters in Scripture embody such suffering and relational anguish (cf. 1 Kings 22:8, 24–28), the prophet Micaiah and the persecutor turned persecuted Saul [Acts 9:16–17]. The suffering in Job is best situated in the earliest stage of God's redemptive program, sometime around the patriarchs. God's covenant name is clearly known (occurring twenty-six times), and sacrifices are used (1:5; 42:8). Long summarizes well what we can learn from Job's suffering:

> [The] marvelous and complex story of Job comes to us as both warning and promise. It warns us away from the presumption that we will find some solution to the theodicy problem that will somehow "make sense" to us independent of our relationship with God. We do not get to draw a line in the sand and say, "OK, God, when I get this problem of suffering worked out in my mind, I'll step over the line toward you." Or, "OK, God, when you begin to honor my sense of justice, then I will trust you." No, we have to step over the line and fall on our knees in prayer and faith. Only in the light of our trust in

God is there anything to see. The promise of the book of Job is that
there is indeed much to see in that light.[5]

God is not detached from Job. Instead, chapters 38–42 present both
parties in candid conversation. We may experience elements of Job's
suffering—physically, emotionally, or spiritually—in our own lives. We
certainly will meet some Job–like people; many, in fact, with profound
and inexplicable suffering, even though they are godly people. The reality of complex suffering should keep us from the common misconception that a lifestyle of wisdom and preparation is a formula for ease
and success. Actually, Job was both a wise and godly man who suffered
horribly, and was also horribly misunderstood (42:7)![6] Yet God even
used Job as an agent for his friends' restoration: "My servant Job will
pray for you, and I will accept his prayer" (42:8 NIV).

The calling of Abram (Gen. 12:1–3) is the *redemptive antidote*, the
"U–turn" for the violence and global disarray of God's creation (Gen.
1–11). The *goal* of his calling is clear: "in you all the families of the earth
shall be blessed" (12:3b). Abraham's family becomes a microcosm of
what God intended for all humanity. God stuck to creation's plan. And
every patriarch afterward is drawn into this redemptive orbit of God's
theo–drama, carrying it forward as the next covenant steward.[7] So this
is the pattern of agents. Flowing through the Abrahamic rubric, God
calls Moses, the Judges, the Davidic kings, the prophets, and finally—
"when the fullness of time had come" (Gal. 4:4)—Jesus, the ultimate
agent of God's redemptive plan.

Pressing toward the rule and rest of creation, Israel itself receives a
charter as a "kingdom of priests" (Ex. 19:3–6).[8] These successive agents
who advance God's redemptive plan each must overcome a new im-
pediment that blocks God's work.[9]

Epoch–Making Mediators, Moses and Elijah

Both Moses (Ex. 3:1–4:18) and Elijah (1 Kings 17–21) are called to
advance the program of God at strategic junctures in Israel's history.

While Moses helps birth the people from national slavery into freedom (Exodus–Deuteronomy), Elijah helps rescue the nation from spiritual slavery to Baal (1 & 2 Kings).

These two mediators, Moses and Elijah, are uniquely defined by God's theophany to each spiritual leader. Theophanies are mission–altering encounters, always on God's terms. God's direct manifestation came in the "un–burning bush" for Moses (Ex. 3:1–6) and the "gentle whisper" for Elijah at Mt. Horeb (1 Kings 19:11–18).

Moses the Deliverer

For all the death surrounding Moses' infancy (Ex. 1:22–2:10), the Israelite nation learns that their human deliverer is really provided by their divine deliverer.[10] YHWH is their warrior–king (15:3, 18). Moses, called to deliver Israel from Egyptian bondage (3:7–10), is also the mediator of unique revelation (20:18–21), the Torah (i.e., Pentateuch), which Israel needs if a traumatized collection of slaves are to have the vision and courage to obey their appointed leader (cf. Numbers 10–36).

And traumatized they are! *The liberated slaves do not know how to trust God.* They threaten to return, and actually call Egypt "a land flowing with milk and honey" (Num. 16:13)! Following the occasions of the golden calf and the spies, their rebellious spirit forced Moses to "talk God down" from destroying them, *twice*! So even the psalmist identifies these key occasions: "They made a calf in Horeb. . . . Therefore he said he would destroy them—had not Moses, his chosen one, stood in the breach before him, to turn away his wrath from destroying them. . . . Then they despised the pleasant land" (Ps. 106:19, 23–24).

Moses' second encounter with God is a more direct experience, leaving his face radiant (Ex. 32–34:8, 29–33). His shining face uniquely marks him as God's authoritative spokesperson.[11] Moses not only advocates for Israel, he is also God's representative. Within redemptive history, *Moses is esteemed most for his unparalleled intimacy with God* (Ex. 33–34; Num. 12:6–8; Deut. 34:10).[12] Later, it is written about Moses: "And there has not arisen a prophet since in Israel like Moses, whom the LORD knew face to face" (Deut. 34:10). Only Jesus surpassed Moses as a better mediator between God and people (Acts 3:17–27; Heb. 3).

Israel's deliverance ultimately serves a far larger redemptive purpose.[13] Under Moses as mediator, Israel is commissioned as a priestly kingdom to extend the blessing of God among the nations (Gen. 12:3). While "kingdom of priests" begins as Israel's *national charter* (Ex. 19:3–6), it culminates in Revelation as the description of the church, ransomed by the blood of Christ (Rev. 1:6).

Who could have imagined that the mediation to the nations would eventually climax in the perpetual doxology of all nations to their Redeemer (Rev. 5:10; 20:6)? In John's theology, Jesus is now the one to whom the nations come for their salvation (Isa. 11:10; 60:3; Rev. 22:16).[14] After observing how Rev. 19:5–6 draws on Genesis 10 and Daniel 7, Bauckham states:

> Less often noticed is that [Rev.] 5:9 alludes to Exodus 19:5: "you shall be my treasured possession out of all the peoples." Instead of taking "out of all the peoples" (מכל־העמים) to mean that God has chosen one of the peoples, John has taken it to mean that members have been drawn from all nations to constitute the church: "by your blood you have purchased for God [people] from (ἐκ) every tribe and language and people and nation."[15]

By this, John has seen a key element in the grand arc of God's redemption. God's redeemed children transcend all ethnic, linguistic, and national boundaries (Rev. 7:9; cp. 13:3–8). Here, God's purposes for history are finally enacted.

Elijah the Mediator

Where Moses brings national *identity*, Elijah brings national *cleansing*. Elijah calls a nation to obey Moses' teaching.

Elijah's name appropriately means "my God is YHWH." Ministering during the reigns of Ahab and Ahaziah (874–852 BC), Elijah was called to bring Israel back from their syncretistic worship of the Phoenician god, Baal. Ahab even built a temple to Baal in Samaria (1 Kings 16:32–33). This state–sponsored religion was utterly incompatible with YHWH's claim to exclusive lordship. It would take a fanatical mediator to heal a nation "limping between two different opinions" (1 Kings 18:21).

Elijah would become a prophet of remarkable energy and candor. During a time of drought and famine, Elijah mediated the aid of God to a widow and her son. While he stayed with her, her food lasted and he also brought her son back from the dead (1 Kings 17:8–24). Only Israel's God, not Baal, had the power to satisfy hunger (1 Kings 17:2–16) and overcome death (vv. 9–24). The mediation of Elijah reveals a couple of key points: (1) YHWH defends the needs of the weak and powerless, and (2) YHWH's concern and help are not confined to the land of Israel; he even works in Baal's territory (cf. Psalm 29)![16]

Having been fed by unclean ravens and living in Gentile territory, Elijah is now prepared for his greatest mediation of God's power. In the third year of the drought, Elijah directly confronts Baal in a contest of strength. Outnumbered 450 prophets to one (1 Kings 18:22), Elijah confronts the other prophets about Baal's specialty of rain. When there is "no voice," no answer, and no response (v. 29) for Baal's prophets, Elijah takes his turn. He reclaims the original site by repairing an abandoned YHWH altar that had been under Phoenician control.[17] He then drenches the altar with water, a priceless sacrifice during drought (vv. 33–35).

God responds, sending from the heavens fire, the symbol of his active presence. Watching with awe, the people admit: "The LORD [YHWH] is God" (v. 39). The real climax comes when God responds to Elijah's prayer, opens the heavens with rain, and ends the drought (vv. 41–46). But royal policy does not change, and a few years later there are enough worshipers of Baal to fill his temple (2 Kings 10:21).

Jezebel soon threatens Elijah's life (1 Kings 19:1–2) and in fear the prophet flees into the wilderness. There he despairs of life (vv. 3–4).

Revived by angelic aid, he receives a sign that his God has not abandoned him. Visiting the same place at Mt. Sinai that Moses had earlier, "there" and "from there" form an *inclusion* highlighting his trip to and from the same sacred place (vv. 9–19). In fact, the same theophany of earthquake, wind, and fire identify the sacred mountain (cf. Ex. 19), but the "sheer silence" (v. 12) that follows shows that YHWH is unlike his rival, Baal. Instead, *YHWH possesses all the attributes of a storm-god, but is above nature, not part of it.*[18] If anything, YHWH was a quiet whisper that could only be heard by one completely devoted to listening for his presence.[19]

Elijah does not die. Because the prophet is taken bodily into heaven, with eyewitnesses (2 Kings 2:9–12), *he continues to live in a special way.* Neither he nor Moses left earthly life in the usual way. God himself buried Moses to conceal his body from the people (cf. Deut. 34:6). So it was believed Elijah could reappear in the future.

In summary, Moses and Elijah were more than mediators; they were *intercessors* who "stood in the breach." They not only extended God's redemptive work, they talked openly with God about the crisis points of their time. As "prophets of the wilderness," they form the backdrop for John the Baptist, another wilderness prophet, calling for national renewal when Jesus, one greater than Moses, came (Heb. 3:1–19).

Isaiah and the Promise of a New Mediator

Isaiah's climactic servant song (Isa. 52:13–53:12) describes the comprehensive work of the Suffering Servant. The *shalom* predicted in the messianic hope (9:6) and anticipated in the good news (52:7) is ultimately achieved by the Servant as God's "shalom–producing rule."[20] God's royal servant is the new *mediator.* A new exodus is achieved by a new agent—but through substitutionary suffering! Creation achieves a massive step of renewal through the identity and accomplishment of the Suffering Servant. This is the Messianic King (Isaiah 1–39) who leads a new exodus (Isaiah 40–55), brings a renewed creation (Isaiah 56–66), and establishes God's kingdom through his atoning death. "In other words, the context of 52:13–53:12 portrays an act of salvation that is *by a servant–king* (identity) and *for a kingdom of servants* (accomplishment). . . . The servant–king is the mediatorial means of establishing God's kingdom."[21]

The servant–king was "lifted up" (*nś'*) and exalted (Isa. 52:13). He is the very one who "has borne (*nś'*) our griefs" (53:4) and "bore (*nś'*) the sin of many" (53:12). The irony could not be greater: "The Servant is exalted through humiliation and victorious through suffering."[22] As Treat explains, The "lifted up" One has "lifted up" our sins onto himself, so that we may be reconciled to God and share in his glory. YHWH's reign restores unfaithful servants to their proper service of the king (cf. Gen. 1:28).[23]

Moses and Elijah at the Close of the Old Testament

The durable presence of both Moses and Elijah is even evident in the way the Old Testament closes. One birthed a nation, the other confronted for repentance. In many ways, biblical history is a series of intensified repetitions. So Malachi ends with a reminder of Moses' teaching, but also the presence of Elijah himself, poised to leap prophetically into the future. Indeed, he does![24] God has not abandoned his redemptive plan and pushes forward. According to Mal. 4:4–6, Elijah would return before the day of the Lord.

> Remember the law of my servant Moses, the statutes and rules that I commanded him at Horeb for all Israel. Behold I will send you Elijah the prophet before the great and awesome day of the LORD comes. And he will turn the hearts of fathers to their children and the hearts of children to their fathers, lest I come and strike the land with a decree of utter destruction.

But the nation does not turn back to God, and so this legendary dramatic mediator is unleashed on the people, again! It is John the Baptist who fulfills this expectation (cf. Matt. 11:14; Luke 1:17), and he will be martyred for it (Matt. 17:13). But the plot thickens.

JOY AND SORROW, DEATH
AND LIFE IN THE NEW TESTAMENT

Jesus' Transfiguration—Glory in Suffering

The New Testament will indicate God's kingdom comes by way of the cross, especially in Mark's theology (Mark 8:22–10:45). The cross is held out as a supreme act of kingly power. This kingdom is redefined by suffering. [25] At the center of Mark's gospel is the full expression of Jesus' messiahship, which forcefully converges with the responsibilities of his disciples.[26] The disciples are slow to understand that their Messiah must suffer (8:28–38). So when Jesus clarifies that his life as Messiah includes a Suffering Servant, they ignorantly protest (8:31–33). It is here that Jesus draws the clearest connection between his own suffering and his followers' responsibility to deny themselves, even to the point of death (8:34–37). This is the lead–up to Jesus' transfiguration (9:2–13).

Well–known themes reappear. In Jesus' transfiguration in Mark 9, we find significant parallels to the theophanies of Moses and Elijah. This helps bridge eras and gather redemptive momentum.

- A high mountain (v. 2), a standard place of divine revelation (cf. Ex. 19:3–25; 1 Kings 19:8). In the transfiguration, the revelation is privately witnessed (Mark 5:37), but also with three witnesses (v. 2; cf. Aaron, Nadab, and Abihu in Ex. 24:1, 9), and mention of "six days" (v. 2; Ex. 24:16).
- Transfiguration–type disclosures are rooted in Jewish apocalyptic thought (2 Cor. 3:18; Phil. 3:21). Dazzling white appearance typically portrays glorification (Dan. 12:3; Rev. 4:4).
- Moses and Elijah—representing the law and prophets—reappear as major Old Testament eschatological figures (v. 4). Moses founded the nation on God's law and predicted that a prophet like himself would come (Deut. 18:15–19). Elijah's ministry pointed to a new era in the future (Mal. 3:1; 4:5–6). Together, they are heralds of the Lord's redemptive work.[27]
- A glory cloud (v. 7) and God's voice (v. 7; Ex. 24:16) often accompa-

nies Old Testament theophanies (Ex. 24:12–18; Ezek. 1:4). Like the disciples' response (v. 6) these typically evoke terror (Ex. 3:1–6; 34:30; Isa. 6:1–5). But unique to Jesus' theophany is the heavenly voice that identifies Jesus as God's unique Son (cf. Mark 1:9–11).

The disciples' questions bring a further explanation from Jesus about the necessity of his many sufferings (vv. 12, 31). The disciples continue to struggle with the necessity of Jesus' suffering, in which they, too, will have a share.

Mark clearly shows how Jesus' transfigured royalty is displayed on the cross. "While the religious leaders oppose this idea and the disciples misunderstand it," writes Treat, "it is only on the cross that Jesus will be properly recognized as the Son of God."[28] In stunning fashion, the *reality* portrayed in Jesus' transfiguration is contrasted with his *appearance* on the cross. (See Chart 4)

Chart 4

TRANSFIGURATION	CRUCIFIXION
Unearthly light (9:2–3)	Supernatural darkness (15:33)
Jesus' luminous clothes (9:2–3)	Jesus stripped of clothes (15:20, 24)
Two OT mediators (9:4)	Two criminals (15:27, 32)
Conversation with Elijah (9:4)	Perceived conversation with Elijah (15:35)
Disciples are present (9:5)	Disciples flee (14:50)
God speaks (9:7)	God is silent

Adapted from Jeremy R. Treat, *The Crucified King* (Grand Rapids: Zondervan, 2014), 99.

While continuity between the transfiguration and crucifixion shows *Jesus is the Messiah who reigns from the cross*, contrast also reveals a paradox in the way his glorious kingship is hidden in a gruesome death: radiance of glory is now seen as darkness, divine power is reduced to profound weakness, and royal kingship has climaxed in a deathly servanthood.[29] In other words, the glimpse of glory (*transfiguration*) is the centerpiece, between Jesus' anointing (*baptism*) and his enthronement (*crucifixion*). Since so many rich themes culminate in the transfiguration account, we can summarize with a few core theological principles.

Theological Truths from the Transfiguration and Crucifixion of Jesus

First, *all followers of Christ must embrace suffering before they can embrace glory*. This is not only evident in the way so many Old Testament mediators faced radical hardship in their own lives, coupled with spiritual defection from those around them; it is most clear in the climactic suffering of Christ, which then leads to his glory. The transfiguration illustrates the implications of the cross. His glory and our ultimate vindication are in the resurrection. This is a profound truth for discipleship, since followers of Christ must accept suffering and sacrifice as they follow the example of their Lord's life. We are only asked to follow where Jesus has already been. Jesus took great care to help his disciples grasp this truth (cf. Mark 8:31–38; 9:30–31), drawing on foundational roles of mediation and suffering from the lives of Old Testament characters.

Second, *the glory of Christ is hidden in his suffering, and vindicated in his resurrection*. The transfiguration actually anticipates the resurrection, since both reveal what is really happening in the crucifixion.[30] These are still scandalous truths. The disciples had misunderstood both the *way* Elijah would come and the *stages* that restoration would take. Jesus clarifies both points in verses 12–13. We need to hear Jesus' words afresh: it is "written of the Son of Man that he should suffer many things and be treated with contempt" (v. 12). Only in the second coming will there be final renewal and restoration of all. A spiritual restoration comes first in Jesus' death (Ps. 118:22; Isa. 52–53).[31] It is a suffering Messiah that Elijah introduces, not a conquering Messiah. Jesus' second clarification is that Elijah has already come (Mark 9:3). Jesus made Elijah into a *type*. "He is John the Baptist, who suffered as Elijah did and as the Son of Man would."[32] The Baptist faced his Jezebel in Herodias (Mark 6:14–29; cf. 1 Kings 19:1–3). Jesus becomes the *antitype* of both in his own suffering and death.

In reality, we are part of the same crowds who were excited about a triumphal king—"Blessed is the coming kingdom of our father David!" (cf. Matt. 21:4–5). Just like the expectations of the ancient masses, we still struggle to understand a kingdom established through so much suffering.[33] But pain is part of the journey in the renewal of the metanarrative. Hurtado is surely right when he says, "Intelligent talk of the glory of Jesus cannot be done apart from emphasis upon his death and resurrection, and that any Christian preaching and devotion that is not centered on the meaning of these events is shallow and confused."[34]

Third, Jesus is the new eschatological Moses and the only mediator for new life. *In the presence of Israel's new leaders, Jesus reenacts the glory that Moses experiences on Sinai, bringing fresh redemptive promises to life in a new exodus that he offers for all enslaved humankind.*[35] In fact, in Luke 9:31, the content of Jesus' discussion with Moses and Elijah is mentioned—Jesus' "departure" (*exodos*)—a new exodus he would lead. Beyond Moses' radiant face (Ex. 34:30) and Daniel's "Ancient of Days" (Dan. 7:9), now the Son of Man displays before the disciples some of God's characteristics, much like Moses' face once shone with God's glory.[36] The Father's words come from another glory cloud (Ex. 19:9), insisting: "This is my beloved Son; listen to him." In these words echoing Deuteronomy 18:15 ("Listen to him"), God himself interrupts the error of Peter (v. 7) and portrays Jesus as their rabbi, in the role of Moses, with vital instruction for others. The combination of these two Old Testament figures, for both Matthew and Mark, was proof that the coming kingdom was in the process of realization.[37] The danger remains that in our false expectations, confusion, and discouragement, we will look for "leaders" that do not have the words of life or know the way out of enslaving patterns of life.

ANTICIPATING A NEW AGE

As we mentioned above, with the coming of the Lord Christ we see a significant jump forward in God's plan and work. Yet, after conversion, we do not live wholly in the new age. While those in Christ are a new creation (2 Cor. 5:17), not all things have been made new yet (Rev. 21:5). The two ages overlap, with the corresponding life and death, joy and tears.

We will look at two key passages. The first, from Romans, speaks of this overlap of ages. It is particularly relevant since Paul compares our current suffering with our future glory. The second, from Revelation, describes the metanarrative wholly renewed, when sin, suffering, and pain are left behind and all is made new.

Romans 8:14–23

We briefly spent some time in this passage in chapter 4, ("A Man of Sorrows"). Following an encouraging teaching about adoption, Paul mentions that as children we should expect suffering in this world, saying,

> For all who are led by the Spirit of God are sons of God. For you did not receive the spirit of slavery to fall back into fear, but you have received the Spirit of adoption as sons, by whom we cry, "Abba! Father!" The Spirit himself bears witness with our spirit that we are children of God, and if children, then heirs—heirs of God and fellow heirs with Christ, provided we suffer with him in order that we may also be glorified with him. For I consider that sufferings of this present time are not worth comparing with the glory that is to be revealed to us. For the creation waits with eager longing for the revealing of the sons of God. For the creation was subjected to futility, not willingly, but because of him who subjected it, in hope that the creation

itself will be set free from its bondage to corruption and obtain the freedom of the glory of the children of God. For we know that the whole creation has been groaning together in the pains of childbirth until now. And not only the creation, but we ourselves, who have the firstfruits of the Spirit, groan inwardly as we wait eagerly for adoption as sons, the redemption of our bodies. (Rom. 8:14–23)

To help us see both the overlap and the great contrast within Romans 8, consider chart 5:

Chart 5

THE CURRENT NARRATIVE	THE RENEWED NARRATIVE
Sons/Children (14–16)	Sons/Children (19)
Sufferings (18); Pains (22)	Glory (18)
Futility (20)	Revelation (18)
Anticipation/Waiting (19, 23)	Heirs (with Christ, 17)
Hope (20)	Freedom (21)
Adoption (15)	Adoption (23)
Bondage and Decay (21)	Redemption (23)
Groaning (22–23)	New Bodies (23)

Much could be said of this rich passage. We restrict ourselves to the following five comments:

First, as mentioned earlier, *the two narratives are not totally disjunctive.* In both we find our adoption and status as children of God. "We are already sons of God, but our sonship is not yet manifest. We have been adopted, but our adoption has yet to be publically proclaimed."[38] Similarly, glory awaits us; but glory has also invaded our current experience. Elsewhere Paul asserts regarding our current progressive sanctification that "we all, with unveiled face, beholding the glory of the Lord, are being transformed into the same image from one degree of glory to another" (2 Cor. 3:18).

Second, *we have anticipation and hope in the first column.* But do we have them in the second? To the Corinthians Paul mentions that faith, hope, and love remain (1 Cor. 13:13), probably meaning that all three are eternal. We will always trust, hope in, and love our heavenly Father. Schnabel is surely right when he says, "Paul obviously wants to emphasize that those who confess Jesus will in the new age be always trusting (faith) and always living for him (hope)."[39] As we trust and have anticipation now, so likewise, in the new heaven and new earth we will anticipate—hope and long for—what he will reveal to us about himself in eternity future.

Third, we should *note carefully the significance of what is present in the first column but absent in the second. In the first we find frustration, or futility.* The word *frustration* "suggests that creation has not been able to attain the purpose for which it was created."[40] It cannot supply us richly as it would like; it is in bondage to decay. The language is similar to Isa. 24:1–6 (in the Septuagint). While Paul says that the creation "itself will be set free from its bondage to decay [*phthoras*] and obtain the freedom of the glory of the children of God" (Rom. 8:21), Isaiah speaks of the judgment that God brings as a result of human sin, saying that the earth will be ruined with decay (*phthora*). Likewise we ourselves—no matter how much faith we have and no matter how holy our lives—will have pain because we, too, are in bondage to decay.

One particular type of suffering Paul mentions is birth pains (v. 22). It is an apt illustration. There we find anxiety and pain mixed with hope. Similar is our existence in our current metanarrative; it longs for glory while it agonizes through our current sinfulness (cf. Mark 13:8; John 16:20–22). Through much pain new life is brought into the world. Paul uses similar language in Gal. 4:19–20, comparing his first evangelization of the Galatians and his subsequent struggles with them to childbirth pains. The image is striking.[41]

As we await new life we groan. To bring out clearly what Paul is saying, Rom. 8:23 should be translated "because we have the Holy Spirit as first–fruit, we groan as we await our full adoption." That is, we groan because the Spirit works in us.[42] So the fruit of the Spirit is joy (Gal. 5:22) for what we have already received, and because we have the Spirit we groan for what we have yet to receive. Green puts it well: "One can say, then, that 'groaning' names (among other things) a *longing* for the eschatological fulfillment of all things, a *travailing* in effort to give life to the new age, and an *agonizing* under the burden of interior frailty and exterior oppression by the forces of sin, death, and injustice."[43]

Fourth, in contrast to our point above, *we should find great joy and hope in the new life* Paul says we await. Our future is described as glory (Rom. 8:30; 2 Thess. 1:12). This is important, for Paul reminds us that we lack the glory we should display as God's image bearers (Rom. 3:23).[44] Psalm 8 gives us a glimpse of what this glory is to be like: God made man "a little lower than the heavenly beings and crowned him with glory and honor" (v. 5). It is not that there is no glory in the present (2 Cor. 3:18; 4:4–6). But Paul has in mind a future glory after resurrection, when Jesus "will transform our lowly body to be like his glorious body, by the power that enables him even to subject all things to himself" (Phil. 3:21). Our destiny as sons of God is to share glory with Christ the Son.[45] Creation awaits that event: the revelation of God's children (v. 19). That is, the children might be seen for who they are. The hope of creation is contingent on the glory given to Christians.

Fifth, *very similar themes are found in 2 Cor. 4:16–5:5.* There Paul says that "this light momentary affliction is preparing for us an eternal weight of glory beyond all comparison" (v. 17). Further, in our current unredeemed bodies "we groan, longing to put on our heavenly dwelling" (5:2). When we change our current dwelling for our eternal home, "what is mortal may be swallowed up by life" (v. 4). We have hope as we await that moment because God "has given us the Spirit as a guarantee" (v. 5).

Revelation 21:1–5a

Then I saw a new heaven and a new earth, for the first heaven and the
first earth had passed away, and the sea was no more. And I saw the
holy city, new Jerusalem, coming down out of heaven from God, prepared as a bride adorned for her husband. And I heard a loud voice
from the throne saying, "Behold, the dwelling place of God is with
man. He will dwell with them, and they will be his people, and God
himself will be with them as their God. He will wipe away every tear
from their eyes, and death shall be no more, neither shall there be
mourning, nor crying, nor pain anymore, for the former things have
passed away." And he who was seated on the throne said, "Behold, I
am making all things new."

In this passage hope, joy, and sheer delight shine through powerfully. The wedding is a happy event. We find the word "new" four times.
Intimacy and transparency are reflected in God himself being with us
and giving his gentle comfort. "The story of the world," Hamilton concludes, "is not a tragedy that ends in death and shame but a comedy
that ends in cosmic renewal and the marriage of the Lamb and his
bride."[46] We see the new metanarrative in the following four points.

First, *John draws on the promises of a new heaven and a new earth*
found in Isaiah 65, especially vv. 17–22. There the themes are "joy (both
God's and his people's) and the removal of sorrow and suffering."[47]

Second, *"the dwelling place of God is with man. He will dwell with
them, and they will be his people."* These words draw on covenant language from the Old Testament. The tabernacle in the wilderness is constructed so that Yahweh would be able to dwell in the midst of his people
(Ex. 25:8). Leviticus 26:12 promises, "I will walk among you and will be
your God, and you shall be my people." Whereas in the past God dwelled
with Israel (Ex. 29:45), now he dwells with all redeemed humanity.

Third, we hear that *"he will wipe away every tear from their eyes, and
death shall be no more, neither shall there be mourning, nor crying, nor
pain anymore, for the former things have passed away."* Here are four

very significant Old Testament words pointing to promises in the New Testament:

- Tears (*dakruon*): The wiping away of tears implies comfort and intimacy. It fulfills Isa. 25:8: "He will swallow up death forever; and the Lord God will wipe away tears from all faces, and the reproach of his people he will take away from all the earth, for the Lᴏʀᴅ has spoken."

- Mourning (*penthos*): We mourn the loss of someone we love, or of a hoped–for goal. In his beatitudes, Jesus said, "Blessed are those who mourn, for they shall be comforted" (Matt. 5:4). Here it happens.

- Crying (*kraugē*): This term may be used positively of the announcement that the bridegroom comes (Matt. 25:6). Here, however, it is negative and reflects heartache, discouragement, or pain as in Heb. 5:7: "In the days of his flesh, Jesus offered up prayers and supplications, with loud cries and tears, to him who was able to save him from death." This end to mourning and crying fulfills Isa. 65:19: "I will rejoice in Jerusalem and be glad in my people; no more shall be heard in it the sound of weeping and the cry of distress."

- Pain (*ponos*): The word is fairly rare in the New Testament, and readers might think it refers to a bodily sensation, such as an ache or soreness, whether mild or harsh. The word primarily refers to work, labor, or other difficult tasks, and then by extension to pain we might encounter in them. Thus at times it can be positive. Paul says of Epaphras, "I bear him witness that he has *worked hard* for you and for those in Laodicea and in Hierapolis" (Col. 4:13, emphasis added). At other times it can be detached from the positive connotation of work and become quite negative. "The fifth angel poured out his bowl on the throne of the beast, and its kingdom was plunged into darkness. People gnawed their tongues in *anguish*" (Rev. 16:10). In this context "pain" more likely refers to the senseless, fruitless, or hopeless pains that we encounter in the old earth.

Fourth, *Revelation gives us a glimpse into our future.* Drawing on earlier prophecy from Isa. 42:9 and 43:19, the One seated on the throne says, "Behold, I am making all things new" (Rev. 21:5). This declaration

from the Lord opens up before us a vista promising endless exploration, where we ceaselessly discover the delights of God's creation, of his
image bearers, and of the Lord himself.

RENEWING OUR CREATOR'S WORLD

The cross of Christ does not culminate redemptive history. Rather, it
enables the renewal of the Creator's world, once called "very good"
(Gen. 1:31). The detailed stories and characters of the Old Testament
show us how desperately sin has corrupted the hearts of humankind
and every kind of relationship. As the metanarrative is renewed, it
points to the patience and persistent love of God, who steps into the
lives of people to heal their brokenness. It is in our hearts, so prone to
self, that Eden has been reformed.

Jesus intentionally steps into these stories, themes, and character
profiles as the very face of God who is "compassionate and gracious . . .
slow to anger, abounding in love and faithfulness," yet who "does not
leave the guilty unpunished" (Ex. 34:6–7 NIV).

With the inauguration of the new covenant (Luke 22:20; 1 Cor.
11:25; Heb. 12:24), we do not find in our world a full restoration to pre–
fall Edenic experience. On the one hand, there is tremendous blessing
in justification, forgiveness, redemption, reconciliation, regeneration,
sanctification, and adoption. Each of these has an *already* and a *not yet*
element. And God continues to use human agents to carry his plan
forward.

AMID PAIN AND SUFFERING

1. Describe the implications of God's constant use of *human agents* throughout Scripture. For example, how do their lives reflect the God who called them?

2. Explain the significance of so many Old Testament themes (e.g., suffering Messiah) and character types (e.g., Moses) flowing into the life and ministry of Jesus.

3. Tell what aspects of the new heaven and the new earth you are groaning for and describe how that groaning plays out in your life.

4. How does this statement make you feel: "All followers of Christ must embrace suffering before they can embrace glory"? Does it strike you as depressing or encouraging? Tell why.

5. Reflect on how this statement is true in your experience: "Truly Christian life means to exist between two worlds: the old world of sin and death and the new world of righteousness and life."

Notes

Introduction: A Different Approach

1. Kushner's book, *When Bad Things Happen to Good People* (New York: Random House, 2004), originally appeared in 1981.

2. Betty R. Ferrell and Nessa Coyle, *The Nature of Suffering and the Goals of Nursing* (New York: Oxford University Press, 2008), 15.

3. Richard J. Mouw, *Called to the Life of the Mind* (Grand Rapids: Eerdmans, 2014), 58.

4. James K. Voiss, *Rethinking Christian Forgiveness* (Collegeville, MN: Liturgical Press, 2015), 281–82; emphasis original.

5. Henri J. M. Nouwen, *The Living Reminder: Service and Prayer in Memory of Jesus Christ* (New York: Seabury Press, 1981), 22.

Chapter 1: The Grammar of Suffering: Basics of Affliction in Scripture

1. Thomas R. Schreiner, *Paul, Apostle of God's Glory in Christ* (Downers Grove, IL: InterVarsity, 2001), 87–102.

2. Walter C. Kaiser, "Eight Kinds of Suffering in the Old Testament," in *Suffering and the Goodness of God*, ed. Christopher W. Morgan and Robert A. Peterson (Wheaton, IL: Crossway, 2008), 65–78.

3. We may have recourse to the term "mental pain." This term is equivalent to "negative emotion" or "emotional pain" (e.g., grief, shame, sorrow, fear, anger, despair).

4. Patrick Wall, *Pain: The Science of Suffering* (New York: Columbia University Press, 2000), 12.

5. Betty R. Ferrell and Nessa Coyle, *The Nature of Suffering and the Goals of Nursing* (New York: Oxford University Press, 2008), 18.

6. R. F. Hurding, "Suffering," in *New Dictionary of Christian Ethics and Pastoral Theology*, ed. David J. Atkinson et al. (Downers Grove, IL: InterVarsity, 1995), 823.

7. Laura M. Parrott, "Anesthetic Management of a Patient with Congenital Insensitivity to Pain: A Case Report," *AANA Journal* 81 (2013): 376. Brand and Yancey call it "congenital indifference to pain"; see Paul Brand and Philip Yancey, *Pain: The Gift Nobody Wants* (New York: HarperCollins, 1993), 5.

8. Brand and Yancey, *Pain*, 5.

9. Russell Nieli, "The Santa Barbara Killings: When Envy Becomes the Deadliest Sin," *Public Discourse* (Witherspoon Institute), August 8, 2014 (http://www.thepublicdiscourse.com/2014/08/13555/).

10. Celicia Vega, "Santa Barbara Killer Smiled before Shooting, Survivor Says," *ABC News*, May 30, 2014 (http://abcnews.go.com/US/
santa-barbara-killer-elliot-rodger-smiled-shooting-survivor/story?id=23923970).

11. A similar perspective is found in Laura Schwecherl, "Why Athletes Can Handle More
Pain: Most Athletes Rely Instinctively on Brain over Body Tricks to Power through
Pain," *Time*, 25 October 2012, available at http://healthland.time.com/2012/10/25/
why-athletes-can-handle-more-pain/.

12. Eric J. Cassell, *The Nature of Suffering and the Goals of Medicine* (New York: Oxford
University Press, 1991), 35.

13. Ibid., 45.

14. Ibid., 44.

15. Gerald W. Peterman, *Joy and Tears: The Emotional Life of the Christian* (Chicago: Moody,
2013), 31. For more on the cognitive theory of emotions, see Matthew A. Elliot, *Faithful
Feelings: Rethinking Emotion in the New Testament* (Grand Rapids: Kregel, 2006); Robert
C. Roberts, *Spiritual Emotions: A Psychology of Christian Virtues* (Grand Rapids: Eerd-
mans, 2007); and *What Is an Emotion? Classic and Contemporary Readings*, ed. Robert
Solomon (New York: Oxford University Press, 2002).

16. Craig S. Keener, *Acts 3:1–14:28* (Grand Rapids: Baker, 2013), 1656.

17. Pamela J. Scalise, "The Way of Weeping: Reading the Path of Grief in Jeremiah," *Word &
World* 22 (2002): 415–22.

18. Walter Brueggemann, "Suffering," in *Reverberations of Faith: A Theological Handbook of
Old Testament Themes* (Louisville: Westminster John Knox, 2002), 203.

19. Rather clumsily, classic theology calls this "the fall," a theological "retrofit" taken from
Paul's writings (Rom. 5:12–21; 1 Cor. 15:21–22, 45–49). Yet the ontological origin of evil
is not Paul's concern. No word for sin is even used in Genesis 1–3! Nor does Genesis
know any "marring" of the image of God (cf. Gen. 9:6). Instead, this biblical text details
the "fallout" of the relational ecosystem, an estrangement that now exists between all
parties: God, ground, animals, humankind, and even the reality of personal shame.

20. F. P. Cotterell, "Suffering," in *New Dictionary of Biblical Theology*, ed. Brian S. Rosner et al
(Downers Grove, IL: InterVarsity, 2000), 802.

21. Brueggemann, "Suffering," 202.

22. Ibid., 202–3.

23. Samuel E. Balentine, "Suffering and Evil," in *New Interpreter's Dictionary of the Bible*, vol.
5 (Nashville: Abingdon, 2009), 391.

24. Ibid., 390.

25. Rosemary Gates Winslow, "Troping Trauma: Conceiving (of) Experiences of Speechless Terror," *Journal of Advanced Composition* 24, Special Issue, Part Two: Trauma and
Rhetoric (2004): 607–33.

26. Some forms of trauma require talking or other forms of active communication as a
means of transferring traumatic experiences that are stored in one part of the brain into
the limbic system, the "feeling" part of the brain. Like defragging a hard drive, this allows
needed integration of event with emotion. Events that are "too painful to talk about"
reflect the great challenge of this integrative process. See Martin H. Teicher, Carol A.
Glod, Janet Surrey, and Chester Swett, "Early Childhood Abuse and Limbic System Rat-
ings in Adult and Psychiatric Outpatients," *The Journal of Neuropsychiatry and Clinical
Neurosciences* 5 (1993): 301–6.

27. Balentine, "Suffering and Evil," 391.

28. Allen P. Ross, *Holiness to the Lord* (Grand Rapids: Baker, 2002), 348.

29. For further discussion, see Warren McWilliams, "Animal Suffering," in *Where Is the God of Justice?* (Grand Rapids: Hendrickson, 2005), 156–70.

30. Balentine, "Suffering and Evil," 390.

31. Ibid.

32. Ibid.

33. Much of the following information comes from Balentine, "Suffering and Evil," 390–91.

34. A helpful study is Andy L. Warren–Rothlin, "Body Idioms and The Psalms," in *Interpreting the Psalms*, ed. David Firth and Philip S. Johnston (Downers Grove, IL: InterVarsity, 2005), 195–212.

35. Rooted in creation theology, the relational ecosystem refers to the interrelationship of all created life: God with humankind, humankind with animals, humankind with the earth, and the man with the woman (Genesis 1–2; Psalm 8). These are core bindings that help define personhood, function, ethics, and the human responsibility as God's vice–regents. Sin's consequences tear apart the relational ecosystem (cf. Rom. 8:19–22).

36. Theodicy attempts to defend God as all–powerful, loving, and just, despite the reality of evil experienced in life.

37. L. Ann Jervis, "Suffering," in *Dictionary of Scripture and Ethics*, ed. Joel B. Green (Grand Rapids: Baker, 2011), 756.

38. Ibid.

39. Walter Brueggemann, *Ichabod Toward Home: The Journey of God's Glory* (Grand Rapids: Eerdmans, 2002), 15.

40. "Grief and Mourning," *The Baker Illustrated Bible Dictionary*, ed. Tremper Longman III (Grand Rapids: Baker, 2013), 708–9.

41. Balentine, "Suffering and Evil," 390.

42. Ibid.

43. The closest we come to this expression is found in the parable of the Good Samaritan where we find that "by chance [*kata sungkurian*] a priest was going down that road" (Luke 10:31).

44. I. Howard Marshall, *The Gospel of Luke* (Grand Rapids: Eerdmans, 1978), 554.

45. Some scholars believe the cry does not reflect despair, asserting that the words must be read "within the context of Psalm 22 as a whole, as a confident prayer of One who did not lose faith even in the midst of his aloneness" (L. P. Trudinger, " 'Eli, Eli, Lama Sabachthani?': A Cry of Dereliction or Victory?" *Journal of the Evangelical Theological Society* 17 [1974]: 235). R. T. France rightly criticizes this view (The Gospel of Matthew [Grand Rapids: Eerdmans, 2007]: 1076) following the seminal work of D. J. Moo, *The Old Testament in the Gospel Passion Narratives* (Sheffield: Almond, 1983), 171–74. See also Bruce D. Marshall, "The Dereliction of Christ and the Impassibility of God," in *Divine Impassibility and the Mystery of Human Suffering*, ed. James F. Keating and Thomas Joseph White (Grand Rapids: Eerdmans, 2009), 246–98.

46. Darrell L. Bock, *Luke 1:1–9:50* (Grand Rapids: Baker, 1994), 848.

47. Taken from "Essentials of Buddhism" at http://www.buddhaweb.org/. See also "Four Noble Truths," in *The HarperCollins Dictionary of Religion*, ed. Jonathan Z. Smith and William Scott Green (San Francisco: HarperCollins, 1995), 366.

48. This richness of emotions is hidden from the reader of the *Dictionary of Jesus and the Gospels*, ed. Joel B. Green (Downers Grove, IL: InterVarsity, 2013). It includes articles on joy, love, and peace but neglects anger, grief, and tears.

49. Many scholars miss the richness of these emotions, choosing to focus only on the pleasant. For example, a recent commentary on Philippians always comments on Paul's joy (sometimes extensively). On the other hand, Epaphroditus's distress (2:26), Paul's reference to "sorrow upon sorrow" (2:27), and Paul's stated desire to "have less anxiety" (2:28 NIV) are ignored. Further, Paul's tears over the enemies of the gospel (3:18) receive only one short paragraph. See G. W. Peterman, "Review of Philippians, by Lynn H. Cohick, The Story of God Bible Commentary," *Journal of the Evangelical Theological Society* 57 (2014): 639–40. This lack reflects a common problem: we like talking about so-called "positive" emotions but not so-called "negative" ones.

50. Mel Schwartz, "Can Your Feelings Be Wrong?" in the blog Shift of Mind, 18 May 2010; available at http://www.psychologytoday.com/blog/shift-mind/201005/can-your-feelings-be-wrong.

51. Thus Roy E. Ciampa and Brian S. Rosner correctly call this "godly sorrow" in *The First Letter to the Corinthians* (Grand Rapids: Eerdmans, 2010), 201 n. 54. To assert that mourning has emotional content, however, is not to deny that appropriate action is also involved.

Chapter 2: Groaning Together: The Relational Ecosystem of Sin and Suffering

1. William Blake, "The Book of Thel II," in *Poetry and Prose of William Blake*, ed. Geoffrey Keynes (London, UK: Nonesuch, 1939), 164.

2. Howard A. Snyder and Joel Scandrett, *Salvation Means Creation Healed: The Ecology of Sin and Grace* (Eugene, OR: Cascade, 2011), 68.

3. Anthony C. Thiselton, *Systematic Theology* (Grand Rapids: Eerdmans, 2015), 102; emphasis added.

4. James K. Mead, *Biblical Theology* (Louisville: Westminster John Knox, 2007), 242.

5. John MacMurry, *Self as Agent* (New York: Humanity Press, 1991), 17.

6. Miroslav Volf, *The End of Memory* (Grand Rapids: Eerdmans, 2006), 99.

7. William P. Brown, *The Ethos of the Cosmos* (Grand Rapids: Eerdmans, 1999), esp. 46–52.

8. Terence E. Fretheim, "Creator, Creature, and Co-Creation in Genesis 1–2," in *What Kind of God?* Literature and Theology of the Hebrew Scriptures, ed. Michael J. Chan and Brent A. Strawn (Winona Lake, IN: Eisenbrauns, 2015), 204–5; emphasis added.

9. This is why, in judgment, God goes silent (Gen. 7:7–8:15)—chaos reasserts itself in *un-creation*.

10. S. D. McBride Jr., "Divine Protocol: Genesis 1:1–2:3 as Prologue to the Pentateuch," in *God Who Creates*, ed. W. P. Brown and S. D. McBride Jr. (Grand Rapids: Eerdmans, 2000), 12.

11. Joseph Blenkinsopp, *The Pentateuch* (New York: Doubleday, 1992), 61–62.

12. John Goldingay, *Old Testament Theology: Israel's Life*, vol. 3 (Downers Grove, IL: InterVarsity, 2009), 640–41; emphasis added.

13. Throughout the Pentateuch, God's "seeing" connotes oversight and judicious discernment (cf. Gen. 6:5, 12; 11:5; 16:13–14; Ex. 2:25; 32:9; Deut. 32:19–20, etc.)

14. Terence E. Fretheim, *God and World in the Old Testament: A Relational Theology of*

Creation (Nashville: Abingdon, 2005), 273.

15. Not surprisingly, the final days of each triad (i.e., Days Three and Six) are the longest. In fact, they have double the amount of words as the other days (69 and 149, respectively; cf. Day 1 [31 words], Day 2 [38 words], Day 3 [69 words], Day 4 [69 words], Day 5 [57 words], and Day 6 [149 words])

16. Fretheim, *God and World*, 275, 278–79; emphasis added.

17. Daniel I. Block, "To Serve and To Keep: Toward a Biblical Understanding of Humanity's Responsibility in the Face of the Biodiversity Crisis," in *Keeping God's Earth*, ed. N. J. Toly and D. I. Block (Downers Grove, IL: InterVarsity, 2010), 130.

18. John Goldingay, *Old Testament Theology: Israel's Life* (Downers Grove, IL: InterVarsity, 2009), 3:642, 461.

19. Fretheim, *God and World*, 316, no. 112; emphasis added.

20. Judgment is evident when these three Mandate–domains of Gen 1:28 are *reversed*, as in Gen. 7:23 (= flood) and Hab. 1:14 (= Babylonian destruction).

21. Henry Cook and John R.Wood, "Looking at Nature through Other Eyes: God's Governance of Nature in the Religion–Science Debate," *Christian Scholar's Review* 39 (2010): 275–90.

22. Ibid., 290.

23. Andrew J. Schmutzer, *Be Fruitful and Multiply: A Crux of Thematic Repetition in Genesis 1–11* (Eugene, OR: Wipf & Stock, 2011), 159–204.

24. John H.Walton, *Ancient Near Eastern Thought and the Old Testament* (Grand Rapids: Baker, 2006), 93–97.

25. S. D. McBride, Jr., "Divine Protocol," 16.

26. J. Richard Middleton, *The Liberating Image: The Imago Dei in Genesis 1* (Grand Rapids: Baker, 2005), 15–90.

27. The Hebrew prefixed verbal form with *waw* conjunctive ("so that they may rule") following the cohortative ("let us make") is a *purpose* construction; R.Van Leeuwen, "Form, Image," in *New International Dictionary of Old Testament Theology and Exegesis*, ed W. A. VanGemeren (Grand Rapids: Zondervan, 1997) 4:645 (so NET, NIV, NEB, and CEB).

28. Terence E. Fretheim, "The Book of Genesis," in *The New Interpreter's Bible: A Commentary in Twelve Volumes* (Nashville: Abingdon, 1994), 1:346; H. J. Zobel, "*radah*" *Theological Dictionary of the Old Testament*, ed. G. J. Botterweck et al. (Grand Rapids: Eerdmans, 1995), 13:335.

29. S. Wagner, "*kavash*" *Theological Dictionary of the Old Testament*, ed. G. J. Botterweck et al. (Grand Rapids: Eerdmans, 1995) 7:54.

30. Ellen J.Van Wolde, "Rhetorical, Linguistic and Literary Features in Genesis 1," in *Literary Structure and Rhetorical Strategies in the Hebrew Bible*, ed. L. J. de Regt, Jan de Waard, and J. P. Fokkelman (Winona Lake, IN: Eisenbrauns, 1996), 149.

31. Patrick D. Miller, "Man and Woman: Toward a Theological Anthropology," in *The Way of the Lord: Essays in Old Testament Theology* (Grand Rapids: Eerdmans, 2007), 311–12.

32. Jürgen Moltmann, *God in Creation: An Ecological Doctrine of Creation* (London: SCM Press, 1985), 279.

33. Miller, "Man and Woman," 312.

34. John Kessler, *Old Testament Theology* (Waco, TX: Baylor University Press, 2013), 254; emphasis original.

35. Ibid.

36. J. Richard Middleton, "Image of God," in *Dictionary of Scripture and Ethics*, ed. Joel B. Green (Grand Rapids: Baker, 2011), 395.

37. Van der Woude, "*panim*," *Theological Lexicon of the Old Testament*, ed. E. Jenni and C. Westermann (Peabody, MA: Hendrickson, 1997), 2:1001.

38. William J. Dumbrell, *The Faith of Israel: A Theological Survey of the Old Testament*, 2nd ed. (Grand Rapids: Baker, 2002), 18; cf. *Dumbrell, The Search for Order* (Grand Rapids: Baker, 1994), 22; emphasis added.

39. Fretheim, *God and World*, 64.

40. Walter Brueggemann, "Sabbath," in *Reverberations of Faith: A Theological Handbook of Old Testament Themes* (Louisville, KY: John Knox Press, 2002), 180.

41. Michael Fishbane, *Text and Texture: Close Readings of Selected Biblical Texts* (New York: Schocken, 1979), 11–13.

42. Bruce K.Waltke, *Genesis* (Grand Rapids: Zondervan, 2001), 68.

43. Jon D. Levenson, "Genesis: Introduction," in *The Jewish Study Bible: Torah, Nevi'im, Kethuvim* (New York: Oxford University Press, 2004), 8.

44. Nahum M. Sarna, *Genesis*. The JPS Torah Commentary (Philadelphia: The Jewish Publication Society, 1998), 27.

45. Walter C. Kaiser et al., *Hard Sayings of the Bible* (Downers Grove, IL: InterVarsity, 1996), 90.

46. Cornelius Plantinga, Jr., *Not the Way It's Supposed to Be* (Grand Rapids: Eerdmans, 1995), 5.

47. Mark E. Biddle, *Missing the Mark: Sin and Its Consequences in Biblical Theology* (Nashville: Abingdon, 2005), xviii.

48. Plantinga, *Not the Way*, 30.

49. Ibid., 25, 26; emphasis added.

50. Biddle, *Missing the Mark*, 96; emphasis added.

51. Ibid., 97.

52. Ibid., 117.

53. Ibid., 120.

54. Ibid., 128.

55. Ibid., 135.

56. Ibid., 130.

57. Plantinga, *Not the Way*, 43.

58. Ibid., 44.

59. Ibid., 44, 45.

60. Alistair McFadyen, *Bound to Sin* (Cambridge, UK: Cambridge University Press, 2000), 221, 223, 237.

61. Bruce C. Birch, Walter Brueggemann, Terence E. Fretheim, and David L.Petersen, *A Theological Introduction to the Old Testament* (Nashville: Abingdon, 1999), 42.

62. Kessler, *Old Testament Theology*, 168.

63. John D. Zizioulas, *Being as Communion* (New York: St.Vladimir's Seminary Press, 1997), 18.

64. Ibid., 170.

65. Kessler, *Old Testament Theology*, 171.

66. Thiselton, *Systematic Theology*, 153.

67. Ibid., 175.

68. Ibid.

69. Veli–Matti Kärkkäinen, *Creation and Humanity, A Constructive Christian Theology for the Pluralistic World*, vol. 3 (Grand Rapids: Eerdmans, 2015), 291–92.

70. Elizabeth Boase, "The Traumatized Body: Communal Trauma and Somatization in Lamentations," in *Trauma and Traumatization in Individual and Collective Dimensions: Insights from Biblical Studies and Beyond*, ed. Eve–Marie Becker, Jan Dochhorn, and Else K. Holt. Studia Aarhusiana Neotestamentica, vol. 2 (Göttingen, Germany: Vandenhoeck & Ruprecht, 2014), 195, 196.

Chapter 3: The Suffering of God: Compassion in Vulnerability

1. Thomas Moore, *Care of the Soul: A Guide for Cultivating Depth and Sacredness in Everyday Life* (New York: HarperPerennial, 1994), 55–65.

2. Craig G. Bartholomew and Michael W. Goheen, *The Drama of Scripture: Finding Our Place in the Biblical Story* (Grand Rapids: Baker, 2004), 12.

3. Aristophanes, *The Frogs*, trans. D. Barrett (London: Penguin Books, 1964), 179.

4. William C. Placher, *Narratives of a Vulnerable God: Christ, Theology, and Scripture* (Louisville: Westminster John Knox, 1994), 4.

5. Allan Aubrey Boesak, *Dare We Speak of Hope? Searching for a Language of Life in Faith and Politics* (Grand Rapids: Eerdmans, 2014), 34.

6. Ibid., 37–38.

7. Ibid., "Dare We Speak of Hope? Only If We Speak of Woundedness," 24–42.

8. Ibid., 42; quoting the phrase by Derrick Bell, *Faces at the Bottom of the Well: The Permanence of Racism* (New York: Basic Books, 1992).

9. See Simon Chan, *Spiritual Theology: A Systematic Study of the Christian Life* (Downers Grove, IL: InterVarsity, 1998), 15–39; also Kazo Kitamori, *Theology of the Pain of God* (Eugene, OR: Wipf & Stock, 1958).

10. See the excellent study of John Kessler, "The Theology of Divine Accessibility," in *Old Testament Theology: Divine Call and Human Response* (Waco, TX: Baylor University Press, 2013), 381–445.

11. L. A. Markos, "Myth Matters," *Christianity Today*, 23 April 2001, 35–36; emphasis added.

12. Walter Brueggemann, *An Unsettling God: The Heart of the Hebrew Bible* (Minneapolis: Fortress, 2009), 1.

13. In *Walking with God through Pain and Suffering* (New York: Dutton, 2013), Timothy Keller acknowledges in the chapter titled "The Suffering of God" that "the suffering of God is indicated already in the Hebrew Scriptures, long before the coming of Jesus into the world" (148). But Keller moves very quickly to the suffering of Jesus, with scant exploration of those Hebrew texts. Some classic biblical texts that disclose the suffering of God include: Gen. 6:5–6; Hos. 9:15; 11:8–9; Isa. 49:15; 63:9, 15; 66:13; Jer. 18:7–10; 31:20; Pss. 78:40–41, 58–59; 103:13. Two of the best volumes addressing the suffering of God are Terence E. Fretheim, *The Suffering of God: An Old Testament Perspective* (Philadelphia: Fortress, 1984), and Richard J. Mouw and Douglas A. Sweeney, *The Suffering*

and Victorious Christ: Toward a More Compassionate Christology (Grand Rapids: Baker, 2013).

14. For celebration of reformed metaphysical austerity, see James Dolezal, *God Without Parts: Divine Simplicity and the Metaphysics of God's Absoluteness* (Eugene, OR: Pickwick, 2011). A classic philosophical theism is Thomas G. Weinandy, *Does God Suffer?* (Notre Dame: University of Notre Dame Press, 2000).

15. Kevin J. Vanhoozer, *Is There a Meaning in This Text?* (Grand Rapids: Zondervan, 2002), 426.

16. G. B. Caird, *The Language and Imagery of the Bible* (Philadelphia: Westminster, 1980), 174. "Thus anthropomorphism is something more than the imposing of man's preconceived and limited images on the divine. There is something that answers back in perpetual dialogue" (182).

17. Terence E. Fretheim, "The Repentance of God: A Key to Evaluating Old Testament God-Talk," in *Horizons in Biblical Theology* 10 (1988): 51; emphasis added.

18. Kenneth A. Mathews, *Genesis 1–11:26*. The New American Commentary, vol. 1A (Nashville: Broadman & Holman, 1996), 344.

19. Terence E. Fretheim, *About the Bible: Short Answers to Big Questions*, rev. ed. (Minneapolis: Augsburg, 2009), 58–59; emphasis added.

20. Brueggemann, *An Unsettling God*, 2.

21. Kevin J. Vanhoozer, *Remythologizing Theology: Divine Action, Passion, and Authorship.* Cambridge Studies in Christian Doctrine 18 (New York: Cambridge University Press, 2010), 60.

22. That said, some appeal to theological syllogism regarding divine ontology to defend impassibility. Paul Helm, for example, argues: (1) God is timelessly eternal; (2) Whatever is timelessly eternal is unchangeable; and (3) Whatever is unchangeable is impassible. (4) Therefore, God is impassible. See "The Impossibility of Divine Passibility," in *The Power and Weakness of God: Impassibility and Orthodoxy*, ed. Nigel M. de S. Cameron (Edinburgh: Rutherford, 1990), 119.

23. Kevin J. Vanhoozer, *First Theology: God, Scripture, and Hermeneutics* (Downers Grove, IL: InterVarsity, 2002), 74; emphasis added.

24. See the insightful cultural critique by Brueggemann, *An Unsettling God*, 1–17.

25. "Patripassianism" was labeled a heresy in the modalism controversy, not because Trinitarian suffering has no biblical basis, but because of Greek philosophical notions of impassibility; see Millard J. Erickson, *Christian Theology*, 2nd ed. (Grand Rapids: Baker, 2009), 360.

26. Roger E. Olson, "God, Existence and Nature of," in *The Westminster Handbook to Evangelical Theology* (Louisville: Westminster John Knox, 2004), 190.

27. Placher, *Vulnerable God*, 5.

28. Richard Bauckham, "'Only the Suffering God Can Help': Divine Passibility in Modern Theology," *Themelios* 99 (1984): 7.

29. Thomas J. Oord, *The Nature of Love: A Theology* (St. Louis: Chalice, 2010), 17.

30. J. Stevenson, *Creeds, Councils, and Controversies* (London: SPCK, 1966), 336.

31. See "Westminster Confession of Faith" (chap. 2) at http://www.reformed.org/documents/wcf_with_proofs/.

32. Erickson, *Christian Theology*, 295 n. 14; emphasis added. Actually, the fault lines run more along Reformed versus Arminian views of divine relationality.

33. Barry L. Callen, *Discerning the Divine: God in Christian Theology* (Louisville: Westminster John Knox, 2014), 23.

34. Olson, "God," *Westminster Handbook*, 190.

35. John S. Feinberg, *No One Like Him* (Wheaton, IL: Crossway, 2001), 31.

36. D. A. Carson, *How Long, O Lord? Reflections on Suffering and Evil*, 2nd ed. (Grand Rapids: Baker, 2006), 165; emphasis added.

37. Nicholas Wolterstorff, "Suffering Love," in *Philosophy and the Christian Faith*, ed. T. V. Morris (Notre Dame, IN: University of Notre Dame Press, 1990), 209, 210; emphasis original.

38. Brueggemann, *An Unsettling God*, 5.

39. Terence E. Fretheim, *The Suffering of God* (Philadelphia: Fortress, 1984), 5–8, 109–13.

40. Mathews, *Genesis*, 344.

41. Fretheim, *The Suffering of God*, 112.

42. Mathews, *Genesis*, 341.

43. Walter Brueggemann, *Genesis: Interpretation: A Bible Commentary for Teaching and Preaching* (Atlanta: John Knox, 1982), 73, 81.

44. Brevard S. Childs, *The Book of Exodus: A Critical, Theological Commentary* (Louisville: Westminster, 1974), 73.

45. Fretheim, *The Suffering of God*, 83, 84.

46. Walter Brueggemann, "Exodus," in *The New Interpreter's Bible*, vol. 1 (Nashville: Abingdon, 1994), 712.

47. Thomas W. Mann, *The Book of the Torah*, 2nd ed. (Eugene, OR: Cascade, 2013), 101.

48. Fretheim, *The Suffering of God*, 110.

49. Ibid., 121.

50. Samuel E. Balentine, *Prayer in the Hebrew Bible*. Overtures to Biblical Theology (Minneapolis: Fortress, 1993), 132–33.

51. If pre–flood humanity had had a mediator like Moses, as Israel experienced in the wilderness period, maybe the suffering would have been modified. Regardless, after the flood we see God in self–limitation (Gen. 8:21). A flood is no longer an option for God.

52. Balentine, *Prayer in the Hebrew Bible*, 134.

53. J. Hausmann, "*salah*," in *Theological Dictionary of the Old Testament*, vol. 10, ed. G. J. Botterweck et al. (Grand Rapids: Eerdmans, 2000), 262.

54. Ibid., 143.

55. Fretheim, *The Suffering of God*, 124–25.

56. K. Seybold, "*haphakh*," in *Theological Dictionary of the Old Testament*, vol. 3 (Grand Rapids: Eerdmans, 1999), 426, 427.

57. Richard D. Patterson, "Hosea," in *Minor Prophets: Hosea–Malachi*. Cornerstone Biblical Commentary (Carol Stream, IL: Tyndale, 2008), 68.

58. Fretheim, *The Suffering of God*, 120.

59. Robert B. Chisholm Jr., *Handbook on the Prophets* (Grand Rapids: Baker, 2002), 362.

60. Fretheim, *The Suffering of God*, 143.

61. David A. Bosworth, "The Tears of God in the Book of Jeremiah," *Biblica* 94 (2013): 25.

62. Ibid.

63. Ibid., 27.

64. J. J. M. Roberts, "The Motif of the Weeping God in Jeremiah and Its Background in the Lament Tradition of the Ancient Near East," in *The Bible and the Ancient Near East* (Winona Lake, IN: Eisenbrauns, 2002), 132–42.

65. Fretheim, *The Suffering of God*, 160–61.

66. Bosworth, "The Tears of God," 33.

67. Peter C. Craigie, Page H. Kelley, and Joel F. Drinkard Jr., *Jeremiah 1–25*. Word Biblical Commentary, vol. 26 (Dallas: Word, 1991), 145.

68. Ibid.

69. Bosworth, "The Tears of God," 38.

70. Roberts, "The Weeping God," 135.

71. Bosworth, "The Tears of God," 40.

72. Ibid., 44–45.

73. Gregory Stevenson, A *Slaughtered Lamb: Revelation and the Apocalyptic Response to Evil and Suffering* (Abilene, TX: Abilene Christian University Press, 2013), 129–30.

74. Richard Bauckham, *The Climax of Prophecy: Studies on the Book of Revelation* (Edinburgh: T&T Clark, 1993), 214.

75. "Looking as if/though it had been slain" (ESV, NIV, CEB) is not clear enough to be helpful. "As advertised" means actually advertised, not just in words. See Gregg K. Beale, *The Book of Revelation* (Grand Rapids: Eerdmans, 1999), 352. The Greek *esphagmenon* (perfect participle, "having been slain") expresses an ongoing condition resulting from a past act. The struggle among translations to reflect this dynamic is obvious: "seemed to have been slain" (JB), "a lamb that appeared to have been killed" (NET), "looked as if it had been slaughtered" (NLT), are interpretively unclear, with "like a slain lamb" (HCSB) or "a lamb with the marks of slaughter upon him" (NEB) being preferable.

76. Stevenson, *A Slaughtered Lamb*, 133.

77. Bauckham, *The Climax of Prophecy*, 215.

78. Ibid.

79. See Herbert W. Bateman IV, Darrell L. Bock, and Gordon H. Johnston, *Jesus the Messiah* (Grand Rapids: Kregel, 2012), esp. "Messiah Confessed: Revelation and the Catholic Epistles," 336–39.

80. Stevenson, *A Slaughtered Lamb*, 133.

81. Ibid., 143.

82. Peter Hicks, *The Message of Evil & Suffering. The Bible Speaks Today* (Downers Grove, IL: InterVarsity, 2006), 75, 76.

83. Ibid., 81–82.

84. Loren T. Stuckenbruck, "Revelation," in *Eerdmans Commentary on the Bible*, ed. James D. G. Dunn (Grand Rapids: Eerdmans, 2003), 1546.

85. This is also the opinion of Daniel Castelo, "Continued Grappling: The Divine Impassibility Debates Today," *International Journal of Systematic Theology* 12 (2010): 364–72; see also Timothy Wiarda, "Divine Passibility in Light of Two Pictures of Intercession," *Scottish Journal of Theology* 66 (2013): 159–73.

86. Wiarda, "Divine Passibility," 71.

87. Jürgen Moltmann, *The Trinity and the Kingdom of God: The Doctrine of God*, trans. Margaret Kohl (London: SCM Press, 1981), 23.

88. Placher, *A Vulnerable God*, 15, quoting Hans Frei, *Types of Christian Theology* (New Haven, CT: Yale University Press, 1992), 126.

89. Michael S. Horton, *A Place for Weakness: Preparing Yourself for Suffering* (Grand Rapids: Zondervan, 2006), 89.

90. Placher, *A Vulnerable God*, 14, 18.

91. Ibid., 20.

92. Ibid., 18, 21.

93. Ibid., 21.

94. Walter Brueggemann, "Suffering," in *Reverberations of Faith: A Theological Handbook of Old Testament Themes* (Louisville: Westminster John Knox, 2002), 203–4.

95. Charles Wesley, "Arise, My Soul, Arise," in *Hymns for the Living Church* (Carol Stream, IL: Hope Publishing Company, 1974), 250. In public domain.

96. Nicholas Wolterstorff, *Lament for a Son* (Grand Rapids: Eerdmans, 1987), 81, as quoted in Jerry Sittser, *A Grace Disguised* (Grand Rapids: Zondervan, 2004), 148.

Chapter 4: A Man of Sorrows: Emotions and the Suffering of Jesus

1. http://www.rottentomatoes.com/m/passion_of_the_christ/.

2. See B. B. Warfield, "The Emotional Life of Our Lord," in *Biblical and Theological Studies* (1912) reprinted in *The Person and Work of Christ* (Philadelphia: Presbyterian and Reformed Publishing, 1970), 93–145. More recently, see G. Walter Hansen, "The Emotions of Jesus and Why We Need to Experience Them," *Christianity Today*, 3 February 1997, 43–47.

3. Frederick Buechner, *Wishful Thinking: A Theological ABC* (New York: Harper & Row, 1973), 15.

4. Walter Bauer, *A Greek–English Lexicon of the New Testament and Other Early Christian Literature*, "splanchnizomai" (Chicago: University of Chicago Press, 2000). In the New Testament we find the verb at Matt. 9:36; 14:14; 15:32; 18:27; 20:34; Mark 1:41; 6:34; 8:2; 9:22; Luke 7:13; 10:33; 15:20, and the noun (*splangchna*) at Luke 1:78; Acts 1:18; 2 Cor. 6:12; 7:15; Phil. 1:8; 2:1; Col. 3:12; Philem. 7, 12, 20; 1 John 3:17.

5. R. T. France, *The Gospel of Matthew* (Grand Rapids: Eerdmans, 2007), 373.

6. D. L. Parkyn, "Compassion," in *New Dictionary of Christian Ethics and Pastoral Theology*, ed. David J. Atkinson et al. (Downers Grove, IL: InterVarsity, 1995), 244.

7. Gerald Peterman, *Joy and Tears: The Emotional Life of the Christian* (Chicago: Moody, 2013), 74–75.

8. Robert H. Stein, *Mark* (Grand Rapids: Baker, 2008), 154.

9. Warfield, "The Emotional Life of Our Lord," 107.

10. E.g., René Lopez, "In the Market" with Janet Parshall radio broadcast, WMBI–FM, 29 March 2013. Reinhold Bonnke in "Was Jesus Afraid?" (http://www.bonnke.net/cfan/en/was–jesus–afraid) asserts that Jesus was never afraid and says, "He rejoiced in everything he did as a warrior rejoices in combat."

11. Denny Burk, professor of biblical studies at Boyce College, Louisville; see Denny Burk, "Did Jesus experience 'doubt' and 'fear'?" 4 April 2012 (http://www.dennyburk.com/president-obama-on-jesus-doubts-and-fears/).

12. The "Christian" perspective that all fear is sinful is probably dependent, in part, on American culture at large. Its growing aversion to fear and its desire to medicate it away is well documented in Allan V. Horowitz and Jerome C. Wakefield, *All We Have to Fear: Psychiatry's Transformation of Natural Anxieties into Mental Disorders* (New York: Oxford University Press, 2012).

13. Brian S. Borgman, *Feelings and Faith: Cultivating Godly Emotions in the Christian Life* (Wheaton, IL: Crossway, 2009), 124.

14. Other examples include Gen. 43:23; 46:3; Josh. 10:25; 11:6; Judg. 4:18; 1 Sam. 4:20; 12:20; 22:23; 28:13; 2 Kings 1:15, 6:16; 19:6; 25:24; 1 Chron. 28:20; Neh. 4:14; Prov. 3:25; Isa. 37:6; Jer. 1:8; 10:5; 40:9; Matt. 14:27; 28:5; 10; John 6:20; Acts 18:9; 27:24.

15. Darrell Bock, *Luke 9:51–24:53* (Grand Rapids: Baker, 1999), 1754.

16. See discussion on "the cup of wrath" in D. T. Lamb, "Wrath," *Dictionary of Old Testament Prophecy*, ed. Mark J. Boda and J. Gordon McConville (Downers Grove, IL: InterVarsity, 2012), 880.

17. Here I depart from the ESV (as well as the NASB and HCSB) and follow the NIV (2011): "All inhabitants of the earth will worship the beast—all whose names have not been written in the Lamb's book of life, the Lamb who was slain from the creation of the world." In support of this translation see Grant R. Osborne, *Revelation* (Grand Rapids: Baker, 2002), 503, and G. K. Beale, *The Book of Revelation* (Grand Rapids: Eerdmans, 1999), 702–3.

18. Scott Bader-Saye, "Fear in the Garden: the State of Emergency and the Politics of Blessing," *Ex Auditu* 24 (2008): 10–11.

19. *Taber's Cyclopedic Medical Dictionary,* 19th ed. (Philadelphia: F. A. Davis Company, 2001), 909.

20. Varna Naidu et al., "Hematohidrosis," *Indian Journal of Dermatology, Venereology & Leprology* 75 (2009): 318. See also H. R. Jerajani, Bhagyashri Jaju, M. M. Phiske, and Nitin Lade, "Hematohidrosis—A Rare Clinical Phenomenon," *Indian Journal of Dermatology* 54 (2009): 290–92; J. E. Holoubek and A. B. Holoubek, "Blood, Sweat and Fear: A Classification of Hematidrosis," *Journal of Medicine* 27 (1996): 115–33; and William D. Edwards, Wesley J. Gabel, and Floyd E. Hosmer, "On the Physical Death of Jesus Christ," *Journal of American Medical Association* 255, no. 11 (1986): 1455–63.

21. Paul Ellingworth answers the question negatively (*The Epistle to the Hebrews* [Grand Rapids: Eerdmans, 1993], 286) as does Luke T. Johnson (*Hebrews* [Louisville: WJKP, 2006], 145). Gareth L. Cockerill says "reference to Gethsemane is suggestive but is not definitive" (*The Epistle to the Hebrews* [Grand Rapids: Eerdmans, 2012], 244). Peter T. O'Brien says the most telling illustration of the words in 5.7 is the Garden (*The Letter to the Hebrews* [Grand Rapids: Eerdmans, 2010], 198).

22. David Allen, *Hebrews* (Nashville: B&H Publishing, 2010), 321–22. Similarly, R. Kent Hughes says, "As he considered the cup he must drink, he was astonished with horror" (*Hebrews Volume One: An Anchor for the Soul* [Wheaton, IL: Crossway, 1993], 141).

23. Our view here runs contrary to most and is close to that of Vincent Taylor, *The Gospel according to Mark* (London: MacMillan, 1952), 355.

24. John Nolland, *The Gospel of Matthew* (Grand Rapids: Eerdmans, 2005), 712.

25. Warfield, "The Emotional Life of Our Lord," 143–44.

Chapter 5: Longing to Lament: Returning to the Language of Suffering

1. W. Sibley Towner, " 'Without Our Aid He Did Us Make': Singing the Meaning of the Psalms," in *A God So Near*, ed. Brent A. Strawn and Nancy R. Bowen (Winona Lake, IN: Eisenbrauns, 2003), 33; emphasis added.

2. George Steiner, *Real Presences* (London, UK: Faber and Faber, 1986), 225.

3. Walter Brueggemann, *An Unsettling God* (Minneapolis: Fortress, 2009), 5.

4. John Goldingay, *Psalms for Everyone, Part 1* (Louisville: Westminster John Knox, 2013), 3.

5. Brueggemann, *An Unsettling God*, 13. Acknowledging the historical and cultural context of Scripture, biblical theology sees God's angelic court surrounding his throne in the plural "us" (cf. 1 Kings 22:19–22; Job 1:6; 2:1; Pss. 29:1–3; 89:5–7; Isa. 6:8; Dan. 10:12–13). Humankind is viewed as the terrestrial counterpart to God's heavenly entourage. See Michael S. Heiser, "Divine Council," in *Dictionary of the Old Testament: Wisdom, Poetry and Writings*, ed. Tremper Longman III and Peter Enns (Downers Grove, IL: InterVarsity, 2008), 112–16; S. Dean McBride Jr., "Divine Protocol: Genesis 1:1–2:3 as Prologue to the Pentateuch," in *God Who Creates*, ed. William P. Brown and S. Dean McBride Jr. (Grand Rapids: Eerdmans, 2000), 16.

6. Bruce C. Birch, Walter Brueggemann, Terence E. Fretheim, and David L. Peterson, *A Theological Introduction to the Old Testament* (Nashville: Abingdon, 1999), 41–53.

7. Jon D. Levenson, *Creation and the Persistence of Evil: The Jewish Drama of Divine Omnipotence* (San Francisco: Harper and Row, 1988), 19.

8. Brueggemann, *An Unsettling God*, 5.

9. Carleen Mandolfo, "Language of Lament in the Psalms," in *The Oxford Handbook of the Psalms*, ed. William P. Brown (Oxford: Oxford University Press, 2014), 114.

10. Claus Westermann, *Elements of Old Testament Theology*, trans. D. W. Scott (Atlanta: John Knox, 1982), 167–74.

11. Brueggemann, *An Unsettling God*, 13–14; emphasis original.

12. Samuel E. Balentine, *Prayer in the Hebrew Bible: The Drama of Divine–Human Dialogue* (Minneapolis: Fortress, 1993), 279.

13. I acknowledge and thank my previous student Adam Bottiglia for sharing some of these observations with me.

14. Nicholas Wolterstorff, "If God Is Good and Sovereign, Why Lament?" *Calvin Theological Journal* 36 (2001): 42; emphasis added.

15. See the helpful discussion of Kevin J. Vanhoozer, *Remythologizing Theology: Divine Action, Passion, and Authorship* (Cambridge, UK: Cambridge University Press, 2010), esp. "Triune dialogics: prayer and providence," 366–86. His discussion of prayer as communicative relationship rather than instrumental rationality—one manipulative of objects and the other the language of understanding between persons—creates helpful categories for prayer.

16. Arthur G. Patzia and Anthony J. Petrotta, *Pocket Dictionary of Biblical Studies* (Downers Grove, IL: InterVarsity, 2002), 70–71.

17. Philip S. Johnston, "The Psalms and Distress," in *Interpreting the Psalms* (Downers Grove, IL: InterVarsity, 2005), 72.

18. Mandolfo, "Language of Lament," 125.

19. Johnston, "The Psalms and Distress," 73.

20. Mandolfo, "Language of Lament," 125.

21. Walter Brueggemann, "The Lament," in *Reverberations of Faith* (Louisville: Westminster John Knox, 2002), 119. Psalms 39 and 88 seem to be the only exceptions to this phenomena, having no positive resolution common to the laments.

22. Tremper Longman III and Raymond B. Dillard, *An Introduction to the Old Testament*, 2nd ed. (Grand Rapids: Zondervan, 2006), 249.

23. Daniel J. Estes, "The Transformation of Pain into Praise in the Individual Lament Psalms," in *The Psalms: Language for All Seasons of the Soul*, ed. Andrew J. Schmutzer and David M. Howard Jr. (Chicago: Moody, 2013), 162.

24. Gregory Mobley, *The Return of the Chaos Monsters: And Other Backstories of the Bible* (Grand Rapids: Eerdmans, 2012), 100.

25. Terence E. Fretheim, *Creation Unbound* (Grand Rapids: Baker, 2010), 131.

26. John Goldingay, *Old Testament Theology: Israel's Gospel*, Vol. 1 (Downers Grove, IL: InterVarsity, 2003), 219.

27. Robin Routledge, *Old Testament Theology* (Downers Grove, IL: InterVarsity, 2008), 206.

28. Mobley, *The Return of the Chaos*, 97.

29. Cf. Pss. 35:22; 38:22; 71:12.

30. Cf. Pss. 22:25; 27:9; 30:8; 69:18; 88:15; 102:3; 143:7.

31. Christopher J. H. Wright, "Giving the Suffering Their Say," interview by Rob Moll, *Christianity Today*, July/August 2015, 67.

32. Bob Becking, "Ex Oriente Silentium," in *Reflections on the Silence of God. Old Testament Studies,* vol 62, ed. B. Becking (Leiden, Netherlands: Brill, 2013), 3, citing the argument of M. C. A. Korpel and J. C. de Moor, *The Silent God* (Leiden, Netherlands: Brill, 2011), 55–70.

33. The healing of Hezekiah powerfully illustrates God's attentiveness to human distress, and His willingness to change—even a stated outcome (2 Kings 20:1)! On the one hand, God says, "Set your house in order, for you shall die; you shall not recover" (2 Kings 20:1b). But after Hezekiah cries out to God, we read, "I have heard your prayer; I have seen your tears. Behold, I will heal you" (20:5b; cf. Ex. 3:9–10).

34. Phil C. Zylla, *The Roots of Sorrow* (Waco, TX: Baylor University Press, 2012), 90.

35. Ibid.; emphasis original.

36. Elna Solvang, "Can the Unrighteous Lament? Lament Speech and Reconciliation," in *Why?. . . How Long? Studies on Voice(s) of Lamentation Rooted in Biblical Hebrew Poetry*. Library of Old Testament Studies 552, ed. Leann Snow Flesher, Carol J. Dempsey, and Mark J. Boda (London: Bloomsbury, 2014), 162.

37. Zylla, *The Roots of Sorrow*, 72.

38. Ibid., 85.

39. See Walter Brueggemann, "The Formfulness of Grief," *Interpretation* 33 (1977): 263–75; Patrick D. Miller, *They Cried to the Lord: The Form and Theology of Biblical Prayer* (Minneapolis: Fortress Press, 1994), 55–177.

40. Mandolfo, "Language of Lament," 123.

41. The psalmists are calling for justice and vindication that operate within God's cosmic moral compass, not mere violence, intimidation, or vengeance (cf. Pss. 5:10; 6:10; 7:9; 8:2; 9:19–20; 28:4; 37:8–10, 35–36; 56:7; 104:35; 137:8; 139:19).

42. John Kessler, "The Theology of Divine Accessibility," in *Old Testament Theology: Divine Call and Human Response* (Waco, TX: Baylor University Press, 2013), 444.

43. Glenn Pemberton, *Hurting with God: Learning to Lament with the Psalms* (Abilene, TX: Abilene Christian University Press, 2012), 65; emphasis added.

44. Ronald Hendel, "Ritual," in *The Oxford Encyclopedia of The Bible and Law*, ed. Brent A. Strawn; vol. 2 Mag–Wom (Oxford: Oxford University Press, 2015), 241.

45. Alan Lenzi, "Invoking the God: Interpreting Invocations in Mesopotamian Prayers and Biblical Laments of the Individual," *Journal of Biblical Literature* (2010): 311.

46. Mandolfo, "Language of Lament," 122.

47. Cf. Pss. 17:9–11; 25:19; 35:14–15; 41:5–6; 140:4–5.

48. See the helpful analysis of W. Derek Suderman, "The Cost of Losing Lament for the Community of Faith: On Brueggemann, Ecclesiology, and the Social Audience of Prayer," *Journal of Theological Interpretation* 6 (2012): 201–18.

49. C. Hassell Bullock, *Psalms: Volume 1: Psalms 1–72*; Teach the Text Commentary Series, ed. Mark L. Strauss and John H. Walton (Grand Rapids: Baker, 2015), 414.

50. Horst D. Preuss, *Old Testament Theology*, vol. 2; OTL (Louisville, KY: Westminster John Knox, 1996), 248.

51. This is a key theme in the recent book by Bruce K. Waltke, James M. Houston, and Erika Moore, *The Psalms as Christian Lament: A Historical Commentary* (Grand Rapids: Eerdmans, 2014).

52. Discussed by Wolterstorff, "If God Is Good and Sovereign, Why Lament?" 50. See Wolterstorff's discussion of some Reformers' views of lament.

53. Ibid., 46. I grew up in South Africa toward the end of national apartheid. I saw firsthand how it was possible to emphasize God's use of destiny, collective force, and nationalist systems to such a degree that the voice of the individual victim was simply shut out.

54. As I write this, a beloved Christian college student headed back to school suffered a fatal accident. She and some friends had stopped at a beach en route to swim in Lake Michigan. The rip current took her away, while her friends were rescued. The parents and faith community need permission to lament their indescribable pain and loss. Much suffering is never courted, nor does it submit to reason.

55. Preuss, *Old Testament Theology*, 124. In the Psalter, נֶפֶשׁ (*nēpēš*) can be used for the whole of the human self, the "I," or simply "life" (Pss. 6:3–4; 7:2; 22:20; 26:9; 42:1–2; 55:18; 57:9), ibid., 124–25.

56. See Deborah van Deusen Hunsinger, *Bearing the Unbearable: Trauma, Gospel, and Pastoral Care* (Grand Rapids: Eerdmans, 2015), 100.

57. Cf. Ps. 44:9; 60:3; 90:15; cf. Ex. 5:22; Job 16:7, 9, 11–12. See the helpful discussion of Philip S. Johnston, "The Psalms of Distress," in *Interpreting the Psalms: Issues and Approaches*, ed. David Firth and Philip S. Johnston (Downers Grove, IL: IVP, 2005), 63–84.

58. R. W. L. Moberly, "Lament," in *New International Dictionary of Old Testament Theology and Exegesis*, ed. W. A. VanGemeren, vol. 4 (Grand Rapids: Zondervan, 1996), 880.

59. Ibid., 873.

60. Suderman, "Losing Lament," 202.

61. Claus Westermann, *Praise and Lament in the Psalms*, trans. Keith R. Crim and Richard N. Soulen (Atlanta: John Knox, 1981), 169.

62. Suderman, "Losing Lament," 208.

63. John D. Witvliet, *The Biblical Psalms in Christian Worship* (Grand Rapids: Eerdmans, 2007), 32.

64. Balentine, *Prayer in the Hebrew Bible*, 276.

65. Patrick D. Miller, "In Praise and Thanksgiving," *Theology Today* 45 (1988): 186–87.

66. Preuss, *Old Testament Theology*, 247.

67. Ibid., 126.

68. Ibid.

69. Mandolfo, "Language of Lament," 122.

70. It should not be surprising that God himself also laments: "And the Lord said to Moses, 'How long will this people despise me? And how long will they not believe in me?'" (Num. 14:11). Preuss states, "And when YHWH himself laments, then this demonstrates something about the God who suffers with his people (Jer. 2:10–13, 31; 3:20; 8:7; 12:7–13; 15:5–9; and 18:13–15a)" (*Old Testament Theology*, 248).

71. Walter Brueggemann, *The Message of the Psalms* (Minneapolis: Augsburg, 1984), 77.

72. William P. Brown, *Psalms* (Nashville: Abingdon, 2010), 140.

73. Walther Zimmerli, *Old Testament Theology in Outline*, trans. David E. Green (Atlanta: John Knox Press, 1978), 155.

74. Zylla, *The Roots of Sorrow*, 88; emphasis added.

75. Ibid., 75.

76. See Moberly, "Lament," 878.

77. See the helpful discussion of Brown, "Psalms as Theological Anthropology," in *Psalms 135–156*; also Patrick D. Miller, "What Is a Human Being? The Anthropology of the Psalter I," in *The Way of the Lord: Essays in Old Testament Theology* (Grand Rapids: Eerdmans, 2004), 226–36.

78. Zylla, *The Roots of Sorrow*, 87; emphasis added.

79. Ibid., 88.

80. Balentine, *Prayer in the Hebrew Bible*, 292.

81. Ibid., 290.

82. Zylla, *The Roots of Sorrow*, 77.

83. Ibid., 86.

84. Balentine, *Prayer in the Hebrew Bible*, 291.

85. Claus Westermann, "The Role of the Lament in the Theology of the Old Testament," *Interpretation* 28 (1974): 22.

86. Moberly, "Lament," 880.

87. Mary Douglas, "Violence," in *Dictionary of Scripture and Ethics*, ed. J. B. Green (Grand Rapids: Baker, 2011), 810.

88. "Knowledge vs. Information: When Trauma Stories Change You," Phil Monroe, 21 January 2015, "Musings of a Christian Psychologist," blog at https://wisecounsel.wordpress.com/2015/01/21/knowledge-vs-information-when-trauma-stories-change-you/.

89. Balentine, *Prayer in the Hebrew Bible*, 290.

90. R. W. L. Moberly, *Old Testament Theology: Reading the Hebrew Bible as Christian Scripture* (Grand Rapids: Baker, 2013), 226. Moberly's chapter on "Faith and Perplexity" (pp. 211–42) is a refreshing relational study in the discipline of OT Theology, which has historically shied away from the existential realities of the Christian life.

91. This discussion draws heavily from the insights of Moberly, *Old Testament Theology*, 233.

92. The interpretive insight of Mandolfo, "Language of Lament," 126.

93. Ibid.

94. Balentine, *Prayer in the Hebrew Bible*, 294–95; also quoting Elie Wiesel, *Souls on Fire* (New York: Vintage, 1973), 111; emphasis added.

95. Zylla, *The Roots of Sorrow*, 80.

96. Moberly, "Lament," 883.

97. Kessler, "The Theology of Divine Accessibility," 444.

98. Ibid., 437.

99. Ibid., 436–37.

100. Ibid., 439.

Chapter 6: Be Angry and Do Not Sin: Suffering and Redemptive Anger

1. *Seneca de Ira* 1.1.1–2. Lucius Annasus Seneca *Seneca's Essays*, vol. 1. *Moral Essays*, trans. John W. Basore (London: W. Heinemann, 1928–1935); http://www.stoics.com/seneca_essays_book_1.html#anger1.

2. Frederick Buechner, *Wishful Thinking: A Theological ABC* (New York: Harper & Row, 1973), 2.

3. There is a long history of such anger elimination. See William V. Harris, *Restraining Rage: The Ideology of Anger Control in Classical Antiquity* (Cambridge, MA: Harvard University Press, 2001).

4. This definition is modified from http://dictionary.reference.com/browse/anger. It defines anger as "a strong feeling of displeasure and belligerence aroused by a wrong; wrath; ire."

5. This section draws significantly from Gerald W. Peterman, *Joy and Tears: The Emotional Life of the Christian* (Chicago: Moody, 2013), 73–81.

6. Andrew D. Lester, *The Angry Christian: A Theology for Care and Counseling* (Louisville: Westminster John Knox, 2003), 206; emphasis original.

7. Matthew R. Schlimm, *From Fratricide to Forgiveness: The Language and Ethics of Anger in Genesis* (Winona Lake, IN: Eisenbrauns, 2011), 173.

8. Derek Kidner, *Ezra & Nehemiah* (Leicester, UK: Inter-Varsity, 1979), 95.

9. Charlie Summers, "Nehemiah 5:1–13," *Interpretation* 65 (2011): 184.

10. The verb (*dakruō*) only appears here in the New Testament. For the noun see Luke 7:38, 44; Acts 20:19, 31; 2 Cor. 2:4; 2 Tim. 1:4; Heb. 5:7; 12:17; Rev. 7:17; 21:4.

11. For example, *aganakteō*—be aroused, be indignant or angry (Mark 14:4; Luke 13:14); *aganaktēsis*—indignation (2 Cor. 7:11); *embrimaomai*—scold, censure (John 11:33, 38; Mark 1:43; 14:5; Matt. 9:30); *diaponeomai*—be (greatly) disturbed, annoyed (Acts 4:2; 16:18).

12. Brian Borgman, *Feelings and Faith: Cultivating Godly Emotions in the Christian Life* (Wheaton, IL: Crossway, 2009).

13. Daniel B. Wallace, "[*Orgizesthe*] in Ephesians 4:26: Command or Condition?" *Criswell Theological Review* 3 (1989): 372.

14. Ibid., 363.

15. See William Werpehowski, "Do You Do Well to Be Angry?" *Annual of the Society of Christian Ethics* (1996): 59–77.

16. Martin Luther King, Jr., in his "Letter from a Birmingham Jail" (16 April 1963), states it this way: "The Negro has many pent up resentments and latent frustrations, and he must release them. So let him march; let him make prayer pilgrimages to the city hall; let him go on freedom rides—and try to understand why he must do so. If his repressed emotions are not released in nonviolent ways, they will seek expression through violence; this is not a threat but a fact of history. So I have not said to my people: 'Get rid of your discontent.' Rather, I have tried to say that this normal and healthy discontent can be channeled into the creative outlet of nonviolent direct action." (Available at http://www.africa.upenn.edu/ Articles_Gen/Letter_Birmingham.html.)

17. B. B. Warfield, "The Emotional Life of Our Lord," in *The Person and Work of Christ* (Philadelphia: Presbyterian and Reformed Publishing, 1970), 107.

18. Schlimm, *From Fratricide to Forgiveness*, 180.

19. Here we draw from much of John Goldingay's "Anger," in *The New Interpreter's Dictionary of the Bible*, ed. Katherine D. Sakenfeld, vol. 1 (Nashville: Abingdon Press, 2009), 156.

20. Ibid.

21. Gerald W. Peterman, *Joy and Tears* (Chicago: Moody, 2013), 86.

Chapter 7: The Lord's Prayer: Suffering, Prayer, and Worldview

1. See the treatment of the subject by Robert L. Mowery, "God, Lord and Father: the Theology of the Gospel of Matthew," *Biblical Research* 33 (1988): 24–36.

2. Especially recommended is Andrew Root, *The Children of Divorce: The Loss of Family as a Loss of Being* (Grand Rapids: Baker, 2010). For a succinct treatment, see Ashley McGuire, "The Feminist, Pro–Father, and Pro–Child Case against No–Fault Divorce," *Public Discourse*, May 7, 2013 (http://www.thepublicdiscourse.com/2013/05/10031/).

3. As Ulrich Luz (*Matthew 1–7* [Minneapolis: Fortress Press, 2007], 316) has pointed out.

4. D. W. Baker, "God, Names of," in *Dictionary of the Old Testament: Pentateuch*, ed. T. Desmond Alexander and David W. Baker (Downers Grove, IL: InterVarsity, 2003), 359–60.

5. For example, Gen. 12:8; Ex. 33:19; 1 Sam. 17:45; 1 Kings 8:20; Luke 1:49; John 12:28; 17:6, 26; Acts 2:21; 4:6; 5:41; Rom. 15:9; Heb. 13:15; Rev. 15:4.

6. John Nolland, *The Gospel of Matthew* (Grand Rapids: Eerdmans, 2005), 287.

7. Note that Israel's first great act of idolatry was asserting of the golden calf, "These are your gods, O Israel, who brought you up out of the land of Egypt!" (Ex. 32:4).

8. John Calvin, *The Institutes of the Christian Religion* 1.11.8, trans. Henry Beveridge (Christian Classics Ethereal Library, n.d.), Kindle Edition locations 2307–15.

9. E.g., George Eldon Ladd, *Gospel of the Kingdom* (Grand Rapids: Eerdmans, 1990); J. Dwight Pentecost, *Thy Kingdom Come* (Grand Rapids: Kregel, 1995); and Bruce Chilton, *Pure Kingdom* (Grand Rapids: Eerdmans, 1996).

10. G. Goldsworthy, "Kingdom of God," in *New Dictionary of Biblical Theology*, ed. T. Desmond Alexander et al. (Leicester, UK: Inter-Varsity, 2000), 618.

11. Tim Ferguson, "World's Worst Rulers: Scratch One Now?" http://www.forbes.com/sites/timferguson/2011/08/22/worlds-worst-rulers-scratch-one-now/.

12. The Borgen Project, "The Five Worst Dictators," May 26, 2014 (http://borgenproject.org/top-5-worst-dictators/).

13. Alankar Kumar, "World's 10 Worst Dictators" (http://www.mensxp.com/special-features/top-10/8298-worlds-10-worst-dictators.html).

14. Gerald Peterman, *Joy and Tears: The Emotional Life of the Christian* (Chicago: Moody, 2013), 104.

15. Donald W. Schriver, Jr., "Prayer that Spans the World—An Exposition: Social Ethics and the Lord's Prayer," *Interpretation* 21 (1967): 282.

16. D. A. Carson, "Matthew," *The Expositor's Bible Commentary*, rev. ed., vol. 9, ed. T. Longman and D. E. Garland (Grand Rapids: Zondervan, 2010), 206.

17. Frederick Dale Bruner, *The Christbook: Matthew 1–12* (Grand Rapids: Eerdmans, 2004), 310.

18. E.g., Jer. 31:34: "And no longer shall each one teach his neighbor and each his brother, saying, 'Know the LORD,' for they shall all know me, from the least of them to the greatest, declares the LORD. For I will forgive their iniquity, and I will remember their sin no more" (see also Isa. 43:25). In "'I Will Remember Their Sins No More': Jeremiah 31, the New Covenant, and the Forgiveness of Sins," *Restoration Quarterly* 53 (2011): 15, Timothy M. Willis says correctly that "the statement regarding forgiveness in Jer 31:34 refers to the cessation of punishment, not the mental act of forgetting wrongs."

19. The noun *peirasmos* can refer to a test or trial (1 Peter 4:12; sometimes performed by God, Heb. 3:8) and also temptation, enticement to sin (Matt. 26:41; Mark 14:38; Luke 8:13; 11:4; 22:40, 46; 1 Tim. 6:9; 2 Peter 2:9; Rev. 3:10; see also "way of tempting," Luke 4:13). Likewise the verb *peirazō* could have the nuance to try, attempt, put to the test (Matt. 16:1; 22:18, 35; Mark 10:2; John 6:6; 1 Cor. 10:3; 2 Cor. 13:5; Heb. 2:18; 11:17; Rev. 2:2; 3:10; sometimes of testing God, Acts 5:9; 15:10; 1 Cor. 10:9; Heb. 3:9). On occasion it has the nuance to tempt or entice to sin (Matt. 4:1, 3; Mark 1:13; Luke 4:2; Gal. 6:1; 1 Thess. 3:5; James 1:13–14; Rev. 2:10). At times temptation arises from our own evil desire (James 1:14) and sometimes from the Evil One (1 Thess. 3:5; Rev. 2:10).

20. The verb appears in Matt. 6:13; 27:43; Luke 1:74; Rom. 7:24; 11:26; 15:31; 2 Cor. 1:10; Col. 1:13; 1 Thess. 1:10; 2 Thess. 3:2; 2 Tim. 3:11; 4:17–18; 2 Peter 2:7, 9.

21. Robert A. Guelich, *The Sermon on the Mount* (Waco, TX: Word, 1982), 297.

22. Carson, "Matthew," 208 (and similarly R. T. France, *The Gospel of Matthew* [Grand Rapids: Eerdmans, 2007], 231, 251).

Chapter 8: A Time to Weep: Leadership and Tears

1. David T. Tsumura, *The First Book of Samuel* (Grand Rapids: Eerdmans, 2007), 572.

2. As Green points out, "We are given no unambiguous guidelines for understanding the cause of her tears"; in Joel B. Green, *The Gospel of Luke* (Grand Rapids: Eerdmans, 1997), 310. They might be tears of remorse or tears of joy for forgiveness or a mixture of the two.

3. See James D. G. Dunn, *Romans 9–16* (Nashville: Nelson, 1988), 746; C. E. B. Cranfield, *Romans 9–16* (London: T&T Clark, 1979), 640; and Robert Jewett, *Romans* (Minneapolis: Fortress, 2007), 767. Cranfield and Jewett, however, use "sympathy" and "sympathize," respectively. According to *The Corsini Encyclopedia of Psychology* 3rd ed. (ed. W. Edward Craighead and Charles B. Nemeroff [New York: Wiley, 2001], 2:496), empathy refers to "one person's vicariously experiencing the feelings, perceptions, and thoughts of another."

4. Martin L. Hoffman, "Empathy and Prosocial Behavior," in *Oxford Handbook of Philosophy of Emotion*, ed. Peter Goldie (repr., New York: Oxford University Press, 2012), 440.

5. For an introduction, see Hoffman, "Empathy," 443–44; for a fuller treatment see C. D. Craig and G. Sprang, "Compassion Satisfaction, Compassion Fatigue, and Burnout in a National Sample of Trauma Treatment Therapists," *Anxiety, Stress & Coping* 23 (2010): 319–39.

6. Nicholas Wolterstorff contrasts any apparent support for lament with the underlying reality in "If God Is Good and Sovereign, Why Lament?" *Calvin Theological Journal* 36 (2001): 42.

   No doubt, most Christians, if asked, would *say* that lament is part of the well-formed Christian life. We all know that there are laments in the Psalms. So it would not feel right to say, flat out, that lament has no place in the Christian life. It is open to question whether we all really believe it. The "victorious living" mentality, currently sweeping through American Christianity, has no place for lament. Likewise, many megachurches have no place for it. Lament does not market well.

7. L. C. Allen, "Jeremiah: Book of," in *Dictionary of the Old Testament Prophets*, ed. Mark J. Boda and J. Gordon McConville (Downers Grove, IL: InterVarsity, 2012), 437.

8. J. A. Thompson, *The Book of Jeremiah* (Grand Rapids: Eerdmans, 1980), 307.

9. Ibid., 304.

10. William L. Holladay, *Jeremiah 1* (Minneapolis: Fortress Press, 1986), 407.

11. Darrell Bock, *Luke 9:51–24:53* (Grand Rapids: Baker, 1996), 1560.

12. Although referring to John's gospel, P. W. L. Walker correctly comments that "Jerusalem is the city at the centre of [Jesus'] 'own country' (4:43–44), but when he 'came to what was his own . . . his own people did not accept him' (1:11). So Jerusalem proves to be the place which epitomizes the 'world' in its hostile response to God's truth and light" ("Jerusalem," in *New Dictionary of Biblical Theology*, ed. T. Desmond Alexander et al. [Leicester, UK: Inter-Varsity, 2000], 591).

13. Brent Kinman, "Parousia, Jesus' 'A-Triumphal' Entry, and the Fate of Jerusalem (Luke 19:28–44)," *Journal of Biblical Literature* 118 (1999): 279–94.

14. Bock, *Luke 9:51–24:53*, 1562.

15. J. Gordon McConville, "Hosea: Book of," in *Dictionary of the Old Testament Prophets*, 348.

16. John Calvin, *The Institutes of the Christian Religion*, trans. Henry Beveridge, Enhanced-Highlight Kindle Loc. 15036–47.

17. We note that similar themes appear in Luke 22:1–38: suffering, vv. 15, 28, 31; death of Jesus, v. 19; leadership, vv. 24–30; and money, vv. 35–36.

18. Eckhard J. Schnabel, *Acts* (Grand Rapids: Zondervan, 2012), 839.

Chapter 9: Joseph's Tears: Suffering from Family Toxins

1. Bruce C. Birch, Walter Brueggemann, Terence E. Fretheim, and David L. Peterson, *A Theological Introduction to the Old Testament* (Nashville: Abingdon, 1999), 94.

2. Claus Westermann, *Genesis 12–36*, trans. John J. Scullion (Minneapolis: Fortress, 1985), 29.

3. In Family Systems Theory, the family is viewed as not just a collection of individuals, but a functional unit of interrelationships between members. Any change in one aspect of the family unit affects everyone. The personal problems of any individual are thought to be symptomatic of problems in broader family functioning (from *The Long Journey*

Home: Understanding and Ministering to the Sexually Abused, ed. Andrew J. Schmutzer [Eugene, OR: Wipf & Stock, 2011], 425). See David L. Petersen, "Genesis and Family Values," *Journal of Biblical Literature* 124 (2005): 5–23.

4. Terence E. Fretheim, "The Book of Genesis," in *Old Testament Survey: The New Interpreter's Bible* (Nashville: Abingdon, 2005), 22; emphasis added.

5. Birch et al., *A Theological Introduction*, 94.

6. Susan Forward, *Toxic Parents: Overcoming Their Hurtful Legacy and Reclaiming Your Life* (New York: Bantam, 2002), 157, 167; emphasis added.

7. Clinton W. McLemore, *Toxic Relationships and How to Change Them* (San Francisco: Jossey–Bass, 2003), 215.

8. Ibid., 19.

9. John Bradshaw, *Family Secrets* (New York: Bantam, 1995), 169; quoting a term by Carl G. Jung.

10. Ibid., 58, 61.

11. Ibid., 233; see especially "Freeing Yourself from the Power of Dark Family Secrets," 230–58.

12. Ibid.

13. McLemore, *Toxic Relationships*, 27.

14. Thomas L. Brodie, *Genesis as Dialogue* (Oxford: Oxford University Press, 2001), 351; emphasis added.

15. Judith L. Herman, *Trauma and Recovery* (New York: Basic, 1992), 33–34.

16. For example, see Meira Polliack, "Joseph's Trauma: Memory and Resolution," in *Performing Memory in Biblical Narrative and Beyond*, ed. Athalya Brenner and Frank H. Polak (Sheffield: Sheffield Phoenix Press, 2009), 65–98.

17. Dirk G. Lange, *Trauma Recalled: Liturgy, Disruption, and Theology* (Minneapolis: Fortress, 2010), 100.

18. Forward, *Toxic Parents*, 158; emphasis added.

19. Gordon J. Wenham, *Exploring the Old Testament: A Guide to the Pentateuch*, vol. 1 (Downers Grove, IL: InterVarsity Press, 2003), 47.

20. Robert Alter, *The Five Books of Moses: A Translation with Commentary* (New York: W.W. Norton & Company, 2004), 139.

21. Ibid., 146.

22. Anthony C. Thiselton, "The Supposed Power of Words in Biblical Writings," *Journal of Theological Studies* 25 (1974): 294.

23. William S. LaSor, *Great Personalities of the Old Testament: Their Lives and Times* (New York: Revell, 1959), 41.

24. R. W. L. Moberly, *The Theology of the Book of Genesis* (Cambridge: Cambridge University Press, 2009), 242.

25. Thomas W. Mann, *The Book of the Torah*, 2nd ed. (Eugene, OR: Cascade, 2013), 82.

26. Marvin A. Sweeney, *Tanak: A Theological and Critical Introduction to the Jewish Bible* (Minneapolis: Fortress, 2012), 77 (cf. Gen. 12, 20, 26, 34).

27. McLemore, *Toxic Relationships*, 209; emphasis added.

28. Ibid., 213.

29. C. Marvin Pate, J. Scott Duvall et al., *The Story of Israel: A Biblical Theology* (Downers Grove, IL: InterVarsity, 2004), 23, 38.

30. Matthew R. Schlimm, *From Fratricide to Forgiveness: The Language and Ethics of Anger in Genesis*; Siphrut 7, Literature and Theology of the Hebrew Scriptures (Winona Lake, IN: Eisenbrauns, 2011), 173.

31. John Goldingay, *Old Testament Theology: Israel's Gospel*, vol. 1 (Downers Grove, IL: InterVarsity, 2003), 280.

32. John Goldingay, *Old Testament Theology: Israel's Life*, vol. 3 (Downers Grove, IL: InterVarsity, 2009), 594, quoting Miroslav Volf, *Exclusion and Embrace* (Nashville: Abingdon, 1996), 125. Saying that "forgiveness gives up the right to justice" is an overstatement. Forgiveness postpones the sharpest edge of justice for the next life, when the "Judge of all the earth" (Gen. 18:25) will issue decisions that are just and restorative.

33. Gregory L. Jones, *Embodying Forgiveness: A Theological Analysis* (Grand Rapids: Eerdmans, 1995), 6.

34. Gary A. Anderson, "Joseph and the Passion of Our Lord," in *The Art of Reading Scripture*, ed. Ellen F. Davis and Richard B. Hays (Grand Rapids: Eerdmans, 2003), 200.

35. Nicholas Wolterstorff, *Justice in Love* (Grand Rapids: Eerdmans, 2011), 170; emphasis original.

36. Donald E. Gowan, *The Bible on Forgiveness* (Eugene, OR: Pickwick Publications, 2010), xv.

37. Walter Brueggemann, "Forgiveness," in *Reverberations of Faith: A Theological Handbook of Old Testament Themes* (Louisville: Westminster John Knox Press, 2002), 87; emphasis added.

38. Brueggemann, "Forgiveness," 87.

39. McLemore, *Toxic Relationships*, 13.

40. Carl R. Bråkenhielm, *Forgiveness*, trans. by Thor Hall (Minneapolis: Fortress, 1993), 27–30.

41. Frank H. Gorman, Jr., *The Ideology of Ritual: Space, Time and Status in the Priestly Theology. Journal for the Study of the Old Testament Supplement Series* 91 (Sheffield: JSOT Press, 1990), 29.

42. Hannah Arendt, *The Human Condition* (Garden City, NY: Doubleday Anchor, 1959), 212.

43. Jerry Sittser, *A Grace Disguised: How the Soul Grows Through Loss* (Grand Rapids: Zondervan, 2004), 107.

44. McLemore, *Toxic Relationships*, 11.

45. Ibid., 27.

46. Jonathan Sacks, *Covenant and Conversation: A Weekly Reading of the Jewish Bible* (New Milford, CT: Maggid Books, 2009), 306; emphasis original.

47. Ibid., 307; emphasis original.

48. Goldingay, *Old Testament Theology: Israel's Gospel*, 281–82.

49. N. R. Whybray, "Genesis," in *The Pentateuch: The Oxford Bible Commentary*, ed. John Barton and John Muddiman (Oxford: Oxford University Press, 2001), 86.

50. The brother's actions were beyond cruel. Their economic decision reflects the price for a slave in the early second millennium, namely, twenty pieces of silver (e.g., Laws of

Hammurapi, cf. Ex. 21:16; K.A. Kitchen, "Genesis 12–50 in the Near Eastern world," in *He Swore an Oath* [Cambridge: Tyndale, 1993], 79–80).

51. Schlimm, *From Fratricide to Forgiveness*, 173.

52. It is important to realize that changes of clothing marked each new stage in Joseph's life (see 37:3, 31–33; 38:14; 39:12–18; 41:14, 42). So giving new clothes to his brothers, as they went home to retrieve his father, was about joy and initiating a new season of relationship.

53. Sacks, *Covenant and Conversation*, 310.

54. Ibid., 309. Jesus and the gospel writers use similar reenactments. For example, the call of Nathan (John 1:47, 51), in which complete integrity and the ascending/descending angels are contrasted with Jacob's deceiving reputation, and the same ascending/descending angels (Gen. 27:1–36; 28:12; 32:28); or Peter's betrayal of Christ and his reinstatement at another "charcoal fire" (Matt. 26:69–75; Luke 22:54–62; John 18:18; 21:9–17).

55. Meir Sternberg, *The Poetics of Biblical Narrative: Ideological Literature and the Drama of Reading* (Bloomington, IN: Indiana University Press, 1985), 308.

56. Sacks, *Covenant and Conversation*, 326.

57. Alter, *Five Books*, 261.

58. Bruce K. Waltke and Michael O'Connor, *An Introduction to Biblical Hebrew Syntax* (Winona Lake, IN: Eisenbrauns, 1990), §23.3c. In 45:3 the ESV reads, "They were dismayed at his presence, or perhaps better, "They became terrified at his presence" (cf. 1 Sam. 28:21). The English translations are trying to capture this with "troubled" (KJV), "terrified" (NIV), and "stunned" (NLT).

59. Robert Longacre, *Joseph: A Story of Divine Providence—A Text Theoretical and Textlinguistic Analysis of Genesis 37 and 39–40* (Winona Lake, IN: Eisenbrauns, 1989), 149.

60. Mann, *Book of the Torah*, 89.

61. Walter Brueggemann, *A Pathway of Interpretation: The Old Testament for Pastors and Students* (Eugene, OR: Cascade Books, 2008), 57.

62. Alter, *Five Books*, 261.

63. Mann, *Book of the Torah*, 90.

64. Goldingay, *Old Testament Theology: Israel's Gospel*, 285. Significantly, Goldingay entitles this section: "God's Involvement with Dysfunctional Families" (285–87).

65. Ibid., 285–86.

66. Anderson, "Joseph," 209.

67. Many scholars recognize that Jacob would have spoken personally to Joseph if he had wanted to address such a significant issue. Jacob has already had private conversations with Joseph (cf. 47:29–48:22). Calling it a "concoction," James McKeoun writes, "It is very unlikely that their report of Jacob's request is genuine, since if Jacob had such worries he would have spoken to Joseph personally," *Genesis*, The Two Horizons Old Testament Commentary (Grand Rapids, Eerdmans, 2008), 192.

68. Goldingay, *Old Testament Theology: Israel's Gospel*, 280.

69. Anderson, "Joseph," 212, n. 23.

70. Birch et al., *Theological Introduction*, 95.

71. Sacks, *Covenant and Conversation*, 327; emphasis original.

72. Wolterstorff, *Justice in Love*, 176–77.

73. Bill T. Arnold, *Genesis*, New Cambridge Bible Commentary (Cambridge, UK: Cambridge University Press, 2009), 388.

74. See Patrick D. Miller, *They Cried to the Lord: The Form and Theology of Biblical Prayer* (Minneapolis: Fortress, 1994), 135–77.

75. Klaus Seybold, "*hshab*," *Theological Dictionary of the Old Testament*, ed. G. J. Botterweck et al. (Grand Rapids: Eerdmans, 1986) 5:238–39.

76. Rolf P. Knierim, *The Task of Old Testament Theology: Method and Cases* (Grand Rapids: Eerdmans, 1995), 439; emphasis added.

77. Anderson, "Joseph," 211.

78. Henri J. M. Nouwen, *The Living Reminder: Service and Prayer in Memory of Jesus Christ* (New York: Seabury Press, 1981), 24–27; emphasis added.

79. R. Schreiter, "Peacemaking and Reconciliation," in *Global Dictionary of Theology*, ed. William A. Dyrness and Veli–Matti Käakkäinen (Downers Grove, IL: InterVarsity, 2008), 640.

80. Sittser, *A Grace Disguised*, 141, 142.

81. Brueggemann, *Pathway of Interpretation*, 59.

82. Sittser, *A Grace Disguised*, 143; emphasis added.

83. N. T. Wright, *Evil and the Justice of God* (Downers Grove, IL: InterVarsity, 2006), 54.

84. Ibid., 55.

85. Adapted from Schreiter, "Peacemaking and Reconciliation," 640–41.

86. D. A. Carson, *For the Love of God*, vol. 1 (Wheaton, IL: Crossway, 1998), Feb 17 reading.

87. Robin Routledge, *Old Testament Theology* (Downers Grove, IL: InterVarsity, 2008), 312.

88. Sittser, *A Grace Disguised*, 118; emphasis original.

Chapter 10: Sexual Abuse: Suffering from a Host of Betrayals

1. Suffering through sexual abuse takes many forms. Some is passively experienced and others, actively. Healing measures must understand this. While one contracts a disease, is caught in an economic downturn, struggles with depression, or is involved in a car accident, sexual abuse: (1) requires another agent (another who), (2) can be passed transgenerationally, (3) imposes moral evil (rather than natural), (4) uses an attack–factor in incest, rape, molestation, and (5) can result in severe emotional (internal) and relational (external) damage, usually among the very family members the victim needs for support.

2. These reductionisms include: pressuring victims to "forgive," confronting the "sin problem" of the victim, shunning any medication, using Scripture for scientific proof texts, and constant blaming of "patriarchy." Many of these have no patience for the process of sanctification, do not understand the depth of trauma, and confuse healing with obedience.

3. See my example of integration and collaboration: Andrew J. Schmutzer, *The Long Journey Home: Understanding and Ministering to the Sexually Abused* (Eugene, OR: Wipf & Stock, 2011).

4. For example, see the helpful terms and discussion of Mark E. Biddle, *Missing the Mark: Sin and Its Consequences in Biblical Theology* (Nashville: Abingdon, 2005), xi–xii.

5. The story of "Brad" is representative to protect individuals. All names, locations, and organizations have been changed.

6. S. R. Dube, R. F. Anda, C. L. Whitfield et al., "Long–term Consequences of Childhood Sexual Abuse by Gender of Victim," *American Journal of Preventive Medicine* 28 (2005): 430–38. See also http://www.netgrace.org; "Child Sexual Abuse" at http://en.wikipedia .org/wiki/ Child_sexual_abuse.

7. G. R. Holmes, L. Offen, and G. Waller, "See No Evil, Hear No Evil, Speak No Evil: Why Do Relatively Few Male Victims of Childhood Sexual Abuse Receive Help for Abuse–related Issues in Adulthood?" *Clinical Psychology Review* 17 (1997): 69–88.

8. Sadly, the medical field has not even drawn up clinical best practices when interacting with male survivors of SA. This tacitly reinforces stereotypes that men are the victimizers, and has directly contributed to the well–known silence of male victims. See Les Gallo–Silver, Christopher M. Anderson, and Jamie Romo, "Best Clinical Practices for Male Adult Survivors of Childhood Sexual Abuse: 'Do No Harm,'" *The Permanente Journal* 18 (2014): 82–87.

9. "Child Sexual Abuse Statistics Fact Sheet," at http://www.stopitnow.org (accessed July 2, 2014).

10. B. H. French, J. D. Tilghman, and D. A. Malebranche, "Sexual Coercion Context and Psychosocial Correlates Among Diverse Males," *Psychology of Men & Masculinity*, March 17, 2014; advance online publication at http://dx.doi.org/10.1037/a0035915; also http://www.apa.org/news/press/releases/2014/03/coerced–sex. Robert A. Dickey, winner of the 2013 Cy Young award as best National League pitcher, was sexually abused by his thirteen–year–old babysitter when only eight years old and struggled with anger at his parents and God. See *Wherever I Wind Up: My Quest for Truth, Authenticity, and the Perfect Knuckleball* (New York: Penguin Group, 2012).

11. Barabara E. Bogorad, "Sexual Abuse: Surviving the Pain," writing for the American Academy of Experts in Traumatic Stress at http://www.aaets.org/article31.htm, accessed July 1, 2014.

12. In 1977, Sandusky started The Second Mile, a nonprofit program for foster and high–risk children. From these, many victims were chosen. On June 22, 2012, he was convicted on forty–five counts of abusing ten boys over a fifteen–year period. "Timeline: The Penn State Scandal," *New York Times*, November 11, 2011, at www. nytimes.com/interactive/ 2011/11/11/sports/ncaafootball/ sandusky.html?_r=0. Jerry Sandusky's wife still claims he's innocent, which is a common response among spouses known as partner collusion.

13. G. Hornor, "Child Sexual Abuse: Consequences and Implication," *Journal of Pediatric Health Care* 24 (2010): 358–64.

14. R. D. Levitan, N. A. Rector, T. Sheldon, and P. Gordon, "Childhood Adversities Associated with Major Depression and/or Anxiety Disorders in a Community Sample of Ontario," *Depression and Anxiety* 17 (2003): 34–42.

15. Richard Rice, *Suffering and the Search for Meaning: Contemporary Responses to the Problem of Pain* (Downers Grove, IL: InterVarsity, 2014), 88.

16. Michelle Boorstein, "Pastor Joshua Harris, an Evangelical Outlier, Heads to Mainstream Seminary," *Washington Post*, January 30, 2015; http://www.washingtonpost. com/local/ long-an-outsider-popular-evangelical-pastor-heads-for-the-mainstream/2015/01/30/31827364-a881-11e4-a7c2-03d37af98440_story.html.

17. One example is a large Christian university that shamed and silenced over six hundred victims of SA on their own campus. See: Richard Perez–Pena, "Bob Jones University

Blamed Victims of Sexual Assaults, Not Abusers, Report Says," *New York Times*, December 11, 2014. In response to the report, the president of the evangelical university subsequently apologized to victims of sexual assault. See Sara Pulliam Bailey, Religious News Service, in "Bob Jones University President Apologizes to Victims of Sexual Assault on Campus," *Washington Post*, December 11, 2014. In a document published in 2015, "Bob Jones University's Response to the GRACE Report Recommendations," the university announced a list of "Core Commitments," including being "committed to providing a place of solace to victims of sexual abuse/assault"; [and] "to communicating with and seeking the forgiveness of any former students or other individuals who came to us in their time of need and did not experience the loving, comforting environment they deserved." The school also announced revised policies to assist victims of abuse. See http://www.bju.edu/grace/response.pdf.

18. From the open letter written by Basyle Tchividjian and signed by the author (Schmutzer) and many others, "A Public Statement Concerning Sexual Abuse in the Church of Jesus Christ"; reproduced at Boz Tchividjian, "A Public Statement Concerning Sexual Abuse in the Church," Religion News Service blog, "Rhymes with Religion," 22 February 2014.

19. Christa Foster Crawford and Glenn Miles, "Why Is Addressing Access of Youth to Pornography So Important to Tackling Demand?" in *Stopping the Traffick: A Christian Response to Sexual Exploitation and Trafficking*, ed. G. Miles and C. F. Crawford (Oxford, UK: Regnum Books, 2014), 134; emphasis added.

20. William M. Struthers, *Wired for Intimacy: How Pornography Hijacks the Male Brain* (Downers Grove, IL: InterVarsity, 2009), 72. Vanessa Williams, former Miss America, was ten when an eighteen–year–old girl molested her. Vanessa admits that her abuse made her sexually promiscuous. See Vanessa Williams and Helen Williams, *You Have No Idea* (New York: Penguin Group, 2012).

21. Thus some churches have support groups for porn addiction, and involvement is considered noble and honest; yet far fewer have support groups for survivors of male and female sexual abuse.

22. The variables in a survivor's life include: the age SA started, parent or additional perpetrator(s), nature of the SA, duration of the abuse, nature of the termination, resilience of the victim, presence of supportive family, adequate (ongoing) treatment, and spiritual support. D. Whitsett, "The Psychobiology of Trauma and Child Maltreatment," *Cultic Studies Review* 5 (2006): 355; and K. Havig, "The Health Care Experiences of Adult Survivors of Child Sexual Abuse," *Trauma, Violence, and Abuse* 9 (2008): 20. See also http://www.hngn.com/articles/36568/20140719/sexual–abuse–childhood–exacerbates–heart–disease–risk–midlife–women.htm.

23. Jennifer E. Beste, *God and the Victim: Traumatic Intrusions on Grace and Freedom* (Oxford: Oxford University Press, 2007), 53.

24. The SA literature is starting to take spouses of survivors more seriously. They can experience secondary trauma, which is no small matter. Even in old age, further psychological problems can emerge in survivors' lives. See Clark Barshinger, "The Spouses of Adult Survivors: How to Respond Christianly," in *The Long Journey Home: Understanding and Ministering to the Sexually Abused*, ed. A. J. Schmutzer (Eugene, OR: Wipf & Stock, 2011), 325–37.

25. Diane M. Langberg, "What Every Minister Should Know about Sexual Abuse," in *The Long Journey Home*, 228; emphasis original.

26. For example, Andrew J. Schmutzer, "Sexual Abuse and the Distortion of Worship," *Society for Christian Psychology* (E–Newsletter) at http://christianpsych.org/wp_scp/sexual–abuse–and–the–distortion–of–worship.

27. Pamela Cooper-White, *The Cry of Tamar: Violence against Women and the Church's Response*, 2nd ed. (Minneapolis: Fortress, 2012).

28. A current study by Lara Stemple and Ilan H. Meyer identifies several factors that perpetuate misperceptions about men's sexual victimization, such as: reliance on worn-out gender stereotypes, outdated and inconsistent definitions of abuse, and methodological sampling biases that exclude inmates. Their study seeks changes that move beyond regressive gender assumptions that are actually harmful to both men and women. See: "The Sexual Victimization of Men in America: New Data Challenge Old Assumptions," *American Journal of Public Health* 104 (2014): 19–26; http://ajph.aphapublications.org.

29. Jocelyn R. Zichterman, *I Fired God: My Life Inside—and Escape from—the Secret World of the Independent Fundamental Baptist Cult* (New York: St. Martin's Press, 2013).

30. Susan Shooter, *How Survivors of Abuse Relate to God: The Authentic Spirituality of the Annihilated Soul* (Farnam, UK: Ashgate, 2012). Shooter squandered a rich opportunity for a quality address of survivors' disillusionment with God, motivated more by her spite for the "all-male God," and animas toward the church in the UK for its lack of ordained female leaders.

31. While key strands of feminism ironically need patriarchy, recent scholarship also acknowledges that the term "patriarchy" is not only anachronistic, but an overgeneralization based on Western concepts of social organization.

32. Ronald Hendel, "Mind the Gap: Modern and Postmodern in Biblical Studies," *Journal of Biblical Literature* 133 (2014): 432.

33. See Andrew J. Schmutzer, "Spiritual Formation and Sexual Abuse: Embodiment, Community and Healing," *Journal of Spiritual Formation and Soul Care* 2 (2009): 67–86.

34. Hilary B. Lipka uses similar terms: "religious," "communal," and "personal boundaries" in *Sexual Transgression in the Hebrew Bible*, ed. D. J. A. Clines, J. C. Exum, and K. W. Whitelam, Hebrew Bible Monographs 7 (Sheffield: Sheffield Phoenix Press, 2006), 16.

35. Christian Gostecnik, "Sexuality and the Longing for Salvation," *Journal of Religious Health* 46 (2007): 589.

36. Alistair McFadyen, *Bound to Sin: Abuse, Holocaust and the Christian Doctrine of Sin* (Cambridge: Cambridge University Press, 2000), 221, 223, 237.

37. Cornelius Plantinga, Jr., *Not the Way It's Supposed to Be: A Breviary of Sin* (Grand Rapids: Eerdmans, 1995), 45.

38. Cathy Caruth, *Trauma: Explorations in Meaning* (Baltimore,: Johns Hopkins University Press, 1955), 151.

39. L. J. M. Claassens and D. G. Garber, "First Words . . . Faith Facing Trauma," *Review and Expositor* 105 (2008): 187.

40. Miroslav Volf, *Exclusion and Embrace: A Theological Exploration of Identity, Otherness, and Reconciliation* (Nashville: Abingdon, 1996), 172.

41. The Hebrew 3ms suffix ("him/it," vv. 27b; cf. 5:1) functions as a collective singular and recent translations now stress this collectivity by translating "them" (per NRSV, NLT, NET, NIV, CEB).

42. Jürgen Moltmann, *God in Creation* (London: SCM Press, 1985), 279.

43. Robert A. Gagnon, "Sexuality," in *Dictionary for Theological Interpretation of the Bible*, ed. K. J. Vanhoozer (Grand Rapids: Baker, 2005), 747.

44. Patrick D. Miller, "Man and Woman: Towards a Theological Anthropology," in *The Way of the LORD: Essays in Old Testament Theology* (Grand Rapids: Eerdmans, 2004), 311–12.

45. Ibid., 311; emphasis added. Marking God's dialogue with "them," plural forms occur fifteen times in four verses (vv. 26–29), an evidence lost in English translations.

46. Volf, *Exclusion and Embrace*, 186.

47. Ibid., quoting Allison Weir, *Sacrificial Logistics* (New York: Routledge, 1996), 3.

48. Ibid., 187.

49. William P. Brown, "Creation," in *Eerdmans Dictionary of the Bible*, ed. D. N. Freedman (Grand Rapids: Eerdmans, 1999), 293.

50. Andrew J. Schmutzer, "A Theology of Sexuality and Its Abuse: Creation, Evil, and the Relational Ecosystem," in *The Long Journey Home*, 115.

51. John Kessler, *Old Testament Theology: Divine Call and Human Response* (Waco, TX: Baylor University Press, 2013), 21.

52. John Goldingay, *Old Testament Theology: Israel's Gospel* (Downers Grove, IL: InterVarsity, 2003), 1:98, n. 90.

53. Ibid., 102.

54. Volf, *Exclusion and Embrace*, 174.

55. Daniel Boyarin, *A Radical Jew: Paul and the Politics of Identity* (Berkeley: University of California Press, 1994), 239.

56. A. Strathern and P. J. Steward, "Embodiment Theory and Performativity," *Journal of Ritual Studies* 22 (2008): 68.

57. Cherith F. Nordling, "The Human Person in the Christian Story," in *The Cambridge Companion to Evangelical Theology*, ed. T. Larson and D. J. Trier (Cambridge: Cambridge University Press, 2007), 71.

58. "The Resurrection Body and Personal Identity: Possibilities and Limits of Eschatological Knowledge," in *Resurrection: Theological and Scientific Assessments*, ed. T. Peters, R. J. Russell, and M. Welker (Grand Rapids: Eerdmans, 2002), 202–18.

59. Volf, *Exclusion and Embrace*, 184; emphasis added.

60. Joel B. Green, *Body, Soul, and Human Life: The Nature of Humanity in the Bible*, STI (Grand Rapids: Baker, 2008), 179.

61. Ibid., 178.

62. E. Schweizer, "*soma*," *Exegetical Dictionary of the New Testament*, ed. H. Balz and G. Schneider (Grand Rapids: Eerdmans, 1981), 3:323.

63. Frank Thielman, *Theology of the New Testament: A Canonical and Synthetic Approach* (Grand Rapids: Zondervan, 2005), 243, 244.

64. Hans Schwarz, *The Human Being: A Theological Anthropology* (Grand Rapids: Eerdmans, 2013), 286.

65. Anthony C. Thiselton, *The Living Paul: An Introduction to the Apostle's Life and Thought* (Downers Grove, IL: InterVarsity, 2009), 70; emphasis original.

66. Thielman, *Theology of the New Testament*, 245.

67. Thiselton, *The Living Paul*, 79.

68. Thielman, *Theology of the New Testament*, 245.

69. Thiselton, *The Living Paul*, 73.

70. Marilyn McCord Adams, *Horrendous Evils and the Goodness of God* (Ithaca, NY: Cornell University Press, 1999), 127.

71. Ralph C. Wood, *The Gospel According to Tolkien: Visions of the Kingdom in Middle-Earth* (Louisville: Westminster John Knox, 2003), 70.

72. Ray S. Anderson, *The Shape of Practical Theology: Empowering Ministry with Theological Praxis* (Downers Grove, IL: InterVarsity, 2001), 302.

73. Thiselton, *The Living Paul*, 79.

74. The phrase of Biddle, *Missing the Mark*, 137.

75. For example, see Andrew J. Schmutzer, Daniel A. Gorski, and David Carlson, *Naming Our Abuse: God's Pathways to Healing for Male Sexual Abuse Survivors* (Grand Rapids: Kregel, 2016).

76. L. J. M. Claassens and D. G. Garber, "First Words…Faith Facing Trauma," *Review & Expositor* 105 (2008): 188.

Chapter 11: Inner Darkness: The Unique Suffering of Mental Illness

1. See http://www.webmd.com/mental-health/.

2. Amy Simpson, "Persistent Stigma," in *Troubled Minds: Mental Illness and the Church's Mission* (Downers Grove, IL: InterVarsity, 2013), 136–65; Stephen P. Hinshaw, "Introduction," in *Breaking the Silence: Mental Health Professionals Disclose Their Personal and Family Experiences of Mental Illness*, ed. Stephen P. Hinshaw (New York: Oxford University Press, 2008), 5.

3. The comment is from Beth Voswinkel, posted 15 August 2010 on the blog "Musings of a Christian Psychologist," in response to 26 June 2007 posting at http://wisecounsel. wordpress.com/2007/06/26/serious-mental-illness-and-faith-what-to-do/.

4. See the brief discussion by Stephen P. Hinshaw, "Introduction," in *Breaking the Silence,* 14–17.

5. Steve and Robyn Bloem, *Broken Minds* (Grand Rapids: Kregel, 2005), Kindle locations 47–50.

6. "Mental Disorder," at http://en.wikipedia.org/wiki/Mental_disorder.

7. Matthew S. Stanford, *Grace for the Afflicted* (Colorado Springs: Biblica, 2008), chaps. 9–11.

8. Mayo Clinic Staff, "Peanut Allergy," http://www.mayoclinic.com/health/peanut-allergy/ DS00710.

9. Jean-Claude Larchet, *The Theology of Illness*, trans. John and Michael Breck (Crestwood, NY: St Vladimir's Seminary Press, 2002), 53.

10. Ibid., 59.

11. This parable has been modified from Jeffery Satinover, *Homosexuality and the Politics of Truth* (Grand Rapids: Baker, 1996), 130–32.

12. Matthew S. Stanford, *Grace for the Afflicted* (Downers Grove, IL: InterVarsity, 2008), 5.

13. Ibid., 7.

14. Ibid., 10.

15. Elyse Fitzpatrick and Laura Hendrickson, *Will Medicine Stop the Pain? Finding God's Healing for Depression, Anxiety, & Other Troubling Emotions* (Chicago: Moody, 2006), 25.

16. *Broken Minds: Hope for Healing When You Feel Like You're "Losing It"* (Grand Rapids: Kregel Publications, 2005), Kindle locations 62, 126, 543, 897, 942, 1000, 1890, 2077.

17. For a survey, see Mina Fazel, Jeremy Wheeler, and John Danesh, "Prevalence of Serious Mental Disorder in 7000 Refugees Resettled in Western Countries," *Lancet* 365 (2005): 309–14. See also Nexhmedin Morina et al., "Psychopathology and Well–Being in Civilian Survivors of War Seeking Treatment," *Clinical Psychology and Psychotherapy* 17 (2010): 79–86.

18. D. A. Carson ("Matthew," in *The Expositor's Bible Commentary*, vol. 8 [Grand Rapids: Zondervan, 1984], 121) prefers "seizures," while R. T. France (*The Gospel of Matthew* [Grand Rapids: Eerdmans, 2007], 659–60 n. 10), prefers "fits."

19. Three to recommend include Nancey Murphy, *Bodies and Souls, or Spirited Bodies?* (New York: Cambridge, 2006); Joel B. Green, *What about the Soul? Neuroscience and Christian Anthropology* (Nashville: Abingdon, 2004); and John W. Cooper, *Body, Soul and Life Everlasting: Biblical Anthropology and the Monism–Dualism Debate* (Grand Rapids: Eerdmans, 1989).

20. Lawson G. Stone, "The Soul: Possession, Part, or Person? The Genesis of Human Nature in Genesis 2:7," in *What about the Soul?*, 49.

21. Kenneth A. Mathews (*Genesis 1–11:26*. The New American Commentary, vol. 1A [Nashville: Broadman & Holman, 1996], 197) says, "To possess the 'breath of life' or 'breath' is to be alive (e.g., Deut 20:16; Josh 10:40; Job 27:3); the absence of it describes the dead (1 Kgs 17:17)."

22. Ibid., 198.

23. John Nolland, *The Gospel of Matthew* (Grand Rapids: Eerdmans, 2005), 436.

24. W. D. Davies and D. C. Allison, *Matthew 8–18,* vol. 2 (Edinburgh: T&T Clark, 1991), 206.

25. G. Gabbard, "Psychodynamic Psychiatry in the 'Decade of the Brain,'" *American Journal of Psychiatry* 149 (1992): 991–98.

26. "Taxi drivers' brains 'grow' on the job," BBC News, World Edition, 14 March 2000; http://news.bbc.co.uk/2/hi/677048.stm.

27. William Hasker, "Emergent Dualism: Challenge to a Materialist Consensus," in *What about the Soul?*, 103.

28. "Medical Symptoms and Complications of Bulimia," an excerpt from Marcia Herrin and Nancy Matsumoto, *The Parent's Guide to Eating Disorders*, 2nd ed. (Carlsbad, CA: Gurze Books, 2007), available at http://www.bulimia.com/client/client_pages/bulimia_medical_symptoms.cfm.

29. Ted Schletter, "Heart Disease and the Environment," *The Collaborative on Health and the Environment* (2005); http://www.healthandenvironment.org/cardiovascular.

30. Jean–Claude Larchet, *Mental Disorders and Spiritual Healing: Teachings from the Early Christian East*, 1st English ed. (Sophia Perennis, 2005), 1. Larchet says the church fathers recognized possible organic, demonic, and spiritual causes for mental illness (8–11).

31. Avshalom Caspi et al., "Influence of Life Stress on Depression," *Science* 301 (2003): 386.

32. "Maternal infections & Flu During Pregnancy Are Associated with Increased Risk of Schizophrenia," http://www.schizophrenia.com/prevention/maternal.html.

33. Presentation at the American Psychiatric Association meeting, May 1–7, 2004, New York City; http://www.schizophrenia.com/new/szup.52704.html$flu.

34. "Causes of Mental Illness," http://www.webmd.com/anxiety-panic/mental-health-causes-mental-illness.

35. The website webmd.com lists loss of a loved one, having a baby, divorce, and being diagnosed with a long-term disease as possible "triggers" for depression. See http://www.webmd.com/depression/tc/depression-causes.

36. Importantly, Larchet informs us that the ancients did not ignorantly assign mental illness to demonic causes. "The celebrated Hippocratic [Hippocrates of Cos, *ca.* 460 BC – *ca.* 370 BC] treatise entitled *On the Sacred Disease* . . . takes to task all those who would attribute to epilepsy and to mental disease in general a divine or demonic cause (chap. III, 15)," *Mental Disorders and Spiritual Healing* 47.

37. See the helpful comments by Larchet, *The Theology of Illness*, 95–108.

38. "Cannabis/Marijuana (and other street drugs) Have Been Linked to Significant Increases in a Person's Risk for Schizophrenia," http://www.schizophrenia.com/prevention/cannabis.marijuana.schizophrenia.html.

39. "Self-Reported Cannabis Use as a Risk Factor for Schizophrenia in Swedish Conscripts of 1969: Historical Cohort Study," *The BMJ* [formerly the *British Medical Journal*], 2002, 325:1199; http://www.schizophrenia.com/ prevention/cannabis.marijuana.schizophrenia.html.

40. "Depression: Prevention," at http://www.webmd.com/depression/tc/depression-prevention-of.

41. Here I draw on the title of Dan Blazer's book *Freud vs. God: How Psychiatry Lost Its Soul and Christianity Lost Its Mind* (Downers Grove, IL: InterVarsity, 1998).

42. "Depression—Treatment Overview"; http://www.webmd.com/depression/tc/treatment-overview-depression.

43. Phil Monroe, "Musings of a Christian Psychologist," 26 June 2007 blog post; http://wisecounsel.wordpress.com/2007/06/26/serious-mental-illness-and-faith-what-to-do/.

Chapter 12: Suffering and God's People: Community, Renewal, and Ethics

1. See, for example, J. L. Brown, D. Sheffield, M. R. Leary, and M. E. Robinson, "Social Support and Experimental Pain," *Psychosomatic Medicine* 65 (2003): 276–83.

2. Robert D. Lupton, *Toxic Charity: How the Church Hurts Those They Help (And How to Reverse It)* (New York: HarperCollins, 2011), Kindle loc. 955–65.

3. Christopher J. H. Wright, *God's People in God's Land: Family, Land, and Property in the Old Testament* (Grand Rapids: Eerdmans, 1990), 63; emphasis original.

4. See *Marriage and the Public Good: Ten Principles* (Princeton, NJ: Witherspoon Institute, 2008).

5. These tithes are sometimes called the first, second, and third tithes; the latter is sometimes called the "Poor Man's" tithe. Whether all three were required every year is open to debate. Certainly amongst Jews Tobit (mid second century BC) and Josephus (late first century AD) held to three tithes, as did Chrysostom (AD 349–407) and Jerome (347–420) among early Christians. See David Henschke, "Tithing," *The Eerdmans Dictionary of Early Judaism*, ed. J. J. Collins and D. C. Harlow (Grand Rapids: Eerdmans, 2010), 1310–12.

6. Patrick Colm Hogan, *The Mind and Its Stories: Narrative Universals and Human Emotion* (Cambridge: Cambridge University Press, 2003), 1–2.

7. Robert D. Bergen, *1, 2 Samuel* (Nashville: B&H Publishing, 1996), 67.

8. David Toshio Tsumura, *The First Book of Samuel* (Grand Rapids: Eerdmans, 2007), 411.

9. Walter Brueggemann, *The Message of the Psalms* (Minneapolis: Augsburg, 1983), 78.

10. Claus Westermann, *Genesis 12–36* (Minneapolis: Augsburg, 1985), 2:474.

11. Ronald M. Enroth, *Churches that Abuse* (Grand Rapids: Zondervan, 1994), 18.

12. See Andrew Jasko, "The Scarlet Letter of Mental Illness: De-Stigmatizing Bipolar Disorder," *Pastoral Psychology* 61 (2012): 299–304. For a more thorough treatment, see D. L. Carlson, *Why Do Christians Shoot Their Wounded?* (Downers Grove, IL: InterVarsity, 1994).

13. See the discussion of Paul's pastoral method in Abraham J. Malherbe, *The Letters to the Thessalonians* (New York: Doubleday, 2000), 309–27.

14. Similar is the assertion that anxiety is founded in unbelief. John Piper says, "Anxiety is one of the evil conditions of the heart that comes from unbelief" (John Piper, "Battling the Unbelief of Anxiety," sermon in Minneapolis, September 25, 1988; http://www.desiringgod.org/sermons/battling–the–unbelief–of–anxiety). Brian S. Borgman writes, "The Bible leaves no room for debate. The source of fear, worry, and anxiety is unbelief" (*Feelings and Faith* [Wheaton, IL: Crossway, 2009], 124).

15. Eric J. Cassell, *The Nature of Suffering and the Goals of Medicine* (New York: Oxford University Press, 1991), 246.

16. Douglas J. Moo, *The Epistle to the Romans* (Grand Rapids: Eerdmans, 1996), 779.

17. S. McKnight, "Collection for the Saints," in *Dictionary of Paul and His Letters*, ed. Gerald F. Hawthorne et al. (Downers Grove, IL: InterVarsity, 1993), 143.

18. Christopher P. Vogt, "Practicing Patience, Compassion, and Hope at the End of Life: Mining the Passion of Jesus in Luke for a Christian Model of Dying Well," *Journal of the Society of Christian Ethics* 24 (2004): 136.

19. Ibid., 149.

20. Ibid., 150.

21. D. A. Carson, *How Long, O Lord? Reflections on Suffering and Evil*, 2nd ed. (Grand Rapids: Baker, 2006), 216.

22. The Voice of the Martyrs, begun in 1967, is "dedicated to assisting our persecuted [Christian] family worldwide" and has among its purposes "to promote the fellowship of all believers by informing the world of the faith and courage of persecuted Christians, thereby inspiring believers to a deeper level of commitment to Christ." See its website http://www.persecution.com.

Chapter 13: Longing for Home: The Metanarrative Renewed

1. For helpful biblical–theological discussions, see J. Richard Middleton, *A New Heaven and a New Earth: Reclaiming Biblical Eschatology* (Grand Rapids: Baker, 2014); also William J. Dumbrell, *The Search for Order: Biblical Eschatology in Focus* (Eugene, OR: Wipf & Stock, 2001).

2. See the helpful volume by Howard A. Snyder and Joel Scandrett, *Salvation Means Overcoming the Divorce between Earth and Heaven* (Eugene, OR: Cascade, 2011); also Albert M. Wolters, *Creation Regained* (Grand Rapids: Eerdmans, 1985), though I prefer more holistic and relational terms to the more classic: creation, fall, redemption.

3. Walter Brueggemann, "Theophany," in *Reverberations of Faith: A Theological Handbook of Theological Themes* (Louisville: Westminster John Knox, 2002), 216.

4. Middleton, *New Heaven and a New Earth*, 60.

5. Thomas G. Long, *What Shall We Say? Evil, Suffering, and the Crisis of Faith* (Grand Rapids: Eerdmans, 2011), 111.

6. Tremper Longman III, *Making Sense of the Old Testament* (Grand Rapids: Baker, 1998), 133.

7. So Abraham (Gen. 12:1–3; 18:17–18; 22:17–18), Isaac (Gen. 26:4–5), and Jacob (Gen. 28:14). God's covenant promise to Jacob is stunning in its wording, "Your descendants [plural] will be like the dust of the earth, and you [singular] will spread out to the west and to the east, to the north and to the south. All peoples on earth will be blessed through you and your offspring" (NIV). Corporate solidarity allows the global impact of Jacob's singular "you" to extend the goal of Abraham's initial calling—"all people on earth will be blessed through you" (cf. Gen. 12:3b).

8. On Israel's national "charter" in Ex.19:3–6, see William J. Dumbrell, *Covenant and Creation: A Theology of Old Testament Covenants* (Exeter, UK: Paternoster Press, 1984).

9. Middleton, *New Heaven and a New Earth*, 62.

10. If Moses' name is understood as Hebrew, it should mean "rescuer from the water," not "rescued from the water," anticipating his role as Israel's deliverer (cf. Isa. 63:11).

11. Dennis T. Olson, "Moses," in *The New Interpreter's Dictionary of the Bible*, vol. 4, ed. Katherine D. Sakenfeld (Nashville: Abingdon, 2009), 148.

12. William H. C. Propp, "Moses," in *Eerdmans Dictionary of the Bible*, ed. David N. Freedman (Grand Rapids: Eerdmans, 2000), 920.

13. Middleton, *New Heaven and a New Earth*, 63.

14. See the stimulating discussion of Richard Bauckham, "The Conversion of the Nations," in *The Climax of Prophecy: Studies on the Book of Revelation* (Edinburgh, UK: T&T Clark, 1993), 325.

15. Ibid., 326, employing a partitive use of the preposition. This fourfold phrase—every tribe, language, people, and nation—occurs seven times in Revelation, in varying expressions (Rev. 5:9; 7:9; 10:11; 11:9; 13:7; 14:6; 17:15).

16. R. Glenn N. Wooden, "Elijah," in *Eerdmans Dictionary of the Bible*, 395. As I write this, the humanitarian crisis of Syrian and Iraqi refugees is reaching catastrophic proportions. Needed resources are now beyond the capability of Lebanon, Jordan, and Turkey to handle. The Middle East, North Africa, and Europe are living in unprecedented times of violence, hunger, poverty, and political unrest. This means the suffering is international and complex. How can the church mediate the aid and love of God to these displaced millions?

17. Ibid., 396.

18. Ibid.; emphasis added.

19. Ibid.

20. Stephen Dempster, *Dominion and Dynasty*, New Studies in Biblical Theology (Downers Grove, IL: InterVarsity, 2003), 175.

21. Jeremy R. Treat, *The Crucified King: Atonement and Kingdom in Biblical and Systematic Theology* (Grand Rapids: Zondervan, 2014), 85; emphasis original.

22. Ibid., 86.

23. Ibid., 85.

24. Brueggemann, "Elijah," in *Reverberations*, 65.

25. Treat, *The Crucified King*, 88.

26. C. Clifton Black, "Mark," in *The New Interpreter's Bible*, ed. Beverly R. Gaventa and David Petersen (Nashville: Abingdon, 2010), 667.

27. Ibid., 668.

28. Treat, *The Crucified King*, 99.

29. Ibid.

30. Grant R. Osborne, *Mark*, ed. Mark L. Strauss and John H. Walton (Grand Rapids: Baker, 2014), 156.

31. Ibid., 155.

32. Darrell L. Bock, *The Gospel of Mark*, Cornerstone Biblical Commentary (Carol Stream, IL: Tyndale, 2005), 476.

33. Mark L. Strauss, *Four Portraits, One Jesus* (Grand Rapids: Zondervan, 2007), 187.

34. Larry Hurtado, *Mark*, New International Biblical Commentary (Peabody, MA: Hendrickson, 1989), 147.

35. Osborne, *Mark*, 156.

36. Craig A. Evans, *Mark 8:27–16:20*. Word Biblical Commentary, 34B (Nashville: Nelson, 2001), 36.

37. Osborne, *Mark*, 153.

38. C. E. B. Cranfield, *The Epistle to the Romans*, vol. 1 (London: T&T Clark, 1975), 419.

39. Eckhard J. Schnabel, *Der erste Brief des Paulus an die Korinther* (Wuppertal, Germany: R. Brockhas, 2006), 782. Similar is C. K. Barrett, *The First Epistle to the Corinthians* (London: 1968), 308: "The life of the age to come will rest on faith as completely as does the Christian life now."

40. Douglas J. Moo, "Eschatology and Environmental Ethics: On the Importance of Biblical Theology to Creation Care," in *Keeping God's Earth: The Global Environment in Biblical Perspective*, ed. N. J. Toly and D. I. Block (Downers Grove, IL: InterVarsity, 2010), 29.

41. Thomas R. Schreiner, *Galatians* (Grand Rapids: Zondervan, 2010), 289.

42. Agreeing with Douglas J. Moo that "a causal interpretation of the participle is to be preferred" (*The Epistle to the Romans* [Grand Rapids: Eerdmans, 1996], 520).

43. Chris E. Green, "The Crucified God and the Groaning Spirit: Toward a Pentecostal *Theologia Crucis* in Conversation with Jürgen Moltmann," *Journal of Pentecostal Theology* 19 (2010): 137.

44. Romans 3:23 is better translated "lack" than "fall short." See Wally V. Cirafesi, "'To Fall Short' or 'To Lack'? Reconsidering the Meaning and Translation of 'ΥΣΤΕΡΕΩ' in Romans 3:23," *Expository Times* 123 (2012): 429–34.

45. Ulrich Wilkens, *Der Brief and die Römer*, vol. 2 (Düsseldorf: Benziger Verlag, 2000), 155.

46. James M. Hamilton Jr., *Revelation* (Wheaton, IL: Crossway, 2012), 382.

47. Grant R. Osborne, *Revelation* (Grand Rapids: Baker, 2002), 729.

Scripture Index

YOU MIGHT ALSO LIKE . . .

From the Word **to Life**

Moody Radio produces and delivers compelling programs filled with biblical insights and creative expressions of faith that help you take the next step in your relationship with Christ.

You can hear Moody Radio on 36 stations and more than 1,500 radio outlets across the U.S. and Canada. Or listen on your smartphone with the Moody Radio app!

www.moodyradio.org